T. Warren ONeill

The Refutation of Darwinism

and the converse theory of development; based exclusively upon Darwin's facts

and comprising qualitative and quantitative analyses of the phenomena of

variation

T. Warren ONeill

The Refutation of Darwinism
*and the converse theory of development; based exclusively upon Darwin's facts and
comprising qualitative and quantitative analyses of the phenomena of variation*

ISBN/EAN: 9783337888176

Printed in Europe, USA, Canada, Australia, Japan

Cover: Foto ©Andreas Hilbeck / pixelio.de

More available books at **www.hansebooks.com**

THE

REFUTATION OF DARWINISM;

AND THE

CONVERSE THEORY OF DEVELOPMENT;

BASED EXCLUSIVELY UPON DARWIN'S FACTS,

AND COMPRISING QUALITATIVE AND QUANTITATIVE ANALYSES OF THE
PHENOMENA OF VARIATION; OF REVERSION; OF CORRELATION;
OF CROSSING; OF CLOSE-INTERBREEDING; OF THE REPRO-
DUCTION OF LOST MEMBERS; OF THE REPAIR OF
INJURIES; OF THE REINTEGRATION OF TISSUE;
AND OF SEXUAL AND ASEXUAL GENERATION.

BY

T. WARREN O'NEILL,

MEMBER OF THE PHILADELPHIA BAR.

———

PHILADELPHIA:
J. B. LIPPINCOTT & CO.

PREFACE.

ALL religious discussion has been studiously avoided in this work, and solely positive processes of discovery have been employed. The argument is founded, exclusively, upon an analysis of the facts of variation, and of selection, as those facts are presented by Mr. Darwin, in his "ORIGIN OF SPECIES," in his "ANIMALS AND PLANTS UNDER DOMESTICATION," and in his "FERTILIZATION OF ORCHIDS."

The design is to show, that the very same facts, which Darwin confesses his inability to explain, yet upon which he relies to sustain his theory, may be explained, to the advantage of every breeder, fancier, horticulturist, and agriculturist; and explained in a way which signally disproves the theory, that Man, and other species of animal, and species of plant, were evolved from lower types.

The arguments herein are all drawn from the phenomena presented by plants, and by the lower animals; it having been deemed more favorable to a temperate and unprejudiced discussion of the subject, to exclude all mention of Man,—upon the understanding, however, that such laws as may be proven to obtain with the lower organisms, must prevail (*cæteris paribus*) also with Man.

Of the cause of Variations, or improvements; of the cause of the good generally resulting from Crossing; of the cause of the evils frequently attendant upon Close-Interbreeding; of the cause of Correlation of Growth; and of the causes of others of his many colligations of facts, Darwin asserts that he is "in profound ignorance." Their explanation, in this work, however, puts a wholly different phase upon the problem of development, from that which Darwin (by merely estimating the ratio of development of seemingly inexplicable variations) has given it; and, further, demonstratively proves that species are normally immutable; that there is, for each species, a physiologically perfect type (capable of being realized by careful selection); and that this type, although it is susceptible of modification, in countless ways, is or may be modified, only at the cost of evil results which soon lead to the sterility, lessened constitutional vigor, and consequent extinction, of the line of those individuals which have so departed from the true moulds of their respective species.

These conclusions are arrived at, simply by making a slightly different apportionment of Darwin's facts, under Darwin's principles.

Mr. Darwin has a body of facts, and a certain set of scientific factors. These facts he distributes under his several factors, conformably to a system of apportionment which leaves a residuum which, in default of ability to explain, he is unwillingly constrained to refer to such confessedly illegitimate factors, or entities, as, "an innate tendency," "spontaneous variability," "the nature and constitution of the being which varies," "some great law of nature," etc.

In this Refutation and Converse Theory, all of Darwin's facts are taken for granted, as are all of his scientific factors. These same facts, however, are differently apportioned, with but a slight variation from Darwin's mode of distribution of them; and they are relegated to the same set of factors, in such relative quantities, as to leave no residuum of facts unexplained; and, thereby, the necessity is obviated, of any reference to such metaphysical and unscientific entities, as "innate tendency," and others, such as Darwin employs.

The result, moreover, of this mode of distribution of the same facts under the same set of principles, is (as the author conceives) to prove, unmistakably, the immutability of each species.

The advantage of the plan herein pursued, is, that no controversy, whatever, can reasonably arise, respecting either the validity of the facts employed, or the legitimacy of the principles assumed. The issue is narrowed down to the mere questions, of the soundness of the mode in which the facts are distributed, and of the significance of the results of such a manner of apportionment.

To avoid the appearance of egotism, and the circumlocution by which such effect might have been avoided, the plural pronoun has been used, instead of the more obtrusive I.

T. WARREN O'NEILL.

PHILADELPHIA, DECEMBER 20, 1879.

CONTENTS.

CHAPTER VIII.

CHAPTER IX.

CHAPTER X.

CHAPTER XI.

CHAPTER XII.

CHAPTER XIII.

REFUTATION OF DARWINISM:

AND THE

CONVERSE THEORY OF DEVELOPMENT, &C.

CHAPTER I.

DARWIN'S THEORY.

TO appreciate a Refutation, it is necessary to know exactly what it is which is refuted. To meet this need, we commence by giving Darwin's theory.

Mr. Darwin's theory of the Origin of Species, as propounded in his works " *The Origin of Species*," and "*Animals and Plants Under Domestication*," is as follows :

As Mr. Darwin professes to base his theory, not upon mere speculation as to the processes which have obtained in the past, but upon obvious inferences from the actual behaviour of things in the present, and from processes now in operation under our very eyes, he takes the reader directly to the barnyard, to the garden, and to the field. Here, under domestication, the individuals of each species, display great variation and

improvement, compared with the state, in which they
were, when first placed under cultivation. The phenomena, here observed, apparently imply an universal
tendency to vary, which ever seems to manifest itself,
under certain changes in the circumstances; that is,
that while the offspring of animals and of plants, taken
from the state of nature, are, in all their main characteristics or features, like their parents, they nevertheless
improve, more or less, upon their parents; and vary
or differ in character, to some degree, from each other.
These variations, and improvements, are also transmitted to the descendants of the varying individuals,
which also go on, from generation to generation, super-
adding to the measure of variation, first displayed.
For, when a modification is acquired by any individual, the law of inheritance transmits the acquired character to the offspring.

Variation, as Darwin remarks, is everywhere seen,
under domestication. Scarcely any species, or individual of any species, either animal or vegetable, has
escaped this tendency. Some species, such as the
Pigeon and the Fowl, display more variation and improvement than others. Some have developed many
important organs not present in the same species,
under nature. Other species have developed few, or no
new features; yet have improved wonderfully and variedly, in the quality and size of the characteristics they
possessed when first placed under domestication. The
improvements, arising in some species, have been
divided or apportioned among different, and widely
distinct varieties. In other species, the improvements

appearing, have been developed in all of the varieties, and each of those varieties is marked solely by the high degree of development to which some one of its features has been carried. Where, in any species, all of the characters arising by variation, have been fixed and retained in each variety, with no one character extraordinarily well developed, in comparison with the others—the breeds or varieties of the species, being distinguishable from each other merely by minute differences in the size or proportion of the features developed—there results convergence of character; which is less frequently met with, than is divergence of character. An instance in point, with respect to the diversity, or divergence of character above mentioned, is the Pigeon; each of whose principal varieties, has some one feature peculiarily characteristic of it. An instance of convergence of character, which Darwin gives, is the Cow, whose varieties, or breeds, have peculiarities which are not very distinct.

Variation also results, through the loss or reduction of some characters which the species had, when taken from the state of nature. Variation, of this kind, is exemplified in the case of the tailless breeds, the earless breeds, turn-spit dogs, niata cattle (with their lips shortened) and, in the case of the "improved" Pig, whose tusks have been greatly reduced, whose bristles and hair have been well-nigh lost, whose legs have been reduced to the smallest possible size compatible with locomotion, and the front of whose head has been rendered short and concave.

While some species, under domestication, such as

the goose, the turkey, the hive-bee, &c., have not
developed features, in their individuals, sufficiently
marked and varied, to serve as the foundation of any
very distinct varieties, a multitude of other species display modifications which form the distinguishing characters of very widely divergent breeds. Many of the
modifications, or improvements, which have arisen
under man's care, and which were not known to the
species, when taken from the state of nature, have led
to the formation of varieties, in such species, with distributed differences distinguishing them, greater even
than those differences which distinguish one species
from another; and, in some cases, greater even than
those which mark one genus from another.

The distinction between species and varieties, should
be thoroughly appreciated, by the reader, that he may
understand Darwin's argument. A species is generally taken to be, that class of organisms which are
known to have a common descent from some ancient
progenitor, and which are capable of indefinitely-
continued, fertile reproduction among each other; but
which, on being crossed with individuals of another
species, are either sterile, or give birth to offspring,
called hybrids, which are sterile. Thus, a horse, and
an ass, are taken to be distinct species. A mule, however, is a hybrid—being the result of a cross between
the two species—and, as is well known, is sterile. A
variety, or breed, on the other hand, is one of a class
of organisms, within a species, distinguished from its
fellow varieties of the same species, by the possession
of some peculiar, negative or positive character; and

which is capable of indefinitely-continued, fertile reproduction, not only among its own individuals, but, peculiarly so, with the individuals of any other variety of
the same species. Thus, an Arab horse, the English
race horse, the dray-horse, the Shetland pony, &c.,
represent varieties, or breeds, of the species horse:
and a Fantail, a Pouter, a Carrier, a Runt, a Barb,
a Jacobin, &c., represent varieties of the Pigeon
species.

The variation, modification, or improvement, occurring
under domestication, Darwin represents truly, as matter
of fact, to be very great. It is proved, by him, conclusively, that there is scarcely any part of the organization of any individual of any species of plant or animal, under domestication, which is not susceptible of
some, and, in the majority of instances, of great modification. Even the bones, and the internal organs—
the liver, the kidneys, the vertebræ, the reproductive
organs, the œsophagus, the intestinal canal—have been
shown to be greatly modified. Cases of increase, and
of decrease in the number of the vertebræ, have been
demonstrated to be of frequent occurrence. There are
improvements, or variations, in the legs, in the tongue,
in the eyes, in the skin, in the hair, in the feathers, in
the hoofs, in the horns, in the tail, and in the
wings. There are the greatest variations in the head.
Even the teeth have varied greatly, in number, size,
and other characters.

Modifications, most favorable, and most different, in
character, have arisen, in a variety of ways, with birds
of the same species; in their head, or crest feathers, in

2*

their wing-feathers, and in their tail-feathers.   In plants, by the process of bud-variation, have been known to arise, in one generation alone, nectarines from the peach, the red magnum-bonum plum from the yellow magnum-bonum; and the moss rose from the Provence rose.   An astonishingly great improvement has taken place in the wild carrot, and the parsnip, which, from mere stringy roots that they were, when taken from nature, have developed into great size and delicacy. Gooseberries also have attained great size and weight: The London Gooseberry being seven and eight times the weight of the wild fruit.   The fruit of one variety of the Curcurbita *pepo*, exceeds, in volume, that of another of the same species, which is less cultivated, by more than 2000 fold !

Whatever part of the plant, man values most, that part has been sure to increase surprisingly, in size, in general development, and in quality.   If it be the flower, to which man attaches value, the most astonishing improvement, in that character, is seen ; while the other parts show little, or no improvement.   The same occurs, where it is the fruit, the leaves, or the root, which man prizes.

Varieties of the fowl, of the turkey, of the canary-bird, of the duck, and of the goose, have developed top-knots, and reversed head feathers, since they have been taken care of by man.   It would be but writing, anew, Darwin's book on *"Animals and Plants under Domestication,"* to record all of the great, and wonderful improvements which have arisen, within a short time, under domestication.

Varieties, or breeds, are formed, in each species, of these variations and improvements. The reader is sufficiently well acquainted with the great improvements which have occurred in the horse, in the sheep, and in cattle, not to need a detailed statement thereof. The Pigeon, however, having displayed, probably, the greatest amount of variation, and as Darwin has not only given the greatest care and attention to this species, but has also used it as the most prominent and striking subject with which to illustrate his view, that divergence of character generates distinct species from the variations of another, a more detailed account of this species, as it exists under man's fostering care, may not be needless.

The progenitor of the pigeons now under domestication, was, Darwin says, the rock pigeon, or Columba *livia;* which, when redeemed from a state of nature, had not the slightest vestige of many of the characters which now form the striking peculiarities of many of the varieties which have descended from it; and, of those characters, which it had, the development was, by no means, so great and pronounced, as is now seen in many of the varieties.

Darwin says, that so great has been the variation or improvement, with the pigeon, that there are now not less than one hundred and fifty distinct varieties, and subvarieties, descended from this original rock pigeon! The wing feathers, head feathers, and tail feathers, in several varieties, have been greatly changed in character and size. The well known, well marked, upwardly expanded tail, which characterizes the variety,

known as the Fantail, has been developed, since the
bird was taken from a state of nature.   The œsophagus
has attained an enormous size, in the Pouter.   A surprisingly large beak marks the Carrier.   A great quantity of eye wattle has arisen, and now adorns the
Barb.   Divergent, and large feathers, along the front
of the neck and breast, have appeared, where not even
a ruffled feather was discernible before, and distinguish the Turbit.   The Jacobin has the feathers so
much reversed, along the back of the neck, that they
form a hood.   These feathers, also, are absent in the
common bird, as found under nature.   Other varieties
have, proportionally to their size, much elongated, or
much shortened, heads, necks, legs, tails, wings, bodies;
and the proportions of the several characters, have
been so much varied, that almost every possible ratio
of the development of the species' characters, is to be
found among the several varieties.   As in the case of
other animals, even the bones, and the internal organs,
have experienced a marked change in size, number,
and other characters.

So great, in fact, has been the range of variation, in
this species, that, as Darwin truly remarks, a naturalist,
did he not know of the community of descent of these
varieties, would be induced to esteem many of them,
as distinct species, and a few of them, as even distinct
genera.

Judging merely by structural differences, and ignoring the physiological effect which the development or
reduction of a character, has upon organisms, there
are many other varieties, under domestication, which

should be regarded as distinct species; and, perhaps, others which a person, so judging, would be not too bold in accounting as belonging to different genera. The argument of Darwin is,

" How possibly can there be fixed species, or immutable species, when the individuals, which represent those species, vary and change so greatly? A species is made up of individuals; and, when those individuals change, the species, also, must necessarily change."

And, again, he argues, if difference in structural build is what alone constitutes the distinction between species, why, then, should not the great differences in structural build, between varieties of what has heretofore been known, or taken, to be one species, be taken as specific distinctions?

Having detailed, at large, these· facts of variation, from which Darwin purposes to deduce his theory, the necessity of some inquiry into the natural forces at work in inducing these improvements, occurred to Darwin. Some aspect of these variations—either founded upon a scientific analysis of the phenomena, or, else, gratuitously assumed—had necessarily to be taken for granted, as a basis for further research. The question, for instance, whether these variations are amenable to any limit; the question, too, whether it be legitimate to estimate the amount of improvement possible to occur in millions of years, by means of these variations, from the amount of development known to have taken place during the last one hundred years; could not be resolved, unless some view was taken. Darwin admits—aye, explicitly states—that he has not made such an analysis; but that he has gratuitously assumed a view, the sole warrant of which, is, he urges, that there is no reasonable, opposing view. He candidly admits that he has made no scientific induction from the facts. He contents himself with the fact alone that these improvements do arise. Conscious, that such a treatment of this subject, at the very inception of his problem, is practically to limit all inquiry at the point where the principles of the inductive philosophy especially require an analysis, he concedes that there must be a law governing them, but that it is seemingly inscrutable; and, all that he can say, on the subject, is, that the reason animals and plants vary, or improve, is because they are possessed of "an innate tendency to vary," or because of a " spontaneous variability!" though this, he admits, " is wholly incorrect, and only serves to show our ignorance of the cause of each particular variation."

In science, in law, in the every day affairs of life, it is fair to presume that, in the absence of all evidence, or other presumption to the contrary, anything which occurs regularly, or at frequent intervals, will ever continue so to recur. This presumption is a valid one, always, if all the preceding points in the problem, of which this presumption enters as an element, have been resolved. If, however, there be an *hiatus* in the chain of reasoning, anterior to the employment of this presumption that things will ever continue as they have been, the presumption is manifestly invalid. In Darwin's problem, he would be fairly entitled to the presumption, that, as variations have ever been occurring, under domestication, they will ever so occur, *if he had resolved the question of the law of variation, and the law were silent on the subject of a limit.*

Darwin, however, takes the fact, viz., that variations do occur, and have occurred, in the past; and holds from this, that he is entitled to the presumption, that these variations will go on forever, or, at least, indefinitely. He reverses the usual canons of logic; appeals to his ignorance (!) of any law of variations; and, hence, to the absence of any such law, imposing a limit to such variations; and complacently assumes, therefore, that there is no limit to variations. He turns the logician's gun against the logician, albeit, most absurdly; and with charming simplicity, declares that the assumption of any such limit is wholly gratuitous —oblivious to the fact that, in the absence of knowledge of the law of variation, his assumption of no-limit is both illegitimate and gratuitous. Variation is ever occurring, now, with all the animals and plants under domestication; and, therefore, the presumption (Darwin holds) is a fair one, that in default of proof to the contrary, those variations ever will occur. What evidence, he triumphantly demands, is there to induce a belief that there is a limit?

Such proof to the contrary, it is the purpose of this work to advance; and full warrant for the belief that there is such a limit, we shall adduce.

It is clear to the reader, that, if there is a law of variation, and it should prescribe a limit, it is happily for Darwin, and for his theory, that his "ignorance of the law of variation" is so "profound."

Darwin, availing himself thus of the presumption of
no-limit (which, other things legitimate would be itself
legitimate) takes the fact, that, during a short period
under domestication, most numerous and important
improvements have sprung up, in animals and plants;
and he concludes therefrom, that the species are not
immutable; that varieties are but incipient species;
that each and every species changes, with the changes
in the individuals of which it is composed; and that,
given a sufficient length of time—he intimates several
millions of generations—it is quite probable, that, at
the same (or even greatly less) rate of improvement
now displayed under our very eyes, the higher forms
will go on progressing, and improving, into still higher
forms; and that the lower forms will develop into the
higher forms :   And that, as these changes of structure,
occurring now with each individual, are accumulated,
and made to form divergent varieties within each species; each variety of such species will further diverge into species, distinct from the parent species;
and evolve, also, into other genera, families and
orders.

In other words, he concludes, from the progress
made with domesticated animals, that a variety of the
Duck species, for example, will diverge into several
distinct types, as high in the order of beings, as the
Fowl, the Goose, the Turkey, the Peacock, the Con-
dor, and the Eagle; and, that, there would be nothing
impossible, but rather probable, in the circumstance of,
another variety of the Duck diverging, successively,
into the Bat, the Flying-Squirrel, the Rabbit, the Pig,

the Cow, the Horse, the Tiger, the inevitable Monkey, and into Man!

This is his conclusion, from the facts of variation, under domestication. This is his reasoning, viz., given, the amount of improvement observed to occur during the last hundred years; and, given, the preservation and accumulation of these variations by Man's Selection, the evolution of any of the lower forms, into any of the higher, is to be considered highly probable, and consistent with all of the analogies of science.

There is no question, with a scientist, that, if his reasoning holds good with the lower animals, it obtains equally well with Man.

Darwin now draws an analogy, between animals and plants under domestication, and all organisms under nature. He declares, and adduces some evidence in support of his statement, that variations occur, also, under nature. As then, he argues, it is possible for such great advances in development, to take place in the future, with respect to the domesticated organisms; so, it is likewise possible, and probable, that Nature has, in the past, brought about similar results; and that such a progression, from simplicity to complexity of structure, has been gradually going on, in the past under nature, by means of accumulated variations, as to have evolved the higher animals (including Man) from the simplest type of structure; or in Darwin's own words, "that all the organic beings which have lived on this earth, have descended from some one primordial form into which life was first breathed."

It is here, at this point, that Darwin anticipates an
3

objection which was possible to be made to his theory
of development. His success in obviating this objection, constitutes his chief claim to the wide reputation
he now enjoys.

It was apparent, that, under nature, and even under
domestication, variability might be frequently displayed;
yet, if the varying individuals were not, in some way,
especially favored; if there were no process or care
employed to fix, and preserve these slight appreciable
variations, as they arose, and render them permanent;
the variations would appear, perhaps, in individuals;
but, if those individuals had not a better chance, than
others, of leaving offspring; or, if they intercrossed
with others displaying different modifications, or none;
the variations most probably would not be transmitted,
nor would any increase in such modification, or any
divergence of character, result.   Under domestication,
such a process, and such a care, is well known to
obtain. This process is Selection by Man. To this
we are greatly indebted, for the great amount of improvement, observable in our domestic animals and
plants. By this, the favorable modifications which
arise (genenally in very small increments of growth),
are preserved and accumulated; and, by this means, is
the great divergence of character effected, in the
varieties of many different species. The modifications,
under domestication, are carefully looked for; and,
when they arise, are distributed to the different varieties of the given species. Those varieties, which present such marked divergence of character, within certain species, result from man's careful selection of those

individuals presenting any modification, or improvement; and from Man's judicious pairing of such individuals, with others with like variations. In this way,
the "tendency to vary," by being combined in pairs
which similarly vary, is strengthened, and fixed; and
an increase in the quality and quantity of the modifications, is insured in the offspring.

By this preservation, and accumulation, of slight,
successive, scarcely appreciable modifications, most distinct varieties are formed; and great differences result,
between the individuals of the same species. Whereas, if Man's intervention did not interpose, the individuals of each of these species would all be of one, uniform character; and the improvements which did arise,
would be sunk again, by the varying individuals' intercrossing with others, of the same species, which had no
like tendency to vary, or which had tendencies of growth,
perhaps, adverse to the continued development of the
said improvements. Under domestication, however, the
individuals, similarly varying, are interbred. Favorable changes are noted by the breeder, or fancier; carefully preserved; and further developed, by the mating
of such individuals, with others displaying a tendency
to a like change of character. The individuals, which
display no variation, or which develop changes, or variations, which are not the recognized peculiarities of
their varieties, are neglected or suppressed. If this
process of Man's selection were not employed, those
individuals, not varying, being in the majority, would
most probably run out the varying ones, or completely
negative, or nullify, the tendency to vary, in others, by

intercrossing with them. Further: even if the "tendency to vary" held its own, the species would probably
go on varying in one, only, line of growth. All the
features which now distinguish the different varieties,
would be suffered to develop themselves in each and
every variety, or individual; and no diversity of character, such as is requisite to explain the great diversity
of forms under nature, would be displayed; as it now
is, through means of Man's selection. Darwin requires
such divergence of character, in order to prove the
evolution of distinct species, one from another. Convergence of character, however, would result, in the
absence of Selection; and the only effect of development
would be to produce, simply, a graduated series of
developments, from his first primordial form. When,
however, under domestication, each new character is
developed, it is allotted by the breeder or fancier, to a
certain variety, of which it is to form the distinguishing
characteristic. In each variety, therefore, especial and
exclusive attention is given to the development of the
character which constitutes the peculiarity, and the
other features which appear, are made to form the
peculiarities of the other varieties. In this way, by
not suffering all the characters which may arise, to become developed in every individual or variety, but by
apportioning these characters among the several varieties of the species, is the required divergence of character effected; and, thus, each variety becomes (as Darwin fancies), a point of divergence, from which similar,
multiplied divergences will also arise, from increased variations, which again will be apportioned or distributed.

Thus, when any individual of the species, Pigeon, displays the variation of the upwardly expanded tail, it is then allotted to a variety, called the Fantail variety; and suffered to be developed in that variety only. All attempts, which individuals, of the other varieties, may make to develop this feature, are discouraged; and all attempts, which any individuals, of this Fantail variety, may make to develop any of the peculiarities of the other varieties, are likewise baffled by the fancier. Again; when an enlargement of the œsophagus appears, it is allotted to the Pouter variety of the Pigeon; and a similar policy of repression of erratic individuals, is pursued. Individuals, presenting very long beaks, are allotted to the Carrier variety. The divergent feathers, along the front of the neck, and on the breast, are developed in the Turbit only; quantity of eye-wattle, in the Barb; and, reversed feathers, along the back of the head, and on the neck, forming a hood, in the Jacobin. Should any individual, of any one of these varieties, evince an inclination to take upon itself the peculiarity of any one of the other varieties, that individual the fancier remorselessly and systematically suppresses; because the standard of character, for each variety, must be maintained. By the careful mating of those individuals, of a variety, which develop the peculiarity of their variety, and which also display no disposition to superadd the peculiarities of other varieties, is this great divergence of character effected, upon which Darwin relies to show that these varieties are but incipient species, and that they diverge by different lines of growth into dis-

3*

tinct species. Occasionally, when any individuals of
any variety, develop some new feature, not known to
any of the other varieties, they are taken from the
variety within which they have been before classed, and
placed within a new category, or variety, carefully
mated, and the accretions of growth, in the new direction, thereby preserved, accumulated, and fixed to a
certain persistency of type.

In this way, by Man's care and selection, has been
occasioned, and rendered possible, the great amount of
variation, which domestication has to show; as, also,
the great divergence of character there seen. To
Darwin's course, in pursuing the analogy of variation
into the domain of nature, objection would have been
taken; for, as it would have been said, even if variations did take place under nature, the improvements
could not have gone on accumulating to any extent, or
effecting any great divergence of character; by reason
of the fact, that these results have been attained, under
domestication, only because Man's selection has guided
and fostered the irregular, and feeble action of variation.

To this, Darwin rejoins, by stating that there is, and
has been, in full and constant operation, under nature,
a process precisely analogous to Man's selection—a
process to the full as efficient, and quite competent
(given, a requisite allowance of time) to effect similar,
great results. This process is Darwin's much-vaunted
principle of Natural Selection.

This Natural Selection, or power of nature to select
the best of the individuals, of any species, for purposes

of breeding, Darwin infers from the Struggle for Existence which, he says, is, under nature, constantly carried on, by all organisms, each with the others; whereby the weak succumb, and those which are the fittest, strongest, and most vigorous survive. Besides the selection of those which are the strongest, there will also be a selection of those which display some new modification; and these mating with their fellow victors in the struggle for life, will attain, through their offspring, to a higher and still higher development. Conformably to the theory of Malthus, he contends, that, under nature, the production of new organisms far outruns the means of their subsistence; that all Nature is at war, one species with another, and the individuals of the same species with each other. The result of this Struggle for Existence, is Natural Selection; by which, the lucky and the stronger prevail, and the weaker and ill-favored perish. As many more individuals are born than can possibly survive, those individuals which possess any variation which contributes to give them an advantage in this warfare, are, in the main, more likely to survive, to propagate, and to occupy the places of their weaker brethren, with their offspring. If but a single variation occurred once in a thousand generations, says Darwin; and that variation were preserved by Natural Selection, until, at the end of another thousand of generations, another variation was superadded, the improvement and diversity of the species would, eventually, be such as to occasion a divergence, by the different individuals favored, into distinct species.

The question of the origination of these improvements, or variations (which are modestly assumed to
occur but once in a thousand generations), is equally
left unresolved by Darwin, and referred, as are the
variations under domestication, to "an innate tendency to vary," or to " spontaneous variability !"

It is impossible to deny, that there is such a Struggle
for Existence, as Darwin pictures ; and, equally impossible to deny, that there is some such process as
Natural Selection, in operation under nature, favoring
at times the preservation of the strongest and most
fitted.   It is scarcely possible, even, to read Darwin's
graphic description of the Struggle for Existence,
among animals and plants, under nature, and not marvel that any survived.   Under nature, he says, organisms are subjected to the greatest vicissitudes, and to
the severest competition with their fellows, with other
species, and with the adverse conditions of nature.
They all enter into competition, for the means of subsistence.   All, almost without exception, he says, have
to struggle against the hard conditions of life, and
against their competitors, from the moment of their
birth, to the hour of their death.   He alleges, that
there is no exception to the rule, that every organic
being naturally increases at so high a rate that, if numbers were not destroyed, the earth would soon be cov-
ered with the progeny of a single pair.   The struggle,
he holds, will almost invariably be the most severe,
between the individuals of the same species ; for, they
frequent the same districts, require the same food, and
are exposed to the same dangers.   Consequent upon

the astonishingly great increase, is the Natural Extinction of large numbers.

Those whom nature exempts from this wholesale destruction, are naturally those which are the fittest to live, the strongest, and most vigorous; and, notably, those who "at intervals of a thousand generations" or so, have developed some character, or modification, which gives them an advantage, in the general contest for life, over their competitors, and over the hard conditions of life.

This selection, of the strongest and fittest, and of the favorably modified organisms, as the ones of the number ordained to live, is what constitutes Darwin's Natural Selection—a factor which depends necessarily upon this Struggle for Existence.

Natural Selection has nothing whatever to do, Darwin says, with the production, or appearance, of any of the variations or improvements. How any favorable modification, or variation, comes to present itself, Darwin insists that he is profoundly ignorant. But, after the variation has appeared, this Natural Selection merely preserves it, insures its transmission to offspring, and so accumulates successive variations which arise, independently of it, owing to "an innate tendency." Natural Selection, Darwin says, does not at all cause the variations which may occur. Their origin is inexplicable to him, he says; but, "it acts exclusively by the preservation and accumulation of those variations after they have arisen." Variations occur in some strange way, by "accident or chance," independently of Natural Selection, though so to refer them to acci-

dent or chance, is, he says, merely to express our
ignorance of the law. Natural Selection but preserves
and accumulates the variations as they arise, and
directs them into favorable lines of growth. "As all the
individuals of each district are struggling together with
nicely balanced forces, extremely slight modifications
in the structure or habits of one individual often give
it an advantage over the others." And (what is part of
the same Natural Selection, called Sexual Selection),
were the individual varying, a male, the acquired modification would doubtless give it an advantage, in a
contest for the most favored, and, perhaps, similarly
varying, females; and, thereby, the modification acquired, would be the more surely impressed upon the
offspring. In "several thousand generations," or a
"million of generations," one of the descendants of
this offspring would, probably, also vary, adding thus
another character to the complexity of its structure.

As, under domestication, Man's care and choice of
those animals and plants, displaying some improvement, tends to the preservation and accumulation of
the characters presenting themselves, and assures the
transmission of those characters to offspring; so, this
Selection by Nature, of the favorably modified animals
and plants, as among those which are suffered to survive and propagate their kind, represents the same
principle.

"Can it be thought improbable," says Darwin, "seeing that variations useful to man, have undoubtedly
occurred, that other variations, useful in some way to
each being in the great and complex battle of life,

should sometimes occur in the course of thousands of generations? If such variations do occur, can we doubt (remembering that many more individuals are born than can possibly survive), that individuals, having an advantage, however slight, over others, would have the best chance of surviving and procreating their kind?" "If," he continues, "a man can, by patience, select variations useful to him, why, under changing and complex conditions of life, should not variations, useful to nature's living products, often arise and be preserved and selected?"

Darwin asks, "What limit can be put to this power, acting during long ages, and rigidly scrutinizing the whole constitution, structure, and habits of each creature—favoring the good and rejecting the bad?" "I can see no limit to this power, in slowly and beautifully adapting each form to the most complex relations of life."

"Selection," continues Darwin, "will pick out, with unerring skill, each improvement. Let this process go on for millions of years, and may we not have a low primordial type" continuing to evolve into higher and still higher forms of life, until, at last, as the result of this "innate tendency to vary," producing improvements, and of this Natural Selection preserving these improvements, all of the higher animals, including Man, are successively evolved, by the gradual operation of strictly natural processes? In this way, Darwin contends, the present development, and diversity of structure, of the several species, have been effected; and in this way "some one low primordial form into which life was first breathed," and its descendants, have been gradually and variously developed, and differentiated, through all intervening species, into the monkey, and thence, by an easy transition, into Man!

The above is a fair statement of Darwin's theory. Condensed, it may be thus stated: Variations, or improvements, or slight, successive advances from simplicity to greater complexity of structure, have, owing to an "innate tendency to vary," occurred with animals and plants, under domestication. Similar, inexplicable modifications may have occurred (and some warrant for this assumption is furnished) with animals and plants, in the state of nature. Under domestication, Man's Selection has so accumulated, and directed these variations or improvements, that, at the same rate of progression from simplicity to complexity of structure, the higher species may continue to improve indefinitely, and each of the lower species may continue to improve into other species, genera, families and orders, as high as the highest in the existing scale of development. By analogy with domestication, the same progression, or evolution, may be said to have occurred in the past under nature; and it is possible, if not probable, that man, and all other animals, have evolved, by means of these inexplicable variations, and with the aid of the process of Natural Selection, from the lowest type of organic structure.

There is—dove-tailed within this theory of the evolution of the species—another theory with which Darwin supplements his main argument. It is, that, besides an advance in development, by means of the slight successive, positive variation, there has been a prodigious amount of degeneration, during the past, under nature. Natural Selection has very frequently simplified and degraded the structure of animals and plants.

So widespread, Darwin says, has been this degeneration, under nature, that there exists now scarcely a single species which has not lost some organs or features.

From changed habits of life, and from the hard conditions of the Struggle for Existence—which needs must be excessively vigorous to give play to Natural Selection—organs, he says, have become of less and less use, and ultimately superfluous; and disuse, and Natural Extinction, acting on the individuals, have gone on reducing the organs, until, finally, they have either become wholly suppressed, leaving not a vestige of their existence (save the power of reappearing which, he says, they are ever competent to do, even after having lain latent for millions of generations); or, they have become only greatly reduced, having the character of rudiments.

With respect to this power of Reversion, in the many long-lost characters ; he says, that characters, proper to both sexes, to both the right and left side of the body, and to a long line of male and female ancestors, separated by hundreds, or even thousands of generations from the present time, frequently lie latent in many individuals, without our being able to detect any signs of their presence; yet that "these characters, like those written on paper with invisible ink, all lie"

4

ever "ready to be evolved, under certain known, or unknown conditions;" and, of the many variations which he adduces, fully nine-tenths are by him explicitly referred to the mere re-appearance of these long lost characters. Of the cause of the appearance of the other tithe, he says that he is in "profound ignorance."

CHAPTER II.

DARWIN'S IGNORANCE OF THE LAW OF VARIATIONS; AND HIS FALSE ASSUMPTION OF NO LIMIT TO IMPROVEMENTS.

After Darwin had adduced his facts, of the improvements among animals and plants, the next step which it behooved him to take, before he assumed that there was no-limit to such improvements, was to generalize those facts; to develop their cause; to discover the law, governing the appearance of the variations; and to ascertain, whether such law fixed a limit to such variations, or was silent on the subject. If, when discovered, the law assigned a limit to the improvements in each species, then, manifestly, no theory of the indefinite accumulation of such variations, would be possible. If, however, the law, when resolved, were to imply that such variations were possible to be carried on to an unlimited extent; or, even if the law were silent on the subject; no exception to the principal postulate of Darwinism (viz., unlimited improvement) could be taken.

But, while the cause, or law, of the improvements, remained unresolved, it was evident, that any theory, based upon such improvements, must needs be illegitimate; not necessarily false, but illegitimate, inasmuch as the assumption of a limit, or the assumption of no-limit, in any theory, would be not only gratuitous, but also in plain derogation of that canon of the inductive philosophy, which enjoins that no principle whatever shall be reasoned from, until it first shall have been reasoned to.

The question, therefore, of the cause, or law of the improvements, is the point where Darwin's claim to the title of a Baconian philosopher should have been made good. A theory, which is to illustrate the signal triumph which "modern thought" has achieved over the ignorance of nineteen centuries, should stand upon a principle, which is as a buttress of adamant, against every assault,—not upon a gratuitous assumption formulated in the teeth of the fact that the law of its data, is yet unresolved; and despite the circumstance (which we shall develop most clearly), that those data conclusively negative such assumption.

What is the law of Variation ?   What is the cause of the improvements ?

Darwin says, the reason that animals and plants vary, and improve, is because they possess "*an innate tendency*" to vary and improve !

This assumption of his, is a barren, metaphysical entity, which, by the concurring testimony of every inductive philosopher, from the time of Bacon down to the present, suffices to vitiate, and wholly invalidate every hypothesis in which it is present.   In his "*Animals and Plants under Domestication*," and in his "*Origin of Species*," he generalizes, and explains (!) the facts of variation, by ascribing them to "an innate, tendency," to "spontaneous or accidental variability," to "an innate tendency," to "the nature and constitution of the being which varies," and, in numerous other portions of his works, to the same "innate tendency," variedly paraphrased.

This is the way in which Darwin resolves the problem of the cause, or law, of improvements, in order to see whether they are amenable, or not, to any limit. This is the manner in which Darwinism stands the test of the principal canon of the inductive philosophy. This "innate tendency" it is, which serves for a foundation stone to his theory;—a foundation upon which every subsequent assumption and deduction of his, depends for its strength and validity. This is the outcome of his peculiar, inductive reasoning: Animals and Plants vary, because they have an innate tendency to vary! A miserable, farcical assumption, which is naught but a restatement of the phenomena to be explained. The foundation of a theory, such as Darwin's, fraught as it would be, if true, with consequences of such moment, ought to be as incontestably established, as the most positive principle within the realm of science. It is not the mere failure to account for phenomena, to which exception is taken. Such failure may well characterize any fair and legitimate hypothesis or theory. But, it is the failure, the signal and avowed failure, to account for phenomena which lie at the very start of the inquiry, and upon which the whole of the superstructure rests for support. Before men should be asked to forswear their past impression of the descent of Man, and required to admit (under pain of ostracism from the ranks of the

4*

learned and scientific), that their derivation is as Darwin would have it, they, beyond question, are entitled to have the ground alleged in support of such an hypothesis, formed of something more substantial than such flimsy material as an "innate tendency." Even though the consequences of the theory were comparatively of no moment whatever, it might well be required in the name of science, and of common sense, that the base of the theory—the base especially —should present at least some semblance of solidity. Most assuredly—even though there were no law, yet discovered, which governed the facts of variation, and though there were no converse theory deducible from that law—Darwin would be bound to find a law of variation, or frame some legitimate induction, before he could rightly mount one step higher in his theory.

It is not, merely, because there is a known, scientific law governing variations, nor because there is a converse theory of development, resting on that law, that Darwin's passing by the facts of variations, with a mere ascription of them to "an innate tendency," is to be deemed unscientific and illegitimate. Those are reasons, to the treatment of which we have not yet come. They are over and beyond the point of the intrinsic illegitimacy of Darwin's first assumption. Darwin's process would be unscientific, and Darwin's theory would be wholly illegitimate, if there were no explanation, of variation, known; and, if science gave, at present, not the faintest glimmering of a promise of one. It may be demurred, that the foundation of Darwin's theory is found in the facts of variation.

Not to quibble and say that the facts and the theory are altogether two different things; it may be admitted, that the facts are a foundation; but, between those facts and Darwin's theory, there is no connection, no intervening support for the superstructure of the theory. A wide hiatus yawns between.

The inductive method, of which Darwin's theory has been lauded to the skies, as the bright exemplar, has, in this ascription of the facts of variation, to an "innate tendency," been ruthlessly violated. That method forbids any principle to be taken for granted (save in a merely tentative hypothesis, avowedly tentative): or assumed at all, unless it represents truly the resolution of the unknown into the known. Thus, had Darwin conceived some law which he fancied governed variations, he might, tentatively only, have assumed it, though the evidence in support of it were very inadequate. But, merely to formulate his ignorance, in some set expression, as he has done, is grossly illegitimate, and never tolerated, when the canons of science are held in any esteem. Had his "innate tendency," not been a mere formula for his ignorance, but a hypothesis; to reason downwards, from such an assumption, which had not withstood all the tests of induction, would have been to violate the very spirit and letter of the scientific method. This method will concede nothing, but insists upon first reasoning upwards; and scoffs at the idea that any theory can be scientific, when based upon a principle which has not complied with the requirements of proof. Yet, Darwin violates all science, by perpetrating something

infinitely worse: He reasons downwards from his
ignorance! which, avowedly, is the first term in his
theory.

He says that he does not know the cause of variations—the law to which his data conform! He,
further, tacitly deprecates all inquiry into the legitimacy of his methods, and requires that all should
accept his metaphysical formula of confessed ignorance,
as matter of necessary belief. Such devices, the advocates of the scientific method say, they leave to tricky
metaphysicians, with which to beguile the ignorant and
superstitious. Yet, this vaunted champion of the inductive method, confesses that his first assumption (or
apology therefor) in a theory which essays to revo-
lutionize all preconceived ideas of the origin and
dignity of the human race, cannot satisfy the requirements of inductive or scientific thought; but, that he
is constrained, at the very outset of such theory, to
deal with his subject on transcendental grounds only.
He himself tacitly concedes, in a mild deprecating
way, that the very base of his theory is sapped, if any
one be so unkind as to take exception to his first
assumption of ignorance; and intimates, in a mode
little short of explicit expression (aye, directly states)
that the sole strength of his theory lies in an assumed
agreement between his deductions from this principle
of ignorance, and the phenomena in hand. You may
read between the lines that he hopes this fancied agreement may atone for his gross violation, at the start, of
the canons of science.

We say fancied agreement; and such it is. For, he,

in illustrating the many phenomena of variation, has adduced a multitude of facts, showing reversion, correlation, crossing, close interbreeding, reproduction, and generation; yet the reader, the breeder, the fancier, the horticulturist, the agriculturist will look in vain to find any one of the facts under either of these heads, explained, or the law of their operation resolved. His theory is confessedly incompetent to explain any of the facts, while numbers of them are irreconcilably at variance with his theory. The sum of his knowledge of them all and each is that they are "peculiar." The facts of variation are "peculiar." The facts of crossing are "peculiar." The facts of close interbreeding are "peculiar," the facts of correlation are "peculiar," and the facts of generation are "peculiar."   .

On page 327, *Origin of Species*, he says:

"How ignorant we are of the precise causes of sterility:" and, again, "in the presence of all the phenomena" (of crossing and close interbreeding) "we must feel how ignorant we are, and how little likely it is that we should understand why certain forms are fertile, and other forms are sterile when crossed." On p. 330, he speaks of "how entirely ignorant we are on the causes of both fertility and sterility." And of the phenomena of Correlation, he says, "this is a very important subject" (p. 170, *Origin of Species*) "most imperfectly understood." And "the nature of the bond of Correlation" (p. 171, *Origin of Species*) "is very frequently quite obscure."

On p. 231, Vol. 2, he says, of the phenomena of Crossing and close interbreeding:

"We are far from precisely knowing the cause; nor

is this surprising seeing how profoundly ignorant we are in regard to the normal and abnormal action of the reproductive organs."

He might, with equal propriety, say (and actually does say it), "seeing how profoundly ignorant" he is, respecting every one of the 100,000 facts of which he treats—how profoundly ignorant he is of variation, of reversion, of correlation, of crossing, &c. His ignorance of the cause of crossing, and of close interbreeding, is not near so surprising as is his temerity, in endeavoring to teach breeders that they are only well developed ourang outangs, when he confesses he cannot inform them of the cause of any of the phenomena with which they are meeting every day of their lives.

His inability, however, to explain these facts, does not necessarily vitiate his theory, as does his inability to give the explanation, or the law, of variation. For in the former case, he simply knows not how to explain the facts; but, in the latter case, he is ignorant of the law to which his data conform. He appears, throughout his works, to plead most pathetically with his readers (and all who are conversant with science, and with his theory, know full well that he has ample occasion to do so), to be so kind as not to be too exacting at the start; and kindly to shut their eyes to the circumstance that he is reasoning, not *to* a first principle, but *from* his ignorance! He also appears to plead with his readers to be considerately blind to the circumstance, that, in default of any resolution of the law of variations, he is is not entitled to the presumption that they go on forever.

He actually endeavors to make a potent factor out of his own ignorance. For, he appeals to his ignorance of any law of variation (therefore, of any law imposing a limit to variation), in justification of his gratuitous assumption of No Limit to Variation.

We do not wish to be understood, as alleging that Darwin, when he assumes this occult quality, this mysterious force which manifests itself in the organism which varies, or this "innate tendency," really affects to explain the phenomena by means of such entity. He confesses (how frankly, we do not know) that this "innate tendency" is the mere symbol of his ignorance of the cause, or law of variation. He stops, for a moment, occasionally to meet the inquiry, of what is the cause of these improvements which arise, and says:

"We can only attribute them to spontaneous or accidental variability, or as due to chance. This, however, is a supposition wholly incorrect and only serves to indicate plainly our ignorance of the cause of each particular variation."

Again, he says (p. 195, *Origin of Species*):

"Our ignorance of the law of variation is profound." "Not in one case out of a hundred can we pretend to assign any reason why this or that differs, more or less, from the same part in the parent."

Again, he says (p. 157, *Origin of Species*):

"I have hitherto sometimes spoken as if the variations—so common and multiform in organic beings under domestication, and, in a lesser degree, in those in a state of nature—had been due to chance. This, of course, is a wholly incorrect expression, but it serves to acknowledge plainly our ignorance of the cause of each particular variation.   *   *   *   Why because the reproductive system is disturbed, this or that part should vary more or less, we are profoundly ignorant. Nevertheless, we can here and there dimly catch a faint ray of light, and we may feel sure that there must be some cause for each deviation of structure, however slight."

Not so much even as a guess lies at the foundation of his theory.

No wonder that he says, respecting his theory (p. 199, *Origin of Species*) :

"A crowd of difficulties will have occurred to the reader.   Some of them are so serious that to this day I can hardly reflect on them without being staggered."

Page 300, Vol. ii.

"Throughout this chapter and elsewhere I have spoken of selection as the paramount power, yet its action absolutely depends on what we, in our ignorance, call spontaneous or accidental variability."

After speaking of those authors who attribute variation to what are manifestly but the *conditions* of variation, such as "an excess of food," "the amount of exercise taken," and "a more genial climate," he says:

"But we must, I think, take a broader view, and conclude that organic beings, when subjected during several generations to any change whatever in their conditions, tend to vary (*sic*); the kind of varying which ensues depends in a far higher degree on the nature or constitution of the being than on the nature of the changed conditions."

Page 302, Vol. ii.

"We will now consider, as far as we can, the causes

of the almost universal variability of our domestic productions. The subject is an obscure one; but it may be useful to probe our ignorance."

It is impossible for Darwin to take refuge behind any presumption, that the facts of variation are ultimate in their character, that they are inscrutable, and that therefore it is no reproach to him, or to his theory, that he has not generalized the facts; for, he precludes himself from the adoption of any such subterfuge by averring that "a cause for each variation must exist."

Thus, the base of Darwin's theory is ignorance!

It is true, that here and there, throughout his works, he seemingly endeavors to convey the impression, that the facts of variation are ultimate, and even forgets himself so far, in his work on *Animals and Plants Under Domestication*, as to assert that the problem of the cause of variations is "a difficulty as insoluble as is that of free will and predestination." (P. 516, Vol. ii, *Animals and Plants, &c.*)

It must be an occasion, for surprise, to the reader, that such an all important matter, as the cause or the law of the improvements, arising all around us, should receive the scant treatment of only a few sentences, scattered here and there, through Darwin's works. One would have thought that the great multitude of facts which he has collated, would have furnished, at least, a clue which the author might have wrought into some conjecture as to the law. He has several chapters on what he terms "The Causes of Variability," which might mislead his readers, if he did not, in the most explicit terms, state that these "causes" are not

5

causes at all, but merely the physical *conditions* of
variability; and that they do not come under the category of laws or causes, in that higher sense in which
the terms indicate a discovered method, under which
natural forces are observed to work. He avers also
that he would be "a bold man," who would esteem
these physical conditions as of any account, in inducing variation, "in comparison with the nature or constitution of the being which varies."

The surprise, of the reader, however, at this neglect
by Darwin of such an important inquiry, would doubtless much abate, were he to scan closely Darwin's
facts, and have to confront him, a well known factor of
development, which, upon Darwin's own showing, and
own admission, fully explains every improvement
which arises; but which, it was antecedently improbable, should find favor in the sight of Darwin, because
that factor unequivocally negatives, and refutes Darwin's next, succeeding, and indispensable assumption,
viz., that these improvements go on forever, or indefinitely. The discovery of this factor or law, might
suggest to the reader, that Darwin, in being so complacently content with his ignorance of any cause for
variation, was governed by the fear, that, if he evinced
any great solicitude to find a cause, the cause might be
only too ready in forthcoming, to the signal discom-
fiture both of himself and of his theory.

Darwin's "innate tendency," is postulated, and the
ignorance, for which this "innate tendency" is confessedly the mere symbol, is assumed, in wanton derogation, and disregard, of a known, scientific law which

explains all the facts of variation, or of improvement, in animals and plants. The cause, or law, of variations and improvements, is not wrapped in such mystery as Darwin asserts it to be. The explanation of the improvements is to be found in his most prominent factor, Reversion; or the law of the regain of positive characters, or organs, once lost by ancient progenitors of the given species.

This law settles the question as to whether there is a limit to the improvements. This known scientific law explaining variations, imposes a definite limit to such variations, and thereby effectively disposes of Darwin's whole theory, which lays claim to being a probable hypothesis, only in the event of those improvements proceeding forever, or indefinitely. Not only is the origin of the improvements, as they occur, under domestication, and under nature, explained by this law of the regain of long lost characters of the respective species, but a full, qualitative, and quantitative analysis of the operation of those improvements after they have arisen is rendered possible; and the phenomena of crossing, of close interbreeding, of correlation, and of generation, in each and several of their many and diverse manifestations, are equally explicable, upon this assumption, viz., that the reason why individuals of any species improve, is because their ancient progenitors have under nature, in the struggle for existence, degenerated; and have lost, or had reduced, those features and organs which, now, when favorable conditions are supplied, reappear.

CHAPTER III.

THE VARIATIONS, OR IMPROVEMENTS, IN EACH SPECIES, LIM-
ITED IN NUMBER AND KIND TO THE NUMBER AND KIND
OF THE CHARACTERS PREVIOUSLY LOST BY SUCH SPECIES,
UNDER NATURE: OR, THE LAW OF REVERSION.

There is no principle, or law, in the whole domain of
Natural History, which Darwin so conclusively establishes, and which is attested by such a multitude of
proofs, as what is known as the law of positive Reversion; or, the principle that each species, under nature,
has suffered greatly from the effects of the Struggle for
Existence, and has lost many characters, features or
organs; and that when, as under domestication, the
conditions of the individuals' environment are propitious, those lost characters, features, and organs reappear.

This law militates against the hypothesis of Darwinism, in two ways, First, a converse theory is
deducible therefrom, which explains all of the phenomena, and so apportions the facts among Darwin's
scientific factors, as to preclude the necessity of referring
any of them to such confessedly objectionable entities
as an "innate tendency," "a spontaneous variability,"
"a law of nature," "vital force," "nature and constitution of the being," etc. Second, this law conclusively
negatives Darwin's gratuitous assumption, that varia-

(48)

tions, or improvements, may go on forever, or indefi-
·nitely; and shows that there exists a limit, within each
species, to the amount of improvement of which its
individuals are susceptible.

Darwin, in treating of this law of reversion, ascribes
to it the appearance of nearly every improvement under
domestication. Almost every character, and organ,
which has been developed, under man's care, and
· those which have arisen induced only by the presence
of favorable conditions of growth, he says, were once
in some period past, in a perfect state, and fully developed in some remote ancestor; that, owing to adverse
conditions, under nature, those characters and organs
had become either wholly lost, or partially reduced;
that those characters and organs lay latent, during the
long interval, ready ever to be evolved again, whenever
the favorable conditions, essential to their growth, were
restored; and that their reappearance, under domestication, is due to this capacity of reversion, which resides
in every individual whose structure has been impaired.
Almost every feature, which has appeared under domestication, he, in detail, ascribes to the mere reappearance
of some character, once lost by an ancient progenitor.
So widespread, he asserts, has been the degeneration
under nature, that there exists scarcely a single species
which has not lost some organs or features. He asserts
that characters which have been lost, may lie in the
organisms, either in a rudimentary state, or with not a
trace of them discernible; and do so lie, for thousands
and millions of generations, with their power of reversion, or of re-development, undiminished; that, when

5*

the individuals of any species, so deprived of some of its characters, are placed under domestication, or under other propitious surroundings, these characters not only may, but do reappear, and resume in a greater or lesser degree, the perfectly developed condition in which they were, originally. He actually shows, whilst affecting profound ignorance of the cause of variation, that the features and organs which were lost by each species under nature, are more than sufficient, in both number and kind, to account for all of the improvements which appear in such species under domestication, or which may appear under nature.

Any doubts, which may arise, in the reader's mind, as to whether Darwin has been truly represented in this connection, will assuredly be dissipated by the following copious and telling extracts, from Darwin's "*Origin of Species*," and from his "*Animals and Plants Under Domestication*."

With respect to past degeneration, or the loss of characters, and to present Reversion, or the regain of such lost characters, Darwin says (p. 126, *Origin of Species*):

"Characters reappear after having been lost for many generations."

"Organs in a rudimentary condition, plainly show that an early progenitor had the organ, in a fully developed state; and this, in some instances, implies an enormous amount of modification in the descendants" (p. 572, *Origin of Species*).

"With species, under a state of nature, rudimentary organs are so extremely common, that scarcely one species can be mentioned which is wholly free from a blemish of this nature" (p. 381, Vol. ii, *Animals and Plants, &c.*).

Why should there be any mystery about the cause of variations, or improvements? In the second extract above, he asserts that these rudimentary organs plainly show, that an early progenitor had the organs in a fully developed state. In the last quotation, he says - that, of species in a state of nature, there is scarcely one which has not these suppressed organs. Will not these assertions of his, cover and explain every favorable or positive variation which has arisen, or which may arise, under domestication, or under nature? When the animal or plant is placed under domestication, it improves solely by reason of the re-development of reduced, or suppressed organs. According to Darwin's own showing, each species is imperfect when taken from a state of nature; and, therefore, it is, that it possesses a certain margin for improvement. Within this margin, Man's care and selection are operative. No greater complexity of structure is ever acquired by an individual under domestication, than that which its species once lost. If any great variation, or change, has taken place under nature, this assertion of Darwin, viz., of the imperfection of each species, shows that such variation, or such change, has not, as he contends, been in the direction of increase of development; but, rather, in the direction of decrease, of degeneration, of devolution, instead of evolution. Indeed, the very conditions, under which he represents his Natural Selection as operating, imply degeneration, rather than any

advance in development. The loss of characters, under
nature, explains the appearance of characters under
domestication. The reduction of characters under
nature, explains the improvement of characters under
domestication. When the characters, lost under nature,
are regained under domestication, Darwin absurdly
argues that, because a certain number of characters
have appeared within a certain time, he need only
multiply such number of characters, by any given
time, to ascertain the number which is possible to
be acquired: Whereas, the fact is, the number of
characters possible to be acquired, within any species,
is not dependent upon any estimate of time, or of selection, but upon the number of the characters which
have been lost by such species.

Continuing his remarks, respecting these rudimentary organs, he says:

"Such organs are generally variable, as several nat-
uralists have observed; for being useless, they are not
regulated by Natural Selection; and they are more or
less liable to reversion. The same rule certainly holds
good with parts which have become rudimentary under
domestication. We do not know through what steps
under nature, rudimentary organs have passed in being
reduced to their present condition; but we so incessantly see, in species of the same group, the finest
gradations between an organ, in a rudimentary and (in
a) perfect state, that we are led to believe that the passage must have been extremely gradual. It may be
doubted whether a change of structure, so abrupt as
the sudden loss of an organ, would ever be of service
to a species in a state of nature; for, the conditions to
which all organisms are closely adapted, usually change

very slowly. Even if an organ did suddenly disappear in some one individual, by an arrest of development, intercrossing with other individuals of the same species, would cause it to reappear in a more or less perfect manner, so that its final reduction could only be effected by the slow process of continued disuse or natural selection. It is much more probable that, from changed habits. of life, organs first become of less and less use, and ultimately superfluous; or their place may be supplied by some other organ; and then disuse, acting on the offspring through inheritance at corresponding periods of life, would go on reducing the organ; but as most organs could be of no use at an early embryonic period, they would not be affected by disuse; consequently, they would be preserved at this stage of growth, and would remain as rudiments."

Again on page 353, Vol. ii, *Animals and Plants*, &c., he says:

"With domesticated animals, the reduction of a part, from disuse, is never carried so far that a mere rudiment is left; but we have good reason to believe that this has often occurred under nature. * * * Structures which are rudimentary in the parent-species, become partially re-developed in their domesticated progeny. * * * They are of interest, as showing that rudiments are the relics of organs once perfectly developed."

"With Plants, the position of the flowers on the axis, and of the seed in the capsules, sometimes leads, through a freer flow of sap, to changes of structure; but these changes are often due to reversion."

" Domesticated races, descended from the same species, are liable to revert to characters derived from their common progenitor."

" Every one would wish to explain to himself, even

in an imperfect manner, how it is possible for a character possessed by some remote ancestor, to reappear in
the offspring." (P. 428, Vol. ii, *Animals and Plants, &c.*)

"I have stated that the most probable hypothesis to
account for the reappearance of very ancient characters, is, that there is a tendency in the young of each
successive generation, to produce the long-lost characters; and that this tendency, from some unknown cause,
sometimes prevails."

"It would be difficult to name one of the higher
animals, in which some organ is not in a rudimentary
condition." (P. 353, *Origin of Species.*)

By this, of course, he means " an organ which has
been perfectly developed in some remote ancestor,"
and subsequently suppressed. When, however, he is
treating of variations which are due to the reappearance of these characters, under domestication, all rec-
ollection of what he here alleges, seems to forsake
him; and he professes himself unable to account for
them. He says, unqualifiedly, without distinction,
that he is ignorant of the cause of the appearance of
variations. As, in his search for the law of variations,
he conveniently forgets these reduced and suppressed
organs, and is so strangely obtuse to the fact, that they
amply supply the cause for which he affects to seek,
there exist, to his seeming, no objection to his settling
down to the conviction, that variations are inexplicable;
and no reason why he should not assume, that these
variations or improvements go on multiplying, indefinitely, or forever. If, however, the variations are to be
explained by the reappearance of long lost characters
of the respective species, it is obvious that there must

be a limit to them. But, strangely enough, the deterioration of each species under nature, and the capacity of each species to regain what it has lost, slip Darwin's memory, in connection with the question of the cause of variations; and, therefore, there exists, for him, no assignable limit to the improvement of animals and plants. He treats of variations under domestication, as if they were clear gain to the species, to which the varying individuals belong, and proceeds to estimate thereupon a ratio of increase of development : Whereas, as he himself shows, variations are but the re-acquisition of what had been lost. Again : Is it not much more scientific, to ascribe variations to a known, scientific factor, such as is Reversion, than to ascribe them to an " innate tendency," or to " profound ignorance" ?

Again he remarks (p. 51, Vol. ii, *Animals and Plants, &c.*):

" From what we see of the power and scope of reversion, both in pure races, and when varieties or species are crossed, we may infer that characters of almost every kind are capable of reappearing, after having been lost for a great length of time."

He might also have remarked : " From what we see of the power and scope of reversion, both in pure races, and when varieties are crossed, we may infer that characters of every kind," which appear under domestication, and positive variations of every kind, which may appear under nature, are not due to any " innate tendency;" but that they may be referred to this well-known scientific factor, Reversion.

On page 382, Vol. ii, *Animals and Plants, &c.*, he says :

"Organs which are naturally rudimentary, in the parent species, become partially re-developed in the domesticated descendants. Thus, cows, like most other ruminants, properly have four active, and two rudimentary mammæ; but, in our domesticated animals, the latter occasionally become considerably developed, and yield milk. * * * The hind feet of dogs include rudiments of a fifth toe, and in certain large breeds, these toes, though still rudimentary, become considerably developed and are furnished with claws. In the common hen, the spurs and comb are rudimentary, but in certain breeds, these become, independently of age, or disease of the ovaria, well developed. The stallion has canine teeth, but the mare has only traces of the alveoli, which, as I am informed by the eminent veterinary, Mr. G. T. Brown, frequently contain minute, irregular nodules of bone. These nodules, however, sometimes become developed into imperfect teeth, protruding through the gums, and coated with enamel; and, occasionally, they grow to a third, or even a fourth, of the length of the canines in the stallion. With Plants, I do not know whether the re-development of rudimentary organs, occurs more frequently under culture, than under nature."

On page 177, *Origin of Species*, he says :

"Rudimentary parts, it has been stated by some authors, and I believe with truth, are apt to be highly variable. * * * Rudimentary parts are left " (*i. e.* subject) "to the tendency to reversion."

On page 380, *Animals and Plants, &c.*, he says :

"With cultivated plants, it is far from rare to find the petals, stamens, and pistils represented by rudiments, like those observed in natural species. So it is with the whole seed in many fruits; thus near Astrakhan there is a grape with mere traces of seeds, 'so small and lying so near the stalk that they are not perceived in eating the grape.' In certain varieties of the gourd, the tendrils, according to Naudin, are represented by the rudiments, or by various monstrous growths. In the broccoli and cauliflower, the greater number of the flowers are incapable of expansion, and include rudimentary organs. In the Feather hyacinth (Muscari *comosum*) the upper and central flowers are brightly colored, but rudimentary ; under cultivation, the tendency to abortion, travels downwards and outwards, and all the flowers become rudimentary ; but the abortive stamens and pistils are not so small in the lower, as in the upper flowers. In the *Viburnum opulus* on the other hand, the outer flowers naturally have their organs of fructification in a rudimentary state, and the corolla is of large size ; under cultivation, the change spreads to the centre, and all the flowers become rudimentary ; thus, the well-known Snow-ball bush is produced. * * * In these several cases we have a natural tendency (!) in certain parts, to become rudimentary, and this under culture spreads either to, or from, the axis of the plant."

Would it not be manifestly fallacious, if, when these rudimentary parts became re-developed (which Darwin asserts they are ever competent so to become) any one were to take such re-growth, and use it as the basis of a calculation of indefinite, or unlimited growth ? If a person had cut his little finger, and then, observing the reparative power displayed, had estimated, from the degree of repair which had occurred, within a week, that, in a year's time, the finger would attain to the thickness of his thumb, he would not commit an ab-

6

surdity any greater than that, of which Darwin is
guilty, when he takes variations which are but the
mere regain of what the given species once lost, and
concludes, from the amount of such improvements,
that such species may develop into another species,
higher in the scale of development.

Again, he says (p. 383, Vol. ii, *Animals and Plants,
&c.*):

"Finally, though organs which must be classed as
rudimentary, frequently occur in our domesticated animals and cultivated plants, these have generally been
formed suddenly, through an arrest of development.
They usually differ, in appearance, from the rudiments
which so frequently characterize natural species. In
the latter, rudimentary organs have been slowly formed
through continued disuse, acting, by inheritance, at a
corresponding age, aided by the principle of the economy of growth, all under the control of natural selection. With domesticated animals, on the other hand,
the principle of economy is far from coming into action,
and their organs, although often slightly reduced by
disuse, are not thus almost obliterated, with mere rudiments left."

Under the heading, "Rudimentary, Atrophied, and
Aborted Organs," he says (p. 533, *Origin of Species*):

"Organs, or parts, in this strange condition, bear-
ing the stamp of inutility, are extremely common,
throughout nature. * * I presume that the 'bas-
tard wing,' in birds, may be safely considered as a
digit in a rudimentary state; in very many snakes,
there are rudiments of the pelvis and hind limbs.
Some of the cases of rudimentary organs are very
curious; for instance, the presence of teeth in fœtal
whales which, when grown up, have not a tooth in

their heads; and the presence of teeth, which never cut through the gums, in the upper jaws of our unborn calves. It has even been stated, on good authority, that rudiments of teeth can be detected in the beaks of certain embryonic birds. Nothing can be plainer than that wings are formed for flight; yet in how many insects do we see wings so reduced in size as to be utterly incapable of flight, and not rarely lying under wing-cases, firmly soldered together! The meaning of rudimentary organs is often quite unmistakable; for instance, there are beetles of the same genus (and even of the same species) resembling each other most closely in all respects, one of which will have full-sized wings, and another mere rudiments of membrane; and here it is impossible to doubt that the rudiments represent wings. * * * In plants of the same species, the petals sometimes occur as mere rudiments, and sometimes, in a well-developed state. In some plants with their sexes separated, the male flowers include a rudiment of a pistil."

When these animals and plants are placed under domestication, or cultivated, the rudimentary organs which "relate to a former condition," become re-developed; and then Darwin proceeds to calculate, thus for instance: If this beetle (say) has developed a pair of wings, within one year, is it not probable that, at the same rate of variation, it may develop into an eagle, in the course of the next million years?

" Rudimentary organs may be utterly aborted," * * with " no trace left " (p. 533, *Origin of Species*).

Darwin adduces variations, or improvements, under domestication, to prove how transitions from lower to higher specific forms may be made, and have been made; but, in the very exposition of his problem, he

shows that, in the past, there have been, in each species, many transitions from a previously higher form
to the lower, degenerate form now extant, under nature ; and, that the improvements, which he adduces to
prove the transition of a species to higher forms, are
but the steps which the organism takes to retrieve its
lost ground, to regain its lost characters, to recover its
lost integrity.

In the consideration of the problem, the reader must
bear in mind, that, even according to Darwin's own
showing, any advance, or improvement, under nature,
is at the best problematical : Darwin urges only, that
it is not improbable that a variation such as those which
occur under domestication, should occur under nature,
" once in a thousand generations ;" whereas, on the
other hand, degeneration, in the past, under nature, is
well attested, unquestionable, and wide-spread, covering every species of animal and plant. So far from
there having been such advance, in development, as is
competent to the evolution of the different species,
there have not been, upon Darwin's own showing,
sufficient improvements or variations, to retrieve a
tithe of the deterioration which many species are
positively known to have suffered !

The above remarks, and quotations, refer principally to lost characters which have left some traces of
their past existence.   There are, however, many more
characters or organs, belonging to the different species,
which have been so entirely suppressed, that not a vestige of them is discernible, before they commence to
reappear.   The prototype of each species, was an

organism of a higher state of development than the type of such species, as now found under nature. Adverse conditions entailed the suppression of the characters; and the mere restoration of the favorable conditions, secures their re-development.

The races of each species, under nature, were formed, exclusively, by the varied modification of the one, original, perfect mould of such species. These races are, all, but various degenerations of the one specific type of the given species. By this, it is not meant to imply any "innate tendency" (such as Darwin postulates) in organisms, to degenerate. Certain conditions were needed for the full and proportionate development of the characters of each species. The withdrawal of some of those conditions, entailed the reduction and suppression of some of the characters—of those characters to which those conditions were immediately correlated. While the conditions remained favorable, the species held its own; when the conditions changed —when the state of affairs ensued, which Darwin represents in his Struggle for Existence—loss of characters, and loss of size resulted. As these adverse conditions varied in degree, and in kind, in different districts and countries, the degree and the manner in which the individuals became modified, were also different. The structure of each race, became slightly different from that of the other races of the same species; because the conditions, in one country, wrought a deleterious effect on one organ or character, and the conditions, in the other countries, wrought injury upon other parts of the organization.

6*

Starting out, therefore, with these degenerate individuals of a species, Darwin essays to prove that their development may proceed *ad infinitum*—and the evidence, he adduces to countenance such an hypothesis, is that, when placed under favorable conditions, those individuals regain the characters which they once lost! The true, and only, induction from his facts, is, that there are no positive characters which appear, which are not due to the principle of reversion. The reader should bear in mind, that the problem is, not how species with all their characters, have been evolved; but, how have been evolved those slight increments of development, which constitute the data of all the prevailing theories of Evolution—those positive variations, or improvements, which arise under domestication, and (perhaps) under nature. The problem, How species have been evolved, is the point to which Darwin addresses himself. But, in the solution of that problem, he has availed himself of these variations, and he professes, that these variations solve the question. If, however, these variations be due to reversion —if they be but the regain of what was once lost— (which he furnishes such ample warrant for believing) then is he mistaken in his belief, that they explain the evolution of species. Therefore it is, that the problem of the evolution of species, gives place, in this controversy, to the problem of the cause of variations; and, to the question whether there be a limit to the improvements of which any species is shown to be capable. If each species is capable of that amount, only, of growth or development, of which it was possessed, at some time in the past; then, there is an end to Darwin's hypothesis, which is tenable, only upon the supposition, that the progress displayed by such species is new growth (*i. e.*, new to the given species) or new development; and upon the supposition that there is no limit to such progress, or variation.

Respecting the degeneration, which has taken place in the past under nature, and the capacity, ever resident in the deteriorated individuals, to recover what they lost, Darwin says (p. 188, *Origin of Species*) :

"No doubt it is a very surprising fact, that characters should reappear, after having been lost for many, perhaps, for hundreds, of generations. * * * In a breed which has not been crossed, but in which both parents have lost some characters which their progenitor possessed, the tendency, whether strong or weak, to reproduce the lost characters, might be, as was formerly remarked, for all that we can see to the contrary, transmitted for almost any number of generations. When a character, which has been lost in a breed, reappears, after a great number of generations, the most probable hypothesis is, not that the offspring suddenly takes after an ancestor some hundreds of generations distant, but that, in each successive generation, there has been a tendency to reproduce the character in question, which, at last, under unknown favorable conditions, gains an ascendancy."

This power of reversion, as he says, is ever operative, and is only kept down by adverse conditions. Each individual of a species would, were the conditions propitious, develop all the positive characters, known to any individual of its species.

Continuing, he says:

"I can see no more abstract improbability in a tendency to produce any character, being inherited for an endless (!) number of generations, than in quite useless and rudimentary organs, being as we all know them to be, thus inherited. Indeed, we may sometimes observe that a mere tendency to produce a rudiment, is inherited."

Again, on p. 27, *Origin of Species*, he says:

"When there has been no cross with a distinct breed, and there is a tendency in both parents to revert to a character which has been lost, during some former generation, this tendency, for all that we can see to the contrary, may be transmitted, undiminished, for an indefinite number of generations."

On page 446, Vol. ii, *Animals and Plants, &c.*, he says:

"What can be more wonderful, than that characters which have disappeared during scores, or hundreds, or even thousands (!) of generations, should suddenly reappear, perfectly developed, as in the case of pigeons and fowls."

The characters lost, do not, in any wise, lie within the organisms, during the interval before their reappearance. The forces of the organization are, when all the characters are fully and proportionately developed, beautifully correlated together, making one, determinate coördination. When a character is lost, the forces so correlated, are capable of reintegrating the lost part, and of restoring the mutual relations of the parts; if the conditions will allow. Cut off the edge of a crystal; the crystal may remain, so impaired, for a hundred or a thousand years, and when placed in a solution, like that in which it was originally formed, it will restore the lost edge.   No one will say, that the lost edge remained in embryo, or in any way, within the crystal, during that period.   It was the correlation of the forces of the crystal, which conspired to effect the reintegration which was so necessary to the normal coördination of the whole.   So is it with organic reversion.   The capacity for reintegrating is, generally to the full as efficient, after a thousand generations, as it would be after the lapse of a day, or of an hour. All of the improvements, effected by breeders, fanciers, horticulturists, and agriculturists, are but reintegrations, partial or complete, of the animals and plants.

"This principle of Reversion is the most wonderful of all the attributes of Inheritance.   *   *   *   Reversion is not a rare event, depending on some unusual or favorable combination of circumstances, but occurs so regularly, with crossed animals and plants, and so frequently, with uncrossed breeds, that it is evidently an essential part of the principle of inheritance.   We know that changed conditions have the power of evoking long-lost characters, as in the case of some feral animals.   The act of crossing in itself possesses this power in a high degree."

The reason, that "changed conditions have the power of evoking long-lost characters," is because, upon a change, those conditions are restored to the individual, the absence of which entailed the loss of those characters.   Crossing "possesses the power in a high degree," because the union, in the offspring, of the two peculiarities, derived respectively from the two parent breeds, so strengthens the correlation of the forces of the organism, as to enable it, the more, to repair its lost integrity.

Continuing, he says:

" Many monstrosities come under this same head, as when rudimentary organs are re-developed, or when an organ which we must believe was possessed by an early progenitor, but of which not even a rudiment was left, suddenly reappears, as with the fifth stamen in some Scrophulariacæ. We have already seen that reversion acts in bud-reproduction; and we know that it occasionally acts during the growth of the same individual animal, especially, but not exclusively, when of crossed parentage—as in the rare cases described of individual fowls, pigeons, cattle and rabbits."

" We are led to believe, as formerly explained, that every character which occasionally reappears, is present in a latent form in each generation. * * * In every (!) living creature, we may feel assured that a host of lost characters lie ready to be evolved under proper conditions. How can we make intelligible, and connect with other facts, this wonderful and common capacity of Reversion—this power of calling back to life long-lost characters !"

" Long-lost characters," break out in mystic refrain, upon almost every page of his works. Why he does not see, that these " long-lost characters " are attuned most harmoniously to the improvements which arise, is a psychological phenomenon which it behooves us not here to explain. Yet, we cannot help suspecting, and cannot refrain from delicately intimating, that either a dim, or a well-defined consciousness, on his part, that the discovery of the harmony of these "long-lost characters," with the variations which he, in his ignorance, attributes to spontaneous variability, would sound the knell of Darwinism; alone prevented him from disclosing the part these "long-lost characters" play, in the grand diapason of Biology. In a future chapter, it will be shown, that each organism is as a sweet bell, jangled and out of tune, if these "long-lost characters" fail to join in that symphony of correlation which, when perfect, alone may make the coördination which is consistent with physiological integrity.

On page 14, Vol. i, *Animals and Plants*, *&c.*, he says:

" By thus adding up variations, he (man) has effected wonderful changes and improvements."

This sum of variations, or improvements, avails his argument just nothing; for, he shows, that the only scientific view is, that this sum of improvements effected, is but the sum, or part of the sum, of characters once lost by the varying species. To show that a species has been divested, by unfavorable conditions, of a number of characters; and then, when·the individuals of that species regain those characters, to proceed to estimate a ratio of indefinitely continued development, is obviously absurd.

On page 54, Vol. ii, *Animals and Plants*, *&c.*, he says, under the heading, " Crossing as a Direct Cause of Reversion ":

" It has long been notorious, that hybrids and mongrels often revert to both or to one of their parent forms, after an interval of from two to seven or eight generations, or, according to some authorities, even a

greater number of generations. But, that the act of
crossing, in itself, gives an impulse towards Reversion,
as shown by the reappearance of long-lost (!) characters, has never, I believe, been hitherto proved. The
proof lies in certain peculiarities which do not characterize the immediate parents, and therefore cannot have
been derived from them, frequently appearing in the
offspring of two breeds when crossed, which peculiarities never appear, or appear with extreme rarity, in
these same breeds, as long as they are precluded from
crossing."

This remark, of his, attests strongly, that he has
settled in his own mind, that all the improvements
which arise, are due to Reversion. He says, "The
proof lies in" the appearance of "certain peculiarities
which do not characterize the immediate parents and
therefore cannot have been derived from them." It
will be observed, that this circumstance, viz., of the
characters not having been derived from the immediate parents, he makes the sole criterion of their being
due to Reversion. The rest of his sentence, has relation to his proof, that crossing gives an impulse to
this Reversion. That is the true law, namely that positive characters, which are not derived from the immediate parents, are due to Reversion. Had he, however,
formulated this rule in set terms, it would have provoked an immediate response to his gratuitous assumption, that there is no limit to variations. This,
his assumption, of no limit to improvements, is the
witching point in the whole controversy. Yet, strange
to say, such assumption is not formulated even once,
but remains a tacit assumption merely, throughout all

his works! To all seeming, he thought it discreet to advance that point in his theory, by implication solely. If he had explicitly stated, that all the characters which arise in each individual, and which did not characterize that individual's immediate parents, are long-lost characters reappearing by Reversion, the fallacy of his theory would immediately have become glaring. For, if each and every variation, or improvement, is but the regain of what was once lost, it is, then, an unavoidable corollary, that variation has a limit, which will be reached in each individual, when all of its lost characters are regained. All of the improvements, which were assumed to be increments of evolution, obeying those mysterious laws, "innate tendency," and "spontaneous variability," are then, manifestly, to be relegated to that known, well-established, scientific factor, Reversion.

Continuing his remarks, respecting the reappearance of long-lost characters, which is occasioned by Crossing, he says, "As this conclusion seems to me highly curious and novel, I will give the evidence in detail." He then gives numerous instances with the pigeon, with the fowl, with the duck, with the rabbit, with the cow, with the horse, and with the ass; and says:

"It would appear, that, with crossed animals, a similar tendency to the recovery of lost characters, holds good with instincts;"

And gives instances, in the case of the fowl, of cattle, of the pig, of the duck, of the horse, and of the ass. Everything is "highly curious," with him, as it must be, with every scientist, who essays to colligate

7

facts, with a theory based upon an assumption which is not only wholly gratuitous, but in wanton deroga- tion of a competent, known, and well-established, scien- tific factor. The phenomenon of the recovery of long- lost characters, by means of crossing, is shown, in a future chapter of this work, to be perfectly explicable.

"In many cases," says he (p. 105, Vol. ii, *Animals and Plants, &c.*), "the failure of the parents to trans- mit their likeness, is due to the breed having been at some former period crossed; and the child takes after his grandparent, or more remote ancestor, of foreign blood. In other cases, in which the breed has not been crossed, but some ancient character has been lost through variation, it occasionally reappears through Reversion, so that the parents apparently fail to trans- mit their own likeness. In all cases, however, we may safely conclude that the child inherits all its characters from its parents, in whom certain characters are latent. * * * When, after a long succession of bud gen- erations, a flower or fruit becomes separated into dis- tinct segments, having the colors or other attributes of both parent forms, we cannot doubt that these charac- ters were latent in the earlier buds, though they could not then be detected, or could be detected only in an intimately commingled state. So it is with animals of crossed parentage, which, with advancing years, occa- sionally exhibit characters, derived from one of their two parents, of which not a trace could at first be per- ceived."

Again he says, on the same page with the above remarks :

"It is assuredly an astonishing fact, that the male and female sexual elements, that buds, and even full- grown animals, should retain characters, during several generations, in the case of crossed breeds, and during thousands of generations, in the case of pure breeds, written as it were in invisible ink, yet ready, at any time, to be evolved under the requisite conditions."

" What these conditions are, we do not in many cases at all know. But, the act of crossing, in itself, apparently from causing some disturbance in the organization, certainly gives a strong tendency to the reappearance of long-lost characters, both corporeal and mental, independently of those derived from the cross."

The purpose in quoting this, and other remarks of Darwin, upon the subject of long-lost characters, is, to show the wide-spread operation of Reversion, and its competency to cover all the variations adduced by Darwin. Having thus furnished full warrant for the assumption of Reversion as the sole cause of all positive variations, or improvements, we shall also enlighten him as to what those mysterious conditions are, of which he speaks, and as to what that curious " some disturbance in the organization," is.

On page 113, Vol. ii, *Animals and Plants*, *&c.*, he says :

" But in all cases " (of crossing different breeds) "there will be, during many subsequent generations, more or less liability to reversion. * * * In considering the final result of the commingling of two or more breeds, we must not forget that the act of crossing in itself tends to bring back long-lost characters, not proper to the immediate parent-forms."

Again, on page 212, Vol. ii, *Animals and Plants*, *&c.*, he speaks of

" The excessive variability of the crossed offspring due to the principle of reversion."

On page 319, Vol. ii, *Animals and Plants, &c.*, it is amusing to remark, with what an air of judicial impartiality, he insinuates, that there are characters independent of reversion.

* * * "It is probable," says he, "that the crossing of two forms, when one or both have long been domesticated or cultivated, adds to the variability of the offspring, independently of the commingling of the characters derived from the two parent forms, and this implies that new characters actually arise."

The implication is, merely, that they are new to either of the crossed *breeds;* and upon this construction, Darwin is right. It is evident, too, that this is the idea he had in his mind. But, the idea he evidently desires to convey, under the shadow of the double meaning of which his words are susceptible, is that they are new to the given *species;* an idea, which he is ever intent upon insinuating, and an idea which is absolutely essential to the support of his theory. Mark the tone of the following sentence—a tone which is ingeniously calculated to convey to the readers' minds, the conviction that they may place implicit confidence in him, and count most securely upon his duly qualifying his remarks, and upon his not overstating the strength of the evidence he adduces.

Continuing :

" But we must not forget the facts advanced in the thirteenth chapter, which clearly prove that the act of crossing often leads to the reappearance or reversion of long-lost characters ; and in most cases, it would be impossible to distinguish between the reappearance of ancient characters, and the first appearance of new characters."

This, again, may mean characters new to either of the crossed *breeds*, or characters new to the *species*. It is, obviously, to the interest of Darwin's theory, that the latter idea be accepted by the reader. If it be so "impossible to distinguish between the reappearance of ancient characters, and the first appearance of new characters," why, in any case, refer them to an "innate tendency," or to "profound ignorance," in derogation of the known, scientific law, Reversion, to which no possible objection can be taken? Assume, as there is so much ground for doing, that all the variations, arising in each species, are but the regain of what that species once lost, and "innate tendency," "vital force," "spontaneous variability," and all the other "metaphysical entities," which clog the path of inquiry, and attest the poverty of scientific thought, may be wholly dispensed with.

Continuing his remarks with reference to the question whether the given characters are "ancient" or "new," he says:

"Practically, whether new or old, they would be new to the breed in which they reappeared."

Doubtless, they would; as a breed formed of the varying offspring of a cross, is, generally, a new breed.

Again he says (page 321, Vol. ii, *Animals and Plants, &c.*):

"We seldom have the means of distinguishing, as previously remarked, between the appearance of really

7*

new characters, and the reappearance of long-lost
characters evoked through the act of crossing."

Darwin in Chap. xxivth, of his *Animals and Plants,
&c.*, reviews all of the *conditions* of development, viz.,
food, exercise, climate, crossing, &c., which divers
authors have ignorantly regarded as the *causes* of
variability ; and he says (p. 303, Vol. ii):

"But we must, I think, take a broader view, and
conclude that organic beings, when subjected during
several generations to any change whatever in their
conditions, tend (!) to vary ; the kind of variation,
which ensues, depending in a far higher degree on the
nature or constitution (!) of the being, than on the
nature of the changed conditions."

On the preceding page, he says:

"The subject (*i. e.*, of "the causes of the almost
universal variability of our domesticated productions")
"is an obscure one ; but it may be useful to probe our
ignorance."

With him, the obscurity arises from this : That he
finds it "impossible" to distinguish between the reappearance of ancient characters, and the first appearance
of "new characters," because, the characters which
arise are *all* "ancient characters."

He says that variation may be accounted for,

"By the more or less complete recovery, through
reversion, of ancestral characters on either side ; but
we thus only push the difficulty further back in time,
for what made the parents, or their progenitors different?"

If the explanation by means of Reversion, only
pushes the difficulty further back in time, why does

he, then, adduce variations as the data for his theory?
He essayed to solve the problem of indefinitely continued development, by means of variations. Variations are then shown to be incapable of sustaining his
theory; because, being but the regain of what was
once lost, they have a limit; and proof of a limit to
the improvements, constitutes complete disproof of his
theory. But, with a coolness most unique, he rejoins,
To explain the variations by means of Reversion is
only pushing the difficulty further back; for, they
need to be explained, when they appeared for the first
time, and effected the development of the different
species; Whereas, this assumption, of his, viz., that
the characters did arise originally, as variations, and
did thereby effect the development of the different
species, is the very point in controversy, and which he
started out to prove.

What puzzles him, and so "obscures" the subject of
the cause of variations, is, that he feels logic prodding
him to know, Why, if reversion is "only pushing the
difficulty further back in time," he does. not meet the
issue at that point further back in time, and there grap-
ple with his problem; and, What business, or concern,
has he with the improvements or variations under domestication, or with those variations, under nature,
which occur at a period subsequent to the great degeneration he has shown, when, by his own confession, the
issue does not hinge where he essays to meet it, but
rests at a point, in the past, respecting which, not a
syllable of evidence, or even a word of mention, is
adduced by him throughout all of his works.

A fair analogue of Darwin's argument, is this : An individual lays claim to a piece of real estate, of which another has long been, and is, in adverse possession. The evidence adduced by the plaintiff to sustain such claim is—the plaintiff's satisfaction of what purported to be a mortgage upon the property, given by the plaintiff; and to the objection, naturally raised, that such evidence is no proof of any acquirement of title, by the plaintiff, to the property, the insensate retort comes, That is "merely pushing the difficulty further back in time." True, true "as proof of Holy Writ;" but make your testimony competent and relevant, by adducing evidence which has some relation to that difficulty further back in time :—would obviously be the response of the defendant.

So, to Darwin it may be said : If Reversion accounts for the improvements under domestication, and for those which are assumed occasionally to appear under nature, and such explanation but pushes the difficulty further back in time, why not adduce, instead, evidence and arguments which meet that difficulty further back in time ?

A true conception of the relation in which Darwin's theory of evolution, stands to the law of Reversion, may be gained, if the reader does but fancy Darwin standing by a canal-lock, immediately subsequent to the passage of a boat, from the river above, to the channel below. He turns to the lock-master, and assures him, that he can explain to him clearly, how the river was originally formed:—If you will notice the action of the water within this lock, you will observe, that the water is rising slowly, by a succession of apparently spontaneous impulses. Since I have been standing here, the water has arisen some four or five feet. Now, it is clear, that this water may arise to any height, if it be confined above, by a wall, as it is below. It is manifestly gratuitous, for any one to assume a limit to the ascension of this water. It has been ascending, during the whole time I have been standing here, and the presumption is, in default of proof to the contrary, that it ever will continue so to rise. · Now, the formation of the whole river, may be clearly demonstrated by analogy with this lock. It is fair to assume that, in the river, also, there exist, and have ever existed, spontaneous impulses of water, similar to what we here observe. Given, then, those ascending, spontaneous impulses, the formation, in the past, of this river, becomes clear.

To the response of the lock-master, that Darwin evidently does not understand the reason, or the cause, why the water so ascends in the lock, he rejoins, that there is the fact—that suffices for him—and that an inquiry into efficient causes is metaphysical. The lock-master explains, that the water has previously fallen below the level of the river above, that it is now returning to that level, and that his theory of the unlimited ascent of the water, is all wrong, for the limit will be reached when the water reaches the plane of the river above.

Darwin recognizes the truth of such explanation, but declares that that is but pushing the difficulty farther back in time; for, how account for these origi-

nal, spontaneous impulses, when they first arose, and
formed the river!

The lock-master declares, that these spontaneous impulses never did form the river, but that Darwin himself started to prove that very point; and now, instead
of proving it, he assumes it to obviate a fatal objection
to that very idea.   He also shows him that he cannot
prove the origin of the river by means of the spontaneous impulses in the lock, for they are due to the action
of a river already formed.   Darwin, however, is proof
against all objections, and departs to assure his friend
Tyndall that his theory, about "giving the religious sen-
timents of mankind, reasonable satisfaction," is altogether Utopian.

So, in his theory of development, he assumes his
very conclusion—viz., that variations formed the different species—to ward off the objection, namely, that
variations did not constitute the process of development, because they are but the regain of developments
lost.

As all of the individuals of a species have, generally, lost the same characters, and all have the same
capacity for regaining such characters, it is to be expected, that the individuals of the several varieties of
such species, will not confine themselves to the development of the peculiarities which man has assigned
them, but will display their power of reversion in characters, of their species, other than those which mark
their respective varieties.   The fact, also, that similar
varieties are produced in different countries, from individuals of the same species, attests strongly, that the

improvements or variations which arise, are due to reversion. Darwin has noted this disposition, on the part of individuals of a species, to develop all of the characters of the given species, and refers it, as he should, to the fact of these characters having once been lost, and to the capacity, in each of the individuals, to regain such characters. As if fearful, that the significance of the phenomenon, should thrust itself upon the reader's attention, to the prejudice of his hypothesis of development without a limit, he assures his readers, that he is " concerned not as hitherto with the *causes* of variation, but with the *results*." He concerns himself about the causes of variation, only when he is engaged upon an enumeration of the conditions of variation (such as food, and climate, and exercise, &c.) which he is able to demonstrate, can furnish no adequate explanation of the appearance of the improvements. When, however, he trenches upon a well-known, scientific law, such as is reversion, he hastens to add, that all discussion upon causes, has been closed!

On page 417, Vol. ii, *Animals and Plants, &c.*, under the heading, "Analogous or Parallel Variation," he says:

"By this term I wish to express that similar characters occasionally make their appearance in the several varieties or races descended from the same species. * * * We are here concerned, not as hitherto with the causes of variation, but with the results; but this discussion could not have been more conveniently introduced elsewhere."

All of the individuals, of a species, are lacking in

characters which their ancient progenitors had; and, of course, each does not tamely submit to the development alone of that character to which the conditions at first gave the ascendant, and which man afterwards made very predominant, but strives ever to regain all of the characters which it lacks, or (as Darwin once happily puts it, when he approaches very near to the true law of development) "to bring all of the parts again into harmony with each other."

Darwin proceeds to arrange the "*results*" into classes:

"The cases of analogous variation, so far as their origin is concerned, may be grouped, disregarding minor sub-divisions, under two main heads; firstly, those due to unknown (*sic*) causes having acted on organic beings with nearly the same constitution, and which consequently vary in an analogous manner; and secondly, those due to the reappearance of characters which were possessed by a more or less remote progenitor."

When a scientist has a body of facts, and has, empirically, or provisionally, arranged them under two heads; one head consisting of facts presumably due to "unknown causes," and the other head comprehending facts acknowledging a known, scientific factor; he, when he is a fair, as well as able scientist, tests all of those facts, and when he finds that the known cause will cover all of the phenomena under either head, and that no possible exception may be taken to the competency of such factor, so to cover all, he relegates them all to one head—to the one known cause; and

dispenses with the services of the "unknown cause."
This is the *modus operandi* of an able scientist who
has not a pet theory, to which a recognition of the
competency of the known cause, to cover all of the
facts, threatens instant explosion.   This, however, is
not the mode of research of a scientist, who has a
theory of the character mentioned.   This is not, as is
manifest, the mode of Darwin.   All of the phenomena
of variation, are, as he concedes, with an unimportant
qualification, possible to be ranged under his second
head, viz., Reversion ; and there is not a single fact, to
be found in any of his works, or within the range of
physiology, ·which militates against such a course.
But, should he so arrange them, and dispense with his
" unknown causes," with his "innate tendency," etc., in
which he fancies he has at least a ghost of a chance of
salvation for his theory; where would be even his
flimsy semblance of support for the hypothesis of indefinitely continued development ?—of variation without any assignable limit ?   One, disposed to suspicion,
and to invidious comment, might doubtless assert, that
Darwin saw there was no earthly necessity for his class
of "unknown causes," and that, to preclude the immediate dissolution of his theory, into the thinnest of
air, with "infinite dexterity of wit," threw in the following remark, to occasion a bewildering doubt, in his
readers' minds, as to whether the problem of the cause
of variation, was so simple as it really is.   He says,
immediately subsequent to his elaboration of the two
heads mentioned,

    " But these two main divisions can often be only

8

conjecturally separated, and graduate, as we shall presently see, into each other."

Now, the only warrant he has for this assertion is, that some changes in an organism, and some varietal types are not due to Reversion. They are not due to Reversion, merely because they are negative changes, negative variations, or types which are formed by modifications of the original perfect type of the species to which they respectively belong. A cat or dog loses its ear : A pig is modified by the reduction, or the suppression of its tusks, its bristles, its tail, its legs, and its snout : These are the kinds of changes to which he appeals, to show that his unknown causes are operative. He fancies, or affects to believe, that the Fantail pigeon, for instance, cannot be due to Reversion, because the species from which it is known to have descended, has produced varieties with a well developed œsophagus, with length of body, with a long beak, with divergent feathers on the neck and breast, &c. But, it is not the *type* which has been regained by Reversion, but those positive characters, or features of development, which enter into such types. *The feature*, fan-tail, is due to reversion. All the positive features of the other varieties of the pigeon, are due to reversion ; the *types* of those varieties are not. There was but one type originally ; that type in which is contained all the positive developments of the given species ; and that type alone is perfect.

Sometimes, it is true, there is a reversion, by an organism, from a positive character, to a negative character. Thus a pig, once under cultivation, has been suffered to run wild; or little care has been taken of it. Its offspring are placed under cultivation, and they return to the condition in which their progenitor was; they have their legs, tusks, bristles, snout, &c., reduced. This is negative reversion, however. This is the dexterous way in which Darwin clouds the subject of the cause of the positive variations, which, as he essays to prove, were successively accumulated, and made to produce all positive developments. . This is the manner in which he redeems his promise of showing that his "two main divisions" of "unknown causes," and of a known cause, graduate into each other.

All of the *positive* variations; all the *positive* changes; all the *positive* improvements; all the *positive* increments of growth or of development; all the advances made by organisms from comparative simplicity to complexity of structure, which Darwin fain would accumulate, *ad infinitum;* are due to Reversion. If the conditions of the growth of a character, are taken away, the character becomes reduced, or suppressed. If Darwin desires to exalt adverse conditions, to the dignity of "unknown causes," and show that species may change one into another, by removes from complexity to simplicity of structure, he stultifies his theory of evolution, which predicates advance in development; but, we are prepared to meet even that issue, and do so meet it; for we show, in the chapters following, treating of crossing and of close interbreeding, that no individual is capable of any remove from complexity to simplicity of structure, and that no

character of any species is possible to be reduced ir
any way, or suppressed, without impairing the constitutional vigor and fertility of the organism; and that
such reduction or suppression of the characters of a
species, may progress to a very slight extent only,
without entailing complete sterility, and a general
breaking up of the whole constitution,—very soon
ending in death.

But, Darwin started to prove the evolution of species
from one another, by means of slight, successive advances in development, or variations. This issue we
meet, by conclusively showing, that the variations to
which he appeals, could not have produced the development in question, because they are amenable to a
limit, very soon reached; and, because every such in-
crement, or every such variation, which is of a positive character, is but the mere regain of a character
lost, by the species in which it occurs, by a process
of degeneration conclusively established by Darwin
himself. But, one-half of the time, Darwin seems to
have forgotten his predicate, and postulates, in the
stead thereof, degeneration. He, instead of showing
the evolution of species, seems rather to contend,
that all the different species have been produced by
degeneration,—that they are all various degenerations
of some higher type. Notably, in his work on the
"*Fertilization of Orchids*," which is a work ancillary
to his "*Origin of Species*," does he argue that the
different species are modifications of one higher type.
But, even the hypothesis of degeneration, is refuted
by the converse theory, propounded in this work. As

above mentioned, it is proven that an animal is not capable of modification in any of its characters, without proportional injury to its physiological integrity; and that a distinct species may not be produced by such a process of degeneration; for, sterility and death ensue, before half of the requisite amount of change, in structure, can be effected.

Speaking of the "similar characters," which "make their appearance in the several varieties or races descended from the same species," he says:

"These facts are important from showing, as remarked in a former chapter, that each trifling variation is governed by law, and is determined, in a much higher degree, by the nature of the organization, than by the nature of the conditions to which the varying being has been exposed."

Darwin confesses, that, of this "law," and of "the nature of the organization," he is wholly ignorant. As he says, "Our knowledge of the cause of variation is profound." For "law," and for "the nature of the organization," read, the power of reversion of characters once lost by the given species; and the above counters for ignorance may be eliminated from the problem.

Again he says (page 502, Vol. ii, *Animals and Plants, &c.*):

"Although every variation is either directly or indirectly caused by some change in the surrounding conditions, we must never forget that the nature of the organization which is acted on, essentially governs the result. Distinct organisms, when placed under similar
8*

conditions, vary in different manners, whilst closely allied organisms under dissimilar conditions, often vary in nearly the same manner. We see this in the same modification frequently reappearing at long intervals of time in the same variety, and likewise in the several striking cases given of analogous or parallel varieties. Although some of these latter cases are simply due to reversion, others cannot thus be accounted for."

The only reason he can advance, for urging that some positive variations "cannot thus be accounted for," is, that he does not know of any individuals of the species under nature, in which the characters which arise, are to be seen. It is clear that, if degeneration has been so rife under nature, then, this objection cannot obtain.

On page 307 (Vol. ii, *Animals and Plants, &c.*), he says:

"Bud-variation, which we fully discussed in a former chapter, shows us that variability may be quite independent of seminal reproduction, and likewise a reversion to long-lost ancestral characters."

In this former chapter, to which he alludes, he says (p. 449, Vol. i, *Animals and Plants, &c.*):

"Nor can we account, in all cases, for the appearance, through bud-variation, of new characters, by the principle of reversion to long-lost characters."

Darwin's inability to account, by reversion, for some of the variations, is due to his idea that varietal *types* d thus to be explained. It is not the *types*, which be explained by reversion; but those positive features which arise. That it is this idea (viz., that varietal types negative the hypothesis of reversion, because such types were never known in the past), which causes him to urge, that there are variations, not due to reversion, is shown in the following remarks of his (p. 488, Vol. i, *Animals and Plants, &c.*):

"Many cases of bud-variation, however, cannot be attributed to reversion, but to spontaneous variability (*sic*), such as so commonly occurs with cultivated plants, when raised from seed. As a single variety of the Chrysanthemum has produced by buds six other varieties, and as one variety of the gooseberry has borne, at the same time, four distinct varieties of fruit, it is scarcely possible to believe that all these variations are reversions to former parents."

The six varietal *types* of the Chrysanthemum, are not due to reversion. Nor are the types of the four varieties of the gooseberry. But the *positive features* which have arisen in the six varieties of the Chrysanthemum, are due to partial reversions to that original perfect type of the Chrysanthemum, which was the sum of all the positive characters of the species. By modifying this original type of the species, it might be possible to obtain a hundred varietal types. What complicates the problem somewhat, is, that these varieties are not the result of direct modifications of the original form. But, that original form has been reduced to the degenerated condition in which the plant is, under nature. Then, it is placed under cultivation; and, because it regains, in different ways, the characters it lost, different varieties or types are formed; and

when the idea of reversion is suggested, in connection
with any variety, the possibility of the type of such
variety, having previously existed, is entertained by
the mind, and rejected under a false conception of
the solution. So, also, the idea, of there having ex
isted in the past, as many types as there are varieties of
the given species, is rejected, and the hypothesis of re
version accordingly suffers. The fact is, that, for each
species, there originally existed a type (then realized
in the members of such species), which included
within it, all of the characters which it was ever pos
sible for any member of that species to develop. This
type, it is possible to modify in an infinity of ways
but, as is shown in future chapters of this work, each
such modified type, suffers physiological evil in pro
portion to the amount of modification it displays.

From the above quotation, it is made manifest to
the reader that, if Reversion cannot account for variation, the only alternative is "Spontaneous Variability!"
Well may Darwin say, "We are (he is) far too ignorant to speculate on the relative importance of the several known and unknown causes of variation." He
cannot lay a *foundation* for a theory of development
but he is an adept in the erection of a *superstructure !*

He says (p. 351, Vol. 2, *Animals and Plants, &c.*):

"To recur once again to bud-variation. When we
reflect on the millions of buds, which many trees have
produced, before some one bud varied, we are lost in
wonder what the precise cause of each variation can
be."

Then after speaking of the improvements which

have arisen in the peach, the plum, the rose, and the camellia, he says:

"When we reflect on these facts, we become deeply impressed with the conviction, that, in such cases, the nature of the variation depends but little on the conditions to which the plant has been exposed, and not in any especial manner on its individual character, but much more on the general nature or constitution, inherited from some remote progenitor, of the whole group of allied beings to which the plant belongs."

This shows that the variations are due to reversion. If they are due to reversion; then, his hypothesis of the community of origin of the species is refuted, because it was by means of these variations, and by means of the assumption, that these variations arose for the first time, that he sought to prove the community of origin of the species. Yet, here he *assumes* the community of origin of the species (which was the *conclusion* at which he professed to arrive by means of the accumulation of variations arising for the first time), to account, by past degeneration and present Reversion, for the appearance of these very variations! Leave out this assumption of the community of origin of the species,—which is the very conclusion which is in dispute(!),—and assume, that the degeneration which has confessedly taken place, has occurred within the limits only of each species; and assume, that the variations, arising in each species, are due to the mere regain of characters lost by such species; and all the phenomena of growth and development will round themselves into a perfect, scientific whole, rigidly exclusive of

all such metaphysical factors as "spontaneous variability," &c.

Darwin evidently sees that, if Reversion may lay
claim to all the variations which arise, his theory is at
an end. As has doubtless been observed, he strives to
show, that Reversion cannot account for "some characters." These "some characters" are the ones upon
which hangs his only hope of salvation for his theory.
One of the devices, to which he resorts, to confound
the problem of reversion, is to appeal to our ignorance
of such and such a character ever having been developed before. Deftly playing upon the prejudice
of the orthodox, to the effect that God made and
placed animals and plants in the existing state of
nature, and that therefore it is derogatory to Infinite
Power, that He should make any of them in an incomplete condition; he affects to deem it a sufficient
answer to the ascription of any variations to Reversion, to refer the reader to the given species as it exists
under nature, and to point to the absence, in it, of any
such character, as the one in question. When it serves
his purpose to refer variations solely to a "spontaneous variability," or to an "innate tendency," he plays
the card above indicated. When he endeavors to
show the great scope of reversion, he coolly contests
any such notion that animals or plants, under nature,
need necessarily, to be complete in structure. What
involves him in such a mesh of inconsistencies, is that
he is endeavoring to arrive at the conclusion, that
species had a common origin, by two different sets of
premises. By one of the two modes of reasoning, he

strives to show a community of origin of species, by showing that variations have arisen, and that such variations have been accumulated, and have evolved all the different species from 'one low, primordial organism. This course necessitates the assumption, that such variations arise for the first time. His other design is, to show a community of origin of the species, by showing that the species have been formed by degeneration; and that they are but the various modifications of some higher type than them all. This, on the other hand, requires him to maintain, that such variations as arise, were once fully developed in a type higher in the scale of development, than is the species in which the variations occur. Would it be believed, were not Darwin's works so easy of reference, that on the one side of his problem of the evolution of species, is arrayed a mass of positive evidence, which is well nigh appalling, showing degeneration to have been wide-spread, and to have invaded every known species; while, on the other hand, to offset this antithesis to evolution, is Darwin's mere assumption of an occasional variation occurring, under nature, "once in a thousand generations!" The *degeneration* of each species, under nature, is positive and incontestably attested; whereas, any *evolution* in any species, under nature, is wholly problematical. When such degeneration, in each species, under nature, is so well established, and when the capacity of each species to regain what it lost, is so fully conceded, is not the presumption an overpowering one, viz., that each and every positive variation, or improvement, occurring under domestication,

or under nature, is due to the regain of characters,
once lost, by the respective species?

Mark the alternative: If included under the head of
reversion, these variations confessedly obey a known,
scientific law.   If taken without the operation of that
law (as Darwin does, without warrant or excuse, and
only to save his theory from signal explosion) they
must be relegated to what? to "innate tendency," to
"spontaneous variability," to "nature and constitution
of the being that varies" and to "unknown causes,"
of all of which "our ignorance is profound."   The
theory of reversion does not rely solely upon this
overpowering presumption; nor upon its competency
to cover all the·facts; nor upon the absurdity of the
alternative explanation (!) of variations.   For, it is
shown, *aliunde*, that an ancient progenitor of each
species, had all the characters fully and proportionately developed.   The proof lies in the circumstance,
that each and every animal and plant, in the world,
is defective (not merely structurally, but physiologically), in proportion as it lacks any positive characters·
of its species; and that the injury, thereby caused,
abates proportionately as it regains the integrity of
its species.   And then, to round this theory of development, there is the sterility of hybrids!

On page 49, Vol. ii, *Animals and Plants, &c.*, he
says:

"When two distinct races are crossed, it is notorious
that the tendency in the offspring, to revert to one or
both parent forms, is strong, and endures for many
generations. I have myself seen the clearest evi-

dence of this, in crossed pigeons, and with various plants. Mr. Sidney states that, in a litter of Essex pigs, two young ones appeared which were the image of the Berkshire boar that had been used twenty-eight years before in giving size and constitution to the breed. I observed in the barn yard at Betley Hall, some fowls, showing a strong likeness to the Malay breed, and was told by Mr. Tollet that he had, forty years before, crossed his birds with Malays, and that, though he had at first attempted to get rid of this strain, he had subsequently given up the attempt, as the Malay characters would appear * * * No rule can be laid down, in cases of a cross, how soon the tendency to reversion will be obliterated * * * But we must be careful, not to confound these cases of reversion to characters gained from a cross, with those given under the first class, in which characters originally common to BOTH parents, but lost at some former period; for such characters may recur, after an almost indefinite number of generations."

Again he says:

"Many sub-varieties of the pigeon have reversed, and somewhat lengthened feathers on the back of the head, and this is certainly not due to the species, under nature, which shows no trace of such a structure, but * * * we may suspect that reversion to some extremely remote form has come into action."

On page 74, Vol. ii, *Animals and Plants, &c.*, he says:

"No doubt it appears, at first sight, in the highest degree improbable that, in every horse, of every generation, there should be a latent capacity and tendency to produce stripes, though these may not appear once in a thousand generations; that in every white, black,

9

or other colored pigeon, which may have transmitted
its proper color, during centuries, there should be a
latent capacity, in the plumage, to become, and to be
marked, with certain characteristic bars; that, in every
child, in a six-fingered family, there should be the
capacity for the production of an additional digit;
and so in other cases. Nevertheless, there is no
more inherent improbability in this being the case,
than in a useless and rudimentary organ, or even in
only a tendency to the production of a rudimentary
organ, being inherited during millions of generations (!),
as is well known to occur with a multitude of organic
beings. There is no more inherent improbability, in
each domestic pig, during a thousand generations, retaining the capacity and tendency to develop great
tusks, under fitting conditions, than in the young calf
having retained, for an indefinite number of generations, rudimentary incisor teeth, which never protrude
through the gums."

Again he says, on page 70, Vol. ii:

"The subject of latent characters is so important,
as we shall see in a future chapter, that I will give
another illustration. Many animals have the right
and left sides of their body unequally developed:
this is well known to be the case with flat fish, in
which the one side differs, in thickness and color,
and in the shape of the fins, from the other; and
during the growth of the young fish, one eye actually travels, as shown by Steenstrup, from the
lower to the upper surface. In most flat fishes, the
left is the blind side, but, in some, it is the right;
though, in both cases, 'wrong fishes,' which are
developed in a reversed manner to what is usual,
occasionally occur, and in Platessa *flesus*, the right
or left side is indifferently developed, the one as
often as the other. With gasteropods, or shell-fish,

the right and left sides are extremely unequal; the far greater number of species are dextral, with rare and occasional reversals of development, and some few are normally sinistral; but, certain species of Bulimus, and many Achitinellæ, are as often sinistral as dextral. I will give an analogous case in the great articulate kingdom: the two sides of Verucca are so wonderfully unlike, that without careful dissection, it is extremely difficult to recognize the corresponding parts on the opposite sides of the body; yet it is apparently a mere matter of chance, whether it be the right or the left side that undergoes so singular an amount of change. One plant is known to me, in which the flower, according as it stands on the one or other side of the spike, is unequally developed. In all the foregoing cases, the two sides of the animal are perfectly symmetrical at an early period of growth. Now, whenever a species is as liable to be unequally developed on the one side, as on the other side, we may infer that the capacity for such development is present, though latent, in the undeveloped side. And as a reversal of development occasionally occurs in animals of many kinds, this latent capacity is probably very common."

After citing a multitude of instances, showing past degeneration; that characters may long lie latent in the individuals of the species; and the capacity, of such individuals, to regain such characters, whenever the conditions of their development are restored to them; he says:

"From these several facts, it must be admitted, that certain characters, capacities, and instincts, may lie latent, in an individual, and even in a succession of individuals, without our being able to detect the least signs of their presence."

If characters may thus lie latent, "without our being able to detect the least signs of their presence," wherein consists the force of the only objection to ascribing characters to Reversion? namely, that the species, under nature, was never known, by man, to have had characters, similar to those arising by variation?

On page 67, Vol. ii, *Animals and Plants, &c.*, he says:

"Finally, we have seen that characters often reappear in purely-bred races, without our being able to assign any proximate cause; but when they become feral, this is either indirectly or directly induced by the change in their conditions of life. With crossbreeds, the act of crossing, in itself certainly leads to the recovery of long-lost characters, as well as of those derived from either parent form. Changed conditions, consequent on cultivation, and the relative position of buds, flowers, and seeds on the plant, all apparently aid in giving this same tendency. Reversion may occur, either through seminal or bud generation, generally at birth, but sometimes only with an advance of age. Segments, or portions of the individual, may alone be thus affected. That a being should be born resembling in certain characters, an ancestor removed by two or three, and in some cases, by hundreds or even thousands of generations, is assuredly a wonderful fact. In these cases, the child is commonly said to inherit such characters directly from its grandparents, or more remote ancestors. But, this view is hardly conceivable. If, however, we suppose that every character is derived exclusively from the father or mother, but that many characters lie latent in both parents, during a long succession of generations, the foregoing facts are intelligible."

It is difficult to conceive, how any one, who looks this evidence fairly in the face, can entertain the slightest doubt that the càuse which Darwin professes to have sought in vain, to explain variations, is furnished by the regain of long-lost characters of the varying species; or, by reversion. The reader will mark, that it is variation which constitutes the problem, not development in general. Development in general, is Darwin's problem; but he chose to solve that problem by the problem of variations. His failure to solve the subordinate problem should alone suffice to demolish his theory of development. *A fortiori*, is his theory destroyed, when there is found a solution of the problem of variations, diametrically opposed to such theory.

To represent, as the author does, that he cannot explain all of the variations or improvements, is to affect an ignorance, simulated under the stress and necessities of his theory. The impression, so widespread and general, that species, taken from a state of nature, are necessarily perfect, after their kind, aids Darwin materially in cloaking the significance of this law of reversion. The current conception, but most erroneous one, is, that all improvements which animals or plants make, after they are placed under domestication, is clear gain, or advance upon what they normally should be. This idea has even been carried so far, as to induce some scientists (?) to maintain, that Providence has introduced something plastic into organisms under domestication, which enables them to vary, in order that they might be of better use to man.

9*

The facts, quoted from Darwin, show that the improvements, or variations, in each species, are but the regain, partial or complete, of an original, normal condition of such species.

On page 447, Vol. ii, he says:

"In every living creature, we may feel assured, that a host of lost characters lie ready to be evolved under proper conditions. How can we make intelligible, and connect with other facts, this wonderful and common capacity of reversion,—this power of calling back to life long-lost characters?"

When he speaks of a "host" of characters, latent in each individual, he is rather overstating the case. But, it places his theory of evolution in a bad light, for it proves that Natural Selection has been engaged in the past, in degenerating organisms, instead of developing them; and, that "the strongest, fittest, and most vigorous," which Natural Selection is said to have preserved, were, instead of being the better for the Struggle for Existence, in a condition only to congratulate themselves, that they were not so completely used up, as were the weakest, which succumbed.

There are not a "host" of such lost characters, in each individual. That is a mere speculative assumption, with Darwin. But, there were a certain number of characters which each species lost under nature, and those characters are represented, in part, by the improvements which arise in each such species under domestication, and at intervals under nature. Even according to Darwin's own showing, there is not a scintilla of evidence, going to prove that one, single, new character, feature, organ, or instinct—nay, one single cell—has been added to the general organic fund, for "millions of generations" past. His facts demonstrate, that every apparent accession of such, has been the mere regain of what was previously lost, by the varying species, at some near, or remote, period in the past.

Darwin, in combating the view of his adversaries, that the existing state of nature is the same state in which each species was originally created, has pursued a suicidal course; for, in revealing the degeneration which has occurred under the state of nature, and in displaying the extent and scope of reversion under domestication, he has swept the ground from under his feet, by furnishing an explanation of the initial developments (variations), with which his argument starts; and thereby puts an imperative veto on that liberty to extend such developments indefinitely, which the improvements under domestication, at first seemingly gave him. What led to Darwin's giving such a suicidal exposition of Reversion, is this: Notwithstanding that there was, to his theory that the species evolve one from another, the insuperable objection, that the species are effectually divided from each other by the sterility of hybrids, he fancied that he had so far sustained his theory, by the view of an indefinite accumulation of variations, that he might corroborate it by a collateral hypothesis. He fancied that, if he showed that a vast number of characters had been lost, then when different species within the same family, developed each a similar long-lost charac-

ter, it might be argued, that all these species inherited
similar characters from some remote, common ancestor from which these several species evolved. But,
the mere possession, of a similar character, by several
species, does not argue a common origin for them.
The turkey, the pigeon, the duck and the chicken,
have tail feathers; but this does not prove they
descended from a common ancestor. If not, then
the loss and regain of such a character by such
species, cannot prove it. If proof, *aliunde*, of a
common origin, had been adduced; then, the possession, or the regain of such common characters
might be advanced as corroborative evidence. If
Darwin had shown that improvements, or variations,
go on indefinitely, and that therefore it was possible
for species to evolve, one from another, this fact of the
possession, or of the re-development of a similar character by different species, might be brought in as cumu-
lative proof. But, standing by itself, it has not the
weight of levity itself. But, while Darwin thought
that he had established the proof, *aliunde*, his collateral hypothesis was sapping that very proof. In
attempting to give extra support to his theory, by
showing this great degeneration and this ever-active
reversion, he undermined his principal theory, by
showing that the variations, which his theory required
should be extended indefinitely, were due to reversion,
and that therefore there was a limit to such variations;
which limit conclusively negatived the idea of a community of origin of the species. Another absurdity,
in which he involved himself, was by displaying the

fact that, instead of there having been evolution in the past, under nature, there has been great degeneration, which is the very antithesis to evolution. Fancy his assumed, slight variation, arising once in "the course of thousands of generations," and dependent upon the fitful action of Natural Selection for its preservation, contending against the wide-spread degeneration which Darwin shows! And when the variation has arisen, and is preserved, who is to tell, whether or not, it is only a lost character regained?

On page 449, Vol. ii, *Animals and Plants, &c.*, Darwin says, that Herbert Spencer's "*Principles of Biology*" "are not brought to bear on reversion; and this is unintelligible to me." It is not unintelligible to Herbert Spencer. He is a wiser man, in his generation, than is Darwin. He had his own sound reasons for not bringing his principles to bear on reversion. Spencer doubtless saw that his synthesis would be shattered in heaps over his head, by his own act, did he not steer clear of all mention of Reversion. Spencer's synthesis requires that variations should be regarded as wholly ultimate facts, inexplicable by any law save the one which Spencer devised for the nonce, viz., "the instability of the homogeneous." Were it admitted, by Spencer, that the varying individuals have degenerated, and that the appearance, in any individual, of characters similar to the ones which such individual's progenitors lost, must be ascribed to the law of reversion, the inevitable outcome must have been, some day, the complete exposition of the fallacy upon which the synthesis rests. The theory,

that Herbert Spencer saw this, and was loth to contribute to the downfall of his gossamer structure, may
alone explain the omission, by a man of his philosophical acumen, of such well known phenomena as
are those of Reversion.

On page 77, Vol. ii, *Animals and Plants, &c.*, Darwin
says:

"Some flowers have almost certainly become more
or less completely peloric through reversion. Corydalis *tuberosa* probably has one of its two nectaries
colorless, destitute of nectar, only half the size of the
other, and therefore, to a certain extent, in a rudimentary state; the pistil is curved towards the perfect
nectary, and the hood, formed of the inner petals,
slips off the pistil and stamens in one direction alone,
so that, when a bee sucks the perfect nectary, the
stigma and stamens are exposed and rubbed against
the insect's body. In several closely allied genera, as
in Dielytra, &c., there are two perfect nectaries, the
pistil is straight, and the hood slips off on either side,
according as the bee sucks either nectary. Now, I
have examined several flowers of Corydalis *tuberosa*, in
which both nectaries were equally developed and contained nectar; in this, we see only the re-development
of a partially aborted organ; but, with this re-development, the pistil becomes straight, and the hood slips
off in either direction; so that these flowers have
acquired the perfect structure, so well adapted for
insect agency, of Dielytra and its allies. We cannot
attribute these coadapted modifications to chance, or
to correlated variability; we must attribute them to a
primordial condition of the species."

Is it not rather inconsistent, in an author, according
to whose theory, every structure, coadaptation, rela-

tion, and dependency, in organic nature, must, at some time, have arisen by variation, to assert, as Darwin does here, that he is compelled to ascribe the improvements to reversion; because it is so difficult to believe that they have arisen in any other way?

On the same, and on the following page, he cites other startling improvements, which he says, he is constrained to refer to reversion. He also says:

"The case of the fifth stamen, in the peloric Antirrhinum, which is produced by the re-development of a rudiment always present, * * * probably reveals to us the state of the flower, as far as the stamens are concerned, at some ancient epoch. It is also difficult to believe, that the other four stamens, and the petals, after an arrest of development, at a very early embryonic age, would have come to full perfection, in color, structure, and function, unless these organs had, at some former period, normally passed through a similar course of growth. Hence it appears to me probable, that the progenitor of the genus Antirrhinum, must, at some remote epoch, have included five stamens, and borne flowers, in some degree resembling those now produced by the peloric form.

"Lastly, I may add that many instances have been recorded of flowers, not generally ranked as peloric, in which certain organs, normally few in number, have been abnormally augmented. As such an increase of parts cannot be looked at as an arrest of development, nor due to the re-development of rudiments, for no rudiments are present, and as these additional parts bring the plant into closer relationship with its natural allies, they ought probably to be viewed as reversions to a primordial condition."

. These quotations, from Darwin's works, showing

Reversion, might be multiplied indefinitely, for he gives several chapters to the subject, and almost every other page of his works, is filled with references to this factor. With one more quotation we will close the direct proofs of Reversion.

On page 80, Vol. ii, *Animals and Plants*, *&c.*, he says:

"On the doctrine of reversion, as given in this chapter, the germ becomes a far more marvelous object; for, besides the visible changes to which it is subjected, we must believe that it is crowded with invisible characters, proper to both sexes, to both the right and left side of the body, and to a long line of male and female ancestors, separated by hundreds, or even thousands, of generations from the present time; and these characters, like those written on paper with invisible ink, all lie ready to be evolved, under certain known or unknown conditions."

Assume but a tithe of the degeneration, which is above implied, and the scope of reversion is sufficiently wide to cover every variation, under domestication, or under nature. Darwin's theory lays claim to be a tenable hypothesis, only in the event, that variations are inexplicable, and may proceed forever, or indefinitely. This assumption of his, is, however, completely negatived by the facts of Reversion, which show that the sole variation possible, is the regain of characters lost, and that when all of the characters, which any species has lost, have been recovered, the limit of positive variation, for that species, is reached.

If it be conceded, that proof of a glaring *hiatus*, intervening between a theory and the facts upon which such theory purports to rest, invalidates that theory ; and, if the filling up of that *hiatus*, with a known, scientific law, diametrically opposed to the assumption essential to such theory, is disproof of the theory; then, the evidence already advanced, constitutes a Refutation of Darwinism. But, the Refutation does not depend upon such mere agreement, of the facts, with the hypothesis of Reversion. Demonstrative proof of the truth of the theory of Reversion is readily available ; which is furnished, in the subsequent chapters, which treat of Crossing, Close-Interbreeding, and Self-Fertilization.

CHAPTER IV.

REVERSION NOT A LAW, *Sui Generis;* BUT A DERIVATIVE LAW, ASSIMILABLE TO OTHER WELL KNOWN LAWS.

We have shown Reversion to be a most potent factor, and proven it to be abundantly able to explain every improvement which has arisen, or which may arise, under Nature, or under domestication. Although it does not explain the origin of the development of each species, it does explain, clearly and fully, what that phase of development is, which, in Biology, has been termed Progress. It does explain,—and explains them in a manner inconsistent with Darwin's theory,— all those slight increments or gradations of growth, called variations or improvements, upon which Darwin endeavors to base his theory.

As heretofore used, the word, Progress, has been simply a metaphysical entity, with as little title to recognition, by science, as have "innate tendency," "inherent aptitude," "vital force," or any of those other, barren terms by which men have shaped ignorance into the semblance of knowledge. There is a law of Progress; but that law, when rightly resolved, is Reversion, or the regain of characters, organs, faculties, instincts and powers which were once lost by the species, now progressing. Thus regarded, Progress is

(106)

a positive, definite, scientific factor; founded upon well established physiological principles, not upon chance, as it has heretofore been, nor upon a "tendency," nor upon any metaphysical entity, or other makeshift of ignorance, nor upon any obscure, fatalistic hypothesis. The advocates of Progress need not abate any of their enthusiasm, for their cherished watchword; for, in each species, and notably in Man, there still remains a wide margin for improvement.

There are, also, four other laws,—three of which are most familiarly known to the vulgar, as well as to the learned,—with which, the identity of Reversion is possible to be fully established. (1). One is the capacity of redintegration, following the disintegration of the tissues. (2). Another is the power of reparation which is manifested, either by what is termed, healing by first intention, or healing with inflammation, upon the occurrence of any wound or abrasion. (3). Another law, with which Reversion is identical, is the power of immediate reproduction of a lost member; a power which is displayed, to the fullest extent, by the lower orders of animals, and, measurably, by even the highest. (4.) The fourth and last law, is Generation, both sexual and asexual.

Of the first,—viz., the repair which is continually making good the waste of the tissue in the organic system,—no evidence is needed, as it is well known by physiologists; and, even the unlearned, in science, attest their knowledge of it, in the current conception, that the body undergoes a complete change, every seven years.

Of the second law, Darwin speaks, at much length, in Chapter XXVII, of Vol. ii, of *Animals and Plants, &c.* This law, also, is matter of common knowledge.

Of the third law,—viz., the reproduction of lost limbs, in the course of the same generation in which they were lost,—evidence perhaps may better be produced, as it is a matter not so generally known.

"It is notorious" (says Darwin) "that some of the lower animals, when cut into many pieces, reproduce so many perfect individuals. Lyonnet cut a Nais, or freshwater worm, into nearly fifty pieces, and these all reproduced perfect animals. It is probable that segmentation could be carried much further in some of the protozoa, and, with some of the lowest plants, each cell will reproduce the parent form" (pp. 429, 430, Vol. ii, *Animals and Plants, &c*).

The power of this reversion, or ability, of any organism to recomplete itself, when any part or parts have been cut off, is such, that a mere fragment, taken from a Begonia leaf, will re-develop the whole plant, if imbedded in fit soil, and kept at an appropriate temperature. So small, frequently, is the fragment which is capable of reproducing for itself the whole plant from which it is torn, that something like a hundred plants, may be produced from the fragments of a single leaf. If this power be kept down by adverse conditions, is it any wonder that, upon the return of the favorable conditions, to a plant which has had a part or organ missing for ten, a hundred, or a thousand generations, it should regain its integrity, by re-developing such part or organ ?

"Now, when the leg, for instance, of a salamander, is cut off, a slight crust forms over the wound, and beneath this crust, the uninjured cells, or units of bone, muscle, nerves, &c., are supposed to unite with the diffused gemmules of those cells which in the perfect leg come next in order; and these as they become slightly developed, unite with others, and so until a papilla of soft cellular tissue, the 'budding leg' is formed; and in time a perfect leg. Thus, that portion of the leg which had been cut off, neither more nor less, would be reproduced. If the tail or leg of a young animal had been cut off, a young tail or leg would have been reproduced, as actually occurs with the amputated tail of the tad-pole" (pp. 450, 451, Vol. ii, *Animals and Plants, &c.*).

"Spallanzani, by cutting off the legs and tail of a salamander, got in the course of three months, six crops of these members; so that 687 perfect bones were reproduced, by one animal, during one season. At whatever point, the limb was cut off, the deficient part, and no more, was exactly reproduced. Even with Man, as we have seen in the twelfth chapter, when treating of polydactylism, the entire limb, whilst in an embryonic state, and supernumary digits, are occasionally, though imperfectly, reproduced after amputation. When a diseased bone has been removed, a new one sometimes gradually assumes the regular form, and all the attachments of muscles, ligaments, &c., become as complete as before" (p. 354, Vol. ii, *Animals and Plants, &c*).

"No doubt, the power of reparation, though not always quite perfect, is an admirable provision, ready for various emergencies, even for those which occur only at long intervals of time" (p. 355, Vol. ii, *Animals and Plants, &c*).

In all of these cases of repair, or reproduction, the
10*

integrity of the organism has been impaired; and, "the coördinating power of the organization" has repaired such integrity.   Darwin speaks of this power, as the

"Reparative power which is common, in a higher or lower degree, to all organic beings, and which was formerly designated by physiologists as the *nisus formativus*" (p. 353, Vol. ii, *Animals and Plants, &c*).

Now, Reversion is, essentially, the same power.   It is but a manifestation of the same law; only, not occurring in the same generation, with that in which the integrity of the organism, was impaired.   The only difference is, that, in the case of reintegration of tissue, in the case of repair of wounds, and in the reproduction of a lost limb, the impaired integrity, consequent, respectively, upon the disintegration of the tissue, upon the infliction of the wound, and upon the dismemberment, is immediately retrieved; while, in Reversion, the return to such state of integrity, is deferred, for one or more generations, owing to unfavorable conditions,—the same conditions, generally, which entailed the loss, or the reduction, of the given part. The relation which Reversion bears to the healing of a wound, is, essentially, that which this same healing, when attended by inflammation, bears to this same healing, when it is effected by what is termed, "first intention."   As, the immediate healing of a wound has been thus termed; and, as it is manifestly implied, that healing, by inflammation, may be called healing by second, third, fourth, fifth, sixth, or twentieth intention; so, Reversion might consistently

be termed, hundredth, thousandth, or ten thousandth
intention; according to the interval of time, during
which, the characters, eventually regained, have remained reduced or suppressed.

The mistake, made by those who have advocated
the evolution of the species, has been, in placing
the fixed type,—that is, the organism, which is in
its full, normal integrity,—in those individuals of the
given species, which have the average structure of the
species, as it exists under nature. The type there, now,
however, is a degenerated type, with its structural integrity impaired, by the loss of some characters, and
by the reduction of others; and, the type of the given
species is not fixed under the existing state of nature.
It is fixed (*i. e.*, normally fixed), at a certain margin of
development, above such structure as it subsists in the
state of nature. The improvement, in each species,
under domestication, is a margin, merely, corresponding with the margin of previous degeneration. The
characters which arise, do but resume their lost, structural integrity, as characters do, when reproduced in a
truncated salamander. The fact, that function takes
precedence of structure, should suffice to indicate that
the power displayed, is Reversion.

All of these powers, of repair, are Reversions to the
primordial integrity of the given organism's species.
The Reversion, which is especially so called, is solely
a different manifestation of the same power which, in
nutrition, replaces the disintegrated tissue; of the same
power, which repairs a wound, or a bruise; of the same
power, which shows itself in the reproduction of a lost

member;—the only difference being, in the amount of time taken to operate. In the one case, the reintegration occurs immediately, or in the same generation, in which the loss of structural integrity occurred; and, in the other case, the reintegration is deferred, owing to the absence of favorable conditions, for several, or for many generations.

"It is notorious," says Darwin, "and we shall immediately adduce proofs, that increased use or action strengthens muscles, glands, sense-organs, &c.; and, that disuse, on the other hand, weakens them. I have not met with a clear explanation of this fact, in works on Physiology. Mr. Herbert Spencer maintains that, when muscles are much used, or when intermittent pressure is applied to the epidermis, an excess of nutritious matter exudes from the vessels, and that this gives additional development to the adjoining parts."

It may be remarked, *en passant*, that Mr. Herbert Spencer never yet failed to explain (?) any phenomena, where language was capable of converting a mere restatement of the facts, into the semblance of a *vera causa*.

The greater efficiency in function, and the greater development in structure, which follow greater activity, are fully explicable, upon the view, that this greater efficiency and greater development, were once part of the perfect coördination of the organism, either in the individual itself, or in its ancestors; that the organism has degenerated; and that the organism has ever been striving,—as Darwin asserts Reversion to be ever striving, in the offspring of each successive generation,—to bring into play its reparative power, or *nisus formativus*, in order to restore the lost integrity. The greater activity does not *cause* the functional, or structural increase. That is but a condition. The absence of such activity has atrophied, or reduced the organ. The subsequent restoration of such condition, occasions the re-development. There is but one normal coördination of the parts of any one species. The absence of any part, or organ, impairs such coördination. By disintegration; by the loss of tissue, consequent upon a wound; or, by the loss or reduction of a character or organ, either suddenly by dismemberment, or by the slow operation of adverse conditions, this coördination is rendered abnormal. Perfect coördination is compatible, only with the sum of all the characters and parts, of a species, fully and proportionately developed. When all the parts are present, and the full complement of tissue is realized, in the individual, the coördination is active, perfect, and normal, in each and every part. When a part is missing, impaired coördination results; but, the remaining parts are correlated to the parts missing; and this correlation, being essentially a coördinating power,—which acts equally when a part is missing, or present,—the reintegration of the lost part results, when the conditions allow. The same force which binds the given part, when present, to the whole, restores it when lost. If a number of parts be missing, or reduced, and the conditions (increased activity, &c.), be exclusively propitious to the re-development of one of such parts; then, that part alone will develop.

The finger-reading of the blind; the exalted ability
of an orchestral conductor, to discriminate delicate
differences of sound; the pronounced development of
a dancer's legs, and of the jockey's crural adductors;
the many instances of high cultivation of the senses,
and of the intellect, either special or general; attest,—
not a development, caused by mere activity,—but the
reparative power, which follows, very late, upon a degeneration suffered by the individual's ancient progenitors. Had the said tactual ability of the blind,
and the other cases of development, been at their
maximum, in an individual; and had they, then, from
some cause, been lost; their regain, by means of the
nisus formativus, or reparative power, would be considered perfectly natural. Why, then, should their
restoration to full integrity, and to full power, be
deemed in anywise singular, when Darwin himself
testifies, that this reparative power is operative, with
the largest and most important organs, after thousands, and even millions, of generations? As a fact,
this functional and structural development does ensue
upon mere activity. But the activity is but the
mere *condition*. The cause is to be sought, elsewhere. To explain it; which is the more scientific'
and reasonable?—to refer it to "evolution," to "pro- ·
gress," to "innate tendency," etc., terms which are,
confessedly, but the mere symbols of a cause unknown; or, to ascribe it to a power, which we see
daily in operation, in the repair of the slightest injury
to the skin?

If an individual should forswear all manner of exercise of his crural appendages, those members would become, either atrophied, or greatly shrunken in size. If, then, he were to indulge in judiciously-increased activity, they would regain their normal, functional, and structural integrity. This regain will not, then, be caused, by such increased activity; but, by the coördinating power of the organism, which ties together all the parts, and which, of itself, never normally changes; but which is changed, or modified, in its efficiency, by the absence of the condition, needful for the exercise of its power. It thus changes and the minimum of such change, to which it is subjected by external conditions, is, doubtless, that flux which it experiences, when the usual process of the disintegration of tissue, is taking place. We are engaged, now, only in establishing our assumption that, after primal Evolution, the only kind of development, or of growth, possible, is Reversion, which is the regain of a species' lost integrity; but it is the purpose of this work, to demonstrate, that the only, normal state of this coördinating (or as some may call it, vital) force, is the state in which it is in the maximum degree of efficiency, possible for any individual of the given species;—and that, within any given species, it is impossible to have any other, normal coördination of parts, than that coördination which comprises all of the characters of such species. All of the differences, between individuals of the same species, are due to the different manners and degrees in which this full integrity of the organism, has been modified; together with the different modes and degrees in which their power of reversion to the full structural build, has been modified by their conditions of life.

That reversion is ever ready to operate,—as are the other powers of repair, in the case of a wound, in the case of interstitial waste, and in the case of the reproduction of a lost member,—Darwin shows, when he says (p. 483, Vol. ii, *Animals and Plants, &c.*):

"That there is a tendency, in the young of each, successive generation, to produce the long-lost characters, and that this tendency, from some unknown cause, sometimes prevails."

This Reversion is, equally with the other powers of repair, but a process of redintegration; and, between it and the others, there is no fundamental distinction. All of the instances, which he adduces, of improvement or positive variation, are merely instances of such reintegration. When Mr. Darwin has furnished his thousands of facts, he has not yet given a scintilla of proof, or of evidence, of the indefinite development of any species. For, all of the improvements, and all of the positive variations, adduced by him, are but regrowth, redintegration, and repair merely, of the specific type; and, upon no principle of logic, or of common sense, may instances of regrowth, or of reintegration, or of repair, or of re-development, or of reversion, serve as *data*, for any theory of unlimited growth, or of unlimited development; for the limit of this repair, reintegration, or reversion, is the form respectively, of the structure, from which the organism, in question, departed. How repair, re-growth, regain, re-development, reproduction, reversion, or redintegration, can, by any possibility, justly enter, as an element, into a process of development, designed to prove unlimited growth, unlimited development or unlimited integration, is a mystery, to every one acquainted with the canons of logic.   Darwin has collected, from various sources, a great number of interesting facts; and·has thereby rendered a great service to science; but, if he had devoted a tithe of the labor, and of the time, to showing the relevancy of those facts, in connection with his theory, he would have furnished his readers, with something of infinitely more value than facts.

He has, however, ingeniously availed himself of an erroneous notion of his adversaries; namely, that, as the state of nature was the state in which the Creator placed the Animals and Plants, when He created them, therefore, the structure, as existing now, in the state of nature, must be the normal, perfect mould,— which is a glaring *non sequitur*.   Darwin, however, though he does not believe in any such alleged, normal structure, derives a great, temporary benefit from the said mistake; for, it allows him to argue thus: If the structure, of any animal or plant, as now existing under nature, is the normal build, then the variations occurring under domestication, are something over and above the development which the Creator established: If so; then, who is to say, that there is a limit to such residual development?   And, if so, it is probable, that the Creator never fixed any structure for any species; but, instead thereof, the species have gone

11

on developing, by means of slow accretions, such as we perceive under domestication.

A most clever trick! He accepts, provisionally,— although not concurring in,—the truth of his adversaries' assumption ; he is suffered, then, to work in his false hypothesis (which he would never have been allowed to do, if his adversaries had not been in error in their said assumption) ; and then arrives at his conclusion, which negatives completely the assumption by which alone it was possible for him to achieve it !

The identity of the several powers, is well shown by the two following quotations, from Darwin's *Animals and Plants, &c.*:

"Between the powers, which repair a trifling injury in any part, and the power which previously was occupied, in its maintenance, by the continued mutation of its particles" (*i. e.*, the reintegration of the tissues), "there cannot be any great difference ; and we may follow Mr. Paget in believing them to be the self-same power. As at each stage of growth, an amputated part is replaced, by one in the same state of development, we must likewise follow Mr. Paget in admitting, 'that the powers of development from the embryo are identical with those exercised for the restoration from injuries'" (p. 430, Vol. ii).

These remarks show the identity of all the powers of repair, which operate in the same generation in which the organism suffered the departure from its proper type. The following quotation, from Darwin, shows, that the repair which occurs in the next, or succeeding generations (that is, Reversion, or appear-

ance of improvements) is also identical with the other
powers of returning to the perfect type :

"No doubt the power of reparation, though not
always quite perfect, is an admirable provision, ready
for various emergencies, even for those which occur
only at long intervals of time" (p. 355, Vol. ii).

In speaking of the power of reproduction of lost
members, he says :

"This power of regrowth does not, however, always
act perfectly; the reproduced tail of a lizard differs in
the forms of the scales from the normal tail" (p. 354,
Vol. ii).

So, with the improvements, arising in animals and
plants under domestication ; this *nisus formativus*, this
reparative power, or Reversion,—as it is especially
so called, when it occurs in a generation following that
in which the injury was caused, or the characters were
lost,—does not always retrieve, in a complete or perfect
state, the characters which were lost by the species.
The conditions are not perfectly supplied.   When they
are perfectly supplied, there will be perfect reparation,
perfect reversion, in those animals and plants, as well
as in the lizard.

This "power is greater in animals, the lower they
are in the scales of organisms," says Darwin (p. 354,
Vol. ii, *Animals and Plants, &c*).

The reason of this lessened reproductive power, in
the higher animals, is, that such animals are more
complex, the conditions of growth are correspondingly
more complex, and less easily supplied; and, therefore,
lost members are less likely to be supplied, when

required. The power, however, ever potentially exists
in these higher animals ; and (with but an abatement,
in degree), actually exists, in the power of repair of
wounds, of reintegration of tissue, and also manifests
itself through Reversion. Darwin quotes quite a
number of authors who, to explain variability, have
formulated a law, *sui generis*, which absolutely requires
offspring to differ, in some degree, from their parents.
This is absurd. Facts are noticed; no explanation
can be furnished to explain them; and then some
genius always steps forward, and complacently declares
that it is a "*law of nature*," that the phenomena should
so be, or so act; and fancies, that he has thereby
added immensely to the body of scientific knowledge.
No such "law" is formulated here. The explanation
requires no such hypothetical, and barren device,
fashioned for the nonce. The offspring, when they
differ, in some positive character, from their parents,
differ, because their reparative power, or capacity to retrieve characters, which were lost by some ancient
progenitor, is, in the said character, manifested
more strongly, than it was, in their parents. Offspring, when they differ, in some negative character,
from their parents, differ, because they, in that character, depart further from the original and perfect type
than their parents have done. Their coördinative
power has been more weakened than has that of their
parents; or, than has that which their parents inherited.

That there is but one, normal mould, for the individuals of any species; and, that the coördination of

an organism is normal, only when it has all of the
positive characters of its species to coördinate; and, is
impaired, proportionally, when there is any disintegration, or loss or reduction of any of the characters of
the given species; are necessary inferences from the
following assertion :

"This subject has been here noticed, because we
may infer, that when any part or organ is either greatly
increased in size, or wholly suppressed, through variation and continued selection, the coördinating power
of the organization will continually tend to bring all
the parts again into harmony with each other" (p. 355,
Vol. ii, *Animals and Plants, &c*).

Had Darwin adhered to this principle, in his treatment of the facts of variation, and of breeding, he
would never have propounded a theory of the evolution of the species, from one another.   For, it shows
that, with each species, there is a certain ratio of
development of its several characters, which cannot
normally be varied from.   How was it possible for
him to be apprised of this principle, and yet fancy that
each variety (of the Pigeon, for instance) could
normally and safely diverge, as it has, both through
having a part, or organ which constitutes its peculiarity,
greatly increased in size ; and by having others wholly
suppressed ? and, how could he ignore the facts, that
the evil results of close-interbreeding, in the pigeon,
are due to this very disproportionate development, and
that the good, which results from crossing, is due to
the parts again being, measurably, brought into harmony with each other?   Are not the varieties of the
    11*

pigeon, each, possessed of a character, of the species, which the others lack? and does not each such variety lack all of those characters of the same species, which respectively constitute the peculiarities of the other varieties? Is not, then, "the coördinating power of the organization" impaired, by such great increase of the one part, and by the suppression of the other parts? Does not the reduction in the pig, of the snout, tusks, bristles, legs, tail, &c., militate against this ."tendency" of "the coördinating power of the organization," "to bring all the parts again into harmony with each other?" Assuredly, the evil results from close-interbreeding the individuals of these varieties, would imply as much ; and, the decline in the measure of those evil effects, when the individuals have all the parts again brought into harmony with each other, looks as if the principle of his, above quoted, was pregnant with more consequences than he has anticipated. Upon what hypothesis, other than that, which holds it necessary to have all of the characters, of a species, developed in each individual, is this " coördinating power of the organization," to be explained? This coördinating power is the bond, which links all the parts of the species together; and, it operates, in Reversion, by again bringing them together, when they have been lost. The same principle holds good, in the slightest wound, and in interstitial waste; the coördinating power reintegrates the parts, and restores the type of the species ; and, all of these powers are but different phases of the one process of coördination.

Darwin's remark, that that portion of the leg of the salamander, which was cut off, " *neither more nor less*," will be reproduced, is, *mutatis mutandis*, applicable to the improvements, or variations, under domestication. Those characters only, no more (though possibly less), will be regained, by a species, which were at one time lost by such species. The like remark, which he makes, when he says, the deficient part, and *no more*, was reproduced, is equally pertinent to the variations which arise. Parts only which are deficient, or absent, where they were once developed, can be acquired, by Man's selection, or by Natural Selection.

To illustrate the absurdity, of taking any of these cases of Reversion, as the basis of an indefinitely-continued development, which is to produce higher animals from lower ones, we shall take the case of redintegration, in the crystal.

It is well known, that, if a crystal has had one of its edges cut off, and the crystal is placed in a solution, similar to that, in which it was first formed, it will reproduce the lost edge, and thus repair its lost integrity. When the edge was absent, there was an imperfect equilibrium of the forces of the crystal. When the coördinating power of the crystal, restored the lost edge, the equilibrium, or coördination, was repaired. The restoration of the part, before cut off, was effected, by correlation with all the other parts, and with the aggregate. The part reproduced, resumes its relations to the other parts, and to the aggregate; and effects a return to the balance, which was impaired by its absence. The reproduction of a part, by the crystal, is precisely analogous to reversion, to the reproduction of a lost member, to the reintegration of tissue, and to the repair of a wound or abrasion. Darwin merely mentions, that he has heard this reparative power of the crystal, likened to the repair of a wound, in an animal. Herbert Spencer also refrains from any extended allusion to this power in the crystal; doubtless, from distrust of the effect its implications would have, upon his hypothesis.

This analogy most happily illustrates the absurdity, of Darwin's adducing the phenomena of variation, to · prove the evolution of the species.

Suppose the same crystal, truncated of its edge. With this edge gone, the crystal is found by Darwin. He places it in a solution, similar to that in which it was first formed. The reproduction of the lost edge, then ensues. He inquires the reason, why this part of the crystal has developed. To this he can answer, only that it develops, because it has an "innate tendency" so to develop. (As Ancient Pistol has it, "*Semper idem, absque hoc nihil est.*") He affects to believe himself forced to conclude that the growth of the edge, is an ultimate fact. He then says that as this development has taken place, he is entitled to the presumption that it will continue forever, or indefinitely. Given, then (he would by analogy, say), a thousand years or a thousand hours; and who is to say, into what, this crystal will not develop? and, may not each of the species, of crystals, evolve one from another? You cannot assume a limit (he would say), other than gratuitously. There cannot, possibly, then, be any such thing as the immutability of the species, of crystals; for, the individual crystals vary, and the species is made up of such individuals.

Such an argument could not be invalidated, if it were conceded, that the growth of the lost edge was absolutely new growth, and that it was not mere repair, or mere reproduction. It is obvious, however, that it is repair only, or reproduction, or Reversion back to the state which existed, in the crystal, previous to its truncation. It is equally obvious, therefore, that there is in the said crystal, no such capacity for unlimited growth, or integration, as Darwin would allege to exist in organisms. It is equally obvious, to a mineralogist, that those forms, of the crystals, which have not been truncated, are normally immutable;—that is, that no change can take place in them, after they have once assumed their specific, determinate form, save in derogation of that peculiar segregation, or coördination, of forces which make up a crystal. It is equally manifest, that all of the different kinds of crystals, ranging from the simplest to the most complex, are not evolved, one from another; that their beautiful subordination, of group under group, which rivals the arrangement of organisms, is no argument, whatever, in favor of a view, that they evolved from one another. They, each and every one, on the contrary, were evolved from independent centres,—centres, possibly, in the same matrix, yet perfectly independent centres, so far as the processes of integration are concerned. The initial force, involved in the deposition of the first molecule, pre-determined the form, shape, and

complexity of the crystal, and controlled the whole
formative process, for that crystal. It is equally manifest, that, when the integration, of the crystal, is once
fully attained, there is a peculiar play, and correlation,
of the forces of the crystal, which constitute a coördinative power, invested with the capacity, to keep all of
the parts together, and capable of repairing any part,
when lost or injured.

It may be well to state, that the organic species, is
not the analogue of what is termed a species, in
crystals; but, it is the analogue of those forms,
which are absolutely alike, when they are not injured, or truncated. Thus, the flowers of snow, in
crystallographic parlance, are termed a species. These,
however, do not correspond to an organic species, but,
rather, to an organic genus; it is those of the flowers
of snow, which are precisely identical, in shape and
form, cleavage, &c., which are analogous to a species
of animal or of plant.

These different flowers of snow did not evolve, from
one another, but they commenced, and completed,
their integration, independently of the others. No
similarity can, with them, afford an argument in favor
of their evolution, one from another. So, with species
of animals and plants. They were evolved, specially,
each from an independent centre. Neither, the similarity of different species, nor their natural subordination, group under group, justly implies that
they evolved, one from another. Kinship is not
necessarily the bond, between the individuals of the
same species. The only necessary tie between them,

is an identical, normal coördination, however derived, whether by descent, or by independent evolution. Organisms, to be of the same species, need not, necessarily, to be descended from a common progenitor; all that is required to class them, within the same species, is to ascertain if their normal coördinations are isochronous. If they have the same number of characters, and the same ratio of development of those characters, when they are free from physiological defects, they belong to the same species. The test by which to determine whether they are free from physiological defect, and of full integrity, is to be found under our chapters, upon Crossing and Close-interbreeding. Near similarities, and such arrangement, group resembling group, may imply, and doubtless do imply, that different species were evolved from a similar matrix, and under similar conditions.

The variations under domestication, are the same with the repair of a lost edge in a crystal,—simply, a regain of lost integrity. With an organic species, however, the individuals composing it are descended, one from another; while, even the individuals, of what, in crystals, is a species, by analogy, are evolved from independent centres.

He says (p. 486, *Origin of Species*):

"From the first dawn of life, all organic beings are found to resemble each other in descending degrees; so that they can be classed in groups under groups."

So, crystals are likewise "found to resemble each other in descending degrees, so that they can be classed in groups under groups;" yet, they were not evolved one from another; but were evolved, each, from an independent centre. Crystals also, may be modified, as are organic beings under nature; and, like them, such modification will be injurious to the coör- dination of their forces. They will also regain a lost edge, as well as organic beings will acquire, by rever- sion, a lost character; and, in proportion as they repair their lost edges, will their coördination approximate its normal type; the same as will the coördination of an organism be repaired, in proportion as Reversion re- stores the lost characters. Although you may trun- cate each individual crystal, after it has attained its full integrity, you do it only in derogation of its coördina- ting, crystallogenic force.

These crystals occur of all sizes, from the merest microscopic point, to a yard, or more, in diameter, and of all degrees of complexity. A single crystal of quartz, now at Milan, is three and a quarter feet long, and five and a half feet in circumference, and its weight is estimated at 870 pounds. Each mineral has its own mode of crystallization, by which it may be dis- tinguished, just as one distinguishes a genus of plant, by its characters, and mode of growth. And it is known, at once, to a mineralogist, of what mineral, a crystal is formed, wherever it may be found, by its angles, and by peculiarities of internal structure, such as its lines of cleavage. A variety of forms is often presented by a single mineral; and this variety may be very great, as with Calc-spar which is found in double pyramid, in prisms, and in rhombohedrons; and so with other species, as they are called; although only those individuals of exactly alike form, and with all their features in common, are, by analogy, with organic species, to be termed species.   But, however great the number of all the forms in each case, they are referable to a single, generic, or family type, and little skill is required to trace out extreme simplicity amid apparent complexity, for all the various modifications are arranged in beautiful order.

Why are they so arranged?   If a mineralogist should argue, as Darwin argues from a like due subordination of group under group, in descending complexity, he would contend for an absurdity; and hold, that they were evolved, the more complex from the simpler. The fact, however, is—not that they were evolved from one another—but that they started from independent centres, and that the degrees of similarity between them, is referable to the circumstance, that they were independently evolved from the like, or the same mineral, and were subject to like conditions of temperature, &c.   The initial force, implied in the deposition of each molecule of each crystal, pre-determined a regular, definite structure, and compelled a form which needed to be attained, or, the correlation of the forces involved in the crystal would have been thrown into disorder, and the forces involved in the crystal would have become so much the less crystallogenic in character.   A truncated crystal may have been long out of a solution; yet, if restored thereto, it will repair the lost part.   If a mineralogist should meet with such a truncated crystal, he, being unconscious that it was truncated, should restore it to a solution, and should proceed to estimate a ratio of integration for that crystal, based upon his observation of the degree of reparative power displayed before his eyes; he would be the perfect analogue of Darwin, who takes truncated organisms, places them under domestication, observes their power of repair, or of Reversion, and then absurdly essays to estimate, what would be the development of such organisms, if a few millions of years were assumed.

No crystal, nor organic species, is possible to be normally modified, after it has been once evolved. You may truncate the crystal; you may deprive the organic species of many of its characters; but a disturbance of the integrity of the forces involved, in either case will inevitably result. The only way, either to modify a crystal normally, or normally to change an organic species, is to resolve either into its original elements, then modify the forces primarily involved in its integration, or evolution, and start a new integration or evolution. That, however, is tantamount, with an organism, to new creation; or to primal evolution from inorganic forces and matter. The test of any abnormal modification of a species, is close interbreeding. The principal differences between a crystal and an organism are: (1). That a crystal is not susceptible to that ebb and flow which we find manifested in an organism, in the waste and repair of its tissue. (2). That the crystal, though capable of integrating a like form when a portion of its substance is detached by force *ab extra*, is not capable of spontaneously exuding or detaching a portion of its substance for the purpose of forming a new, like coördination; as, is an organism, when it evolves, or exudes sexually, or asexually, a reproductive element.

Not a little prejudice exists against a perfect type. This prejudice is, in a measure, justified; owing to the vague and gratuitous manner in which it is generally assumed,—and, owing to the fact, that those, assuming it, cannot give any definite idea of what they mean by it. But, such prejudice cannot be extended to the perfect type, which we show.   This of ours, is an individual in which all the characters of its species, are fully and proportionately developed.   It is no Platonic idea; and is no more metaphysical, than the assumption of a specific shape, for a truncated crystal, which, at the time, falls short of that shape, in the matter of a lost edge.

Thus, we have furnished, at least, warrant for assuming, that there is but one coördination, which is normal, for each species; that, when the structural integrity, of any individual, is impaired, such coördination is proportionally impaired; that this coördination is capable of restoring the lost, structural integrity; that the reintegration of tissues wasted by function, that the repair of a wound, that the reproduction of a lost member, that the regain of characters lost in some preceding generation, and that the reproduction of a lost edge in a crystal, are all merely different phases of one and the same power,—*i. e.*, the power, of any body whose parts are correlated together with reference to a definite form of structure, to recomplete itself, when any of its correlated parts have, by influences *ab extra*, been reduced or suppressed.   As before intimated, we do not rely upon the mere capacity of the assumption to explain all of the facts. Proof, approximating demonstration, is to be found in the chapters on Crossing and close-interbreeding, where a crucial test is furnished, by which it is possible ever, to ascertain, with respect to organisms, whether the structure is complete, and whether the coördination is of full integrity; or, how far such structural integrity, and such full, normal coördination have been departed from. Before proceeding to develop this test, it is incumbent upon us to show what a *petitio principii*, the argument from Natural Selection (Darwin's potent factor) is.

It is possible, also, to establish the similarity of the Law of Generation, with that of Reversion. Generation is, equally, a process of repair. A portion of an organism is exuded by an individual, and this portion at once proceeds to complete, for itself, the type of the given species. The reproductive element differs but little, essentially, in its operation, from the part (spoken of by Darwin), which is cut off from a Nais, or fresh-water worm, and which then reproduces the whole. The only difference lies in the manner in which the parts are separated from the parent organism, and in the necessity which, in some modes of Generation, there is, that the reproductive element should be united to that of the other sex.

The point, sought to be illustrated, is, that every mode of growth and of development (save that process which controlled the evolution of the first member, or members, of each species), is but a regain of the lost integrity of the given species.

CHAPTER V.

THE FALLACIES OF DARWIN'S ARGUMENT FROM NATURAL SELECTION.

It is possible, without, in the least, questioning the potential efficiency of Natural Selection, to show that Darwin's argument from Natural Selection begs the whole question at issue. For it gratuitously assumes that the variations (which Darwin would have Natural Selection to preserve and accumulate to an indefinite or unlimited extent) are not restricted to the number and kind which the varying species once lost.

Darwin says, that the higher species have been evolved from the lower, by means of the preservation and accumulation of slight, successive increments of development, and by means of the preservation and accumulation of those marked variations which are assumed to spring up mysteriously, under nature, "once in the course of thousands of generations."

The reader will perceive that there are thus two ways in which Darwin gets the units of development which, he purports to prove, are accumulated indefinitely, or without limit.

The one mode is by attempting, by argument, to *prove* that slight advances in development necessarily result from Natural Selection. Under nature, there has been

12* (133)

ever recurring, he alleges, a fearful struggle for Existence (brought on by adverse conditions, want of food,
and the severe competition consequent upon the ratio
of increase of living beings), in which the weak succumb, and "the strongest and most vigorous" survive.
These "strongest and most vigorous" being the ones,
exclusively, which continue the line of descent, increase in development, he contends, must obviously
follow. The indefinitely-continued accumulation of
increments of development so occasioned, explains, he
says, the process by which the lower species have
been evolved into the higher.

Darwin's other mode of getting units of development for Natural Selection to accumulate to an indefinite extent, is, not by any argument from Natural
Selection, but by *assuming* that marked variations—
similar to the "sports" which appear under domestication—arise under nature, at least once in the course of
thousands of generations. Then he contends that
Natural Selection preserves and accumulates these
marked variations to an unlimited or indefinite extent,
and so evolves the species one from another.

Now, it is intended to show, in this chapter,   •

First : That Natural Selection, or "the survival of
the stronger and more vigorous," does not *prove* any,
even the slightest advance in development, or any,
even the slightest variation.

Second : It is intended to show that even though
slight advances in development, or variations, were
proven by "the survival of the stronger and more vigorous," or were proven in any way; and even though

Natural Selection were proven to be perfectly competent, in itself, to preserve and accumulate such advances in development, or such variations; the accumulation of such advances in development, or such
variations, by means of Natural Selection, could not
proceed to the extent necessary to evolve one species
into another, because the presumption—which arises
from Darwin's very detail of the operation of Natural
Selection—which arises from the many rudimentary
organs adduced by him—which arises from the many
features which he admits have been reduced or simplified by the action of the conditions of Natural Selection—which arises from the many characters which,
Darwin says, have been so wholly suppressed, under
nature, that not a vestige of their past development
remains—which arises from the multitude of organs
and features which he confesses are due to Reversion—and which arises from the fact that there is,
confessedly, no other scientific explanation of variations than Reversion—is, that any such advances in development, and any such slight variations, are but the
regain of what was previously lost by the varying
species; and, being restricted, therefore, in amount, to
the amount lost by such species, the amount preserved
and accumulated by Natural Selection must necessarily
be commensurately restricted.

Third : With respect to Darwin's assumption, that
an occasional, marked variation may probably "arise
once in the course of thousands of generations;" it is
not intended to gainsay this point, but,

Fourth : It is intended to show that even though these

occasional, marked variations did arise under nature, and as many arose there as are known to arise under domestication, and even though Natural Selection were proven to be fully competent, in itself, to preserve and accumulate these variations; the accumulation of such variations, by means of Natural Selection, could not proceed to the extent necessary to evolve one species into another; because the presumption, before adverted to—arising from the very conditions under which, Darwin says, Natural Selection works,— arising from rudimentary, reduced and wholly suppressed organs which, Darwin admits, are so rife among all animals and plants—and arising from the absence of any other scientific explanation of the variations—is, that such occasional variations are due to Reversion; that, in consequence, they are limited to the number and kind which the given species once lost; and that their accumulation by Natural Selection, beyond the number and kind once lost, is impossible.

First : Now, with respect to the first point, Does the extinction of the weakest, and the selection of "the strongest and most vigorous" *prove* any, even the slightest advance in development?

As Darwin alleges Natural Selection to be the analogue of Man's Selection, it is well, first, to ascertain the conditions under which Man's Selection works; and, to see whether Man's Selection implies any advance in development.

The Selection of certain inviduals, under man's care, for breeding purposes, is generally held to induce the improvement of the animals.

Is it·the Selection which causes such advance?

Manifestly, it is not.   The advance in development is produced, independently of the Selection.   Man's Selection does but preserve and accumulate the developments.

Selection either does but preserve those which progress the fastest; or, where some alone of the individuals improve, it does but preserve those which have improved; or, where none improve, but some degenerate, and some hold their own, it does but preserve those which hold their own; or, where all have degenerated, it does but preserve those which have degenerated the least.

Obviously, then, the fact, that those selected have increased in development, must first, either be assumed, or be proven; before any argument may be drawn from Selection, designed to prove any ratio of accumulation of slight successive increments of development.

Therefore, it is, that we contend that Darwin cannot justly prove the needful, slight advances in development, by means of Selection; for, that process never even implies advance in development, unless advance in development is first assumed, or proven, *aliunde !*

If, in any generation, the individuals, of a species, under nature, do but hold their own; or, if they degenerate, it is manifest, that Natural Selection, *per se,* cannot imply any advance in development.   Advance in development must be established, independently, as a fact; or, inferred from the circumstance, that the conditions, to which the individuals of the given species are subjected, are favorable; that the organisms have an abundance of food, a healthy climate and all the other requisites of a propitious *habitat;* and, that they suffer not from a ruinous competition. Even these circumstances, however, would but argue, that the individuals held their own.

If, however, the fact be; or, if the presence of unfavorable conditions imply; that all of the individuals, of such species, are degenerating, the mere Selection of those which are the least degenerate, cannot argue any advance in development. If, again, the fact be; or the nature of the conditions imply; that some of the individuals have degenerated, and that some do but hold their own, the mere selection of those, which do but hold their own, cannot argue advance in development.

Now, Darwin, represents the conditions, under nature, to be very unfavorable. In fact, it was absolutely incumbent upon him to picture them, as well nigh fearful, in order that they should work the extinction of those which prove the weakest. Yet, those individuals, the elect, which have been, similarly with the weakest, subjected to these conditions, he pretends, are advancing in development!

Let the reader fancy his emotion, were he the owner of live stock, and were his farmer to assure him that he "reckoned," that the stock were improving, because (*sic*) the conditions, to which all of the herd were subjected, had long been so hard and rigorous, that all of the weaker ones were being killed off; and, as the strongest and most vigorous (?) were the only individuals, of the herd, which could endure, at all, the effects of the climate, of the rough treatment, of the insufficient food, and of the bitter competition prevailing to obtain the necessaries of life, the breed must eventually offer many prize animals; because, "the strongest and most vigorous," only, would survive, to produce offspring. Even if the reader cared, only to raise a few, from the herd, which might be capable of taking a prize, would not his fears be justly and reasonably provoked for these, by such a statement? and would not he be thankful, under the circumstances, if the result showed, that "the strongest and most vigorous" had but managed to hold their own? It would be absurd, in the absence of a special excuse, to fancy any farmer talking and arguing, in such a manner. Yet, such a farmer would display, to the full, as much intelligence and sense, as does Darwin, in propounding his theory of Natural Selection.

The problem of Selection resolves itself into the question: What are the conditions? do they imply development? or do they imply degeneration? or, do they imply any more than that the individuals hold their own?

Ask any farmer, of even inferior intelligence, if the mere Selection of the best animals, of a herd, will produce advance in development; and, he will, before answering, desire to know, under what conditions, favorable or adverse, the herd is placed. If the whole herd be degenerating, and if the elect are but those which are least degenerated, he will laugh at the idea of advance in development; and assure his questioner that mere Selection, by itself, does not argue any advance in development. If, he were told, that it was not Man's agency which wrought the Selection; but that such Selection was effected through the extinction of the weaker animals, by means of unfavorable conditions to which all the animals were alike subjected, he would doubtless guffaw most vulgarly, at the idea of even the possibility of any advance being inferred from Selection so occasioned.

Advance in development is usually, or ordinarily, implied by Man's Selection; because, usually, or ordinarily, there is an advance in development, among the select of animals, under domestication, owing to the favorable conditions there generally prevailing. In extending the idea of Selection to animals and plants, under nature, Darwin has gratuitously carried, along with such idea, this implication of an advance in development,—an implication which arose, under domestication, from the favorable conditions under which the animals and plants are there placed. Before applying the idea of Selection, to animals and plants, under domestication, it was known, that, with them, there *was* advance in development ; and, even if it were not known, as a fact, the favorable conditions, there generally prevailing, implied it. Before, however, Darwin could be justified, in carrying, to the state of nature, this implication, raised by the facts, and by the favorable conditions under domestication, it was necessary that he should adduce full warrant for such implication of advance under nature. Proof was needed, either, of the fact, or of favorable conditions.

But, he has, neither, the fact, nor the favorable conditions.

He has not the fact, required to warrant such an implication; for, *this very point of advance in development under nature, is what he is endeavoring to prove, by means of an argument from Natural Selection, into the premises of which argument, he has surreptitiously conveyed this very implication which issues forth, with such éclat, as his conclusion!* Advance in development, figures, both, in his assumption, and in his conclusion. What he inserts in his premises, he, with ease, extracts in the conclusion.

Neither, is he able to establish such an implication, by proof of favorable conditions, under nature; for, he shows that the very converse there obtains. *By the very terms of his argument, the conditions, under nature, to which, he says, all of the organisms, without exception, are subjected, are absolutely required to be adverse, and very unfavorable to development, in order to work the very Selection, which is designed to prove advance in development!* Insufficient food, and all the other elements of the Struggle for Existence, are required to operate upon all, in order to kill off the weaker; and such conditions obviously cannot establish an implication of advance in development, when their effect is death and extinction, to myriads of the numbers exposed to them. For; given, the effect of such conditions, upon the latter individuals, to be death and extinction; what will, presumptively, be the effect upon the development of those which Natural Selection preserves? Will not Natural Selection be doing all that
13

may reasonably be required of it, if it enable its select to hold their own?

Such implication is negatived, not only by the unfavorable conditions under nature, but by all of the facts which bear upon the problem. The many "rudimentary organs," which, he says Natural Selection has reduced to their present condition; from a perfectly developed state; and the many "long-lost characters," which, he says, lie latent in organisms, militate against his assumption.

The very order, in which he arrays his argument, exposes the above fallacies, and reveals still others.

1. The first proposition which he lays down, is, that there is an ever-recurring Struggle for Existence, among all animals and plants under nature, entailing the extinction of many such animals and plants; which Struggle for Existence, in the order of time, precedes the Selection, and is absolutely necessary to such Selection.

He avers, that all organisms, under nature, have had to struggle hard for their existence.

"More individuals are born, than can possibly survive. A grain in the balance will determine which individuals shall live, and which shall die" (p. 552, *Origin of Species*).

Even "the strongest and most vigorous" have had to enter into competition with their fellows, and with other species, for the means of existence; and have had to withstand, in each generation, the action of adverse climatic influences, of want of food, and of the other hard conditions which entailed the extinction of their weaker brethren.   An idea of the battle for life, which Darwin pictures, as the ordeal through which all organisms have to. pass, may be derived from the extracts given below.   The tale which the picture tells, it must be acknowledged, is not the happiest possible inducement to an argument, designed to prove advance in development—*net* advance, too.   It is, however, the misfortune with Darwin, in his exposition of his theory of Evolution, that, at each stage, as he advances, he has been constrained to a choice between rival absurdities.   Darwin's description of the Struggle for Existence, shows conclusively, that, so far from animals and plants, having advanced in development, the most that it has been possible for them to do, has been to hold their own; and, that, when they have not remained stationary (which, as the reader will see, is quite difficult of performance, in the face of such conditions), their movement has been in the direction of degeneration.   It must be conceded, that the adverse conditions under nature, are sufficiently strongly portrayed, in the following quotations, to prompt an estimate, rather, of how much even "the strongest and most vigorous" have deteriorated, than of how much they have advanced in development.

In his *Origin of Species*, Darwin says:

"Nothing is easier than to admit, in words, the truth of the universal struggle for life, or more difficult,—at least I have found it so,—than constantly to bear this conclusion in mind.   Yet, unless it be thoroughly ingrained in the mind, I am convinced that the whole economy of Nature, with every fact on distribution, rarity, abundance, extinction, and variation, will be dimly seen, or quite misunderstood. We behold the face of Nature, bright with gladness; we·often see superabundance of food; we do not see, or we forget, that the birds which are idly singing around us, mostly live on insects or seeds, and are thus continually destroying life; or, we forget how largely these songsters, or their eggs, or their nestlings, are destroyed by birds and beasts of prey; we do not always bear in mind that, though food may be now superabundant, it is not so at all seasons of each recurring year."

Again he says:

"Climate plays an important part in determining the average numbers of a species; and periodical seasons of extreme cold or drought, I believe to be the most effective of all checks. I estimated that the winter of 1854–55 destroyed four-fifths of the birds on my own grounds; and this is a tremendous destruction when we remember that ten per cent. is an extraordinarily severe mortality from epidemics with man. The action of the climate seems at first sight to be quite independent of the struggle for existence, but in so far as climate chiefly acts in reducing food, it brings on the most severe struggle between the individuals, whether of the same or of distinct species, which subsist on the same kind of food. Even when climate, for instance, extreme cold, acts directly, it will be the least vigorous, or those which have got least food, through the advancing winter, which will suffer most. When we travel from south to north, or from a damp region to a dry, we invariably see some species gradually getting rarer and rarer, and finally disappearing; and the change of climate being conspicuous, we are tempted to attribute the whole effect to its direct action. But, this is a very false view; we forget that each species, even where it most abounds, is constantly suffering enormous destruction at some period of its life, from enemies or competitors for the same place or food; and if these enemies or competitors be in the least degree favored by any slight change of climate, they will increase in numbers, and as each area is already stocked with inhabitants, the other species will decrease. When we travel southwards and see a species decreasing in numbers, we may feel sure that the cause lies quite as much in other species being favored, as in this one being hurt. So it is, when we travel northward, but in a somewhat lesser degree, for the number of species of all kinds, and therefore of competitors, decreases northward; hence, in going northward, or in ascending a mountain, we far oftener meet with stunted forms, due to the *directly* injurious action of climate, than we do in proceeding southward, or descending a mountain. When we reach the Arctic regions, or snow-capped summits, or absolute deserts, the struggle for life is almost exclusively with the elements."

Again he says :

"Battle within battle must ever be recurring, with varying success; and yet, in the long run, the forces are so nicely balanced, that the face of Nature remains uniform, for long periods of time, though assuredly the merest trifle would often give the victory to one organic being over another. Nevertheless, so profound is our ignorance, and so high our presumption, that we marvel when we hear of the extinction of an organic being; and, as we do not see the cause, we invoke cataclysms to desolate the world, or invent laws on the duration of the forms of life."

Speaking of a forest, in order to exemplify the Struggle for Existence, he says:

"What a struggle between the several kinds of trees, must here have gone on during long centuries, each annually scattering its seeds, by the thousand;

13*

what wars between insect and insect,—between insects, snails and other animals, with beasts and birds of prey,—all striving to increase, and all feeding on each other, or on the trees, or their seeds and seedlings, or on the other plants which first clothed the ground, and thus checked the growth of the trees!"

What is the obvious outcome, of such a condition of affairs?   Is it not, manifestly, degeneration?

But, the effect of this Struggle for Existence, is not left to presumption alone, strong as is that presumption.   Darwin shows the actual effect of the action of this factor, in the many "rudimentary organs," which "plainly show that an early progenitor had the organ in a fully developed state; and this, in some instances, implies an enormous amount of modification in the descendants." He shows the actual effect of this factor, when he says, that " Rudimentary organs are so extremely common throughout nature, that scarcely a single species can be mentioned, which is free from such a blemish." He shows the actual effect of this factor, in the multitude of "long-lost characters," to which he so frequently refers. He shows the actual effect of this factor when he admits that, " Not but that it" (the Struggle for Existence) "may and will leave many creatures, with simple and unimproved structures, fitted for simpler conditions of life, and in some cases will even degrade and simplify the organization.   *   * "

Now, we have not moved beyond the first stage in the order, in which he arrays his argument, before we find that, at that stage,—in the very inducement to his argument,—degeneration (which is the converse and refutation of the conclusion, at which his argument aims), is established, beyond question, by, both, an overwhelming presumption, arising from the very terms used in the inducement to such argument, and by facts conceded by Darwin, to be incident to the conditions under which works the main factor that he employs.

The reader doubtless fancies, that, assuredly, the very first care, with Darwin, will be to obviate,—or, at least to endeavor to obviate,—this strong and apparently insuperable objection to his argument. But, no ; Darwin proceeds with his ratiocination,—or induction, for it is always well nigh impossible to determine how he reasons,—as serenely and complacently, as if he had essayed, exclusively, to prove the descent of a mouse from an elephant, instead of the descent of an elephant from a mouse.

By the methods with which he argues, the outcome may be, as of old, the evolution of a ridiculous, little mouse ; but it will never be the evolution of any other organism.

2. His next proposition, in order, is that, in this Struggle for Existence, "the strongest and most vigorous" alone survive.

There is a fallacy, lying *perdu*, in these terms, "strongest and most vigorous." They beg the whole question; and they beg it, in the face of a state of facts, which wholly disprove the gratuitous assumption.

Viewed with reference to the circumstances of the fearful "battle for life," to which, Darwin says, all organisms have been subjected, the terms, "strongest and most vigorous," are, even in a grammatical sense, incorrect.

Viewed with reference to the same circumstances of the Struggle for Existence, and viewed with reference to the inference, intended to be drawn from the application of such terms, the terms "strongest and most vigorous," are wholly false, in the connection in which Darwin uses them.

"The strongest and most vigorous survive!" Let us define terms. Are these elect, which have survived, to be styled "strongest and most vigorous;" when, the sole idea possible to be gained, of the state of their strength, or of their weakness, is that which is to be gathered from the conditions, to which they, similarly with those which succumbed, have been subjected? and when such conditions are represented, by the very argument, to be adverse, and wholly unfavorable to strength or to development? According to the argument, the Struggle for Existence has acted upon those styled "the strongest and most vigorous," as well as upon those, yclept, the "weakest." Those, in which the conditions induced such impaired constitutions as were incompatible with prolonged existence, were, evidently, to be termed the weakest and most degenerate. What then, manifestly are the survivors correctly to be styled, which were alike subjected to such adverse conditions, and which owe their prolonged existence to a mere "grain in the balance?" What do even merely grammatical principles prescribe, that these should be called, which had also to fight the con-

ditions which proved too much for their weaker
brethren? Should not they, in view of the unfavorable conditions so graphically described by Darwin, be styled, the least degenerate, or the least weakened?

In the use of terms of comparison, regard must be
had to surrounding circumstances. If the surrounding
circumstances of Natural Selection had conveyed the
idea of strength, then, "strongest or most vigorous"
would be proper. But, when the conditions of Natural
Selection are confessedly so adverse, and when the
effect of the operation of such conditions, is, obviously,
to induce weakness and degeneration, terms of comparison, in harmony with such conditions, alone should
be used. Darwin's use, therefore, of such terms as
"strongest and most vigorous," is, in connection with
the idea of such a fearful Struggle for Existence, clearly
improper, irrespective of any argument which may
follow. Usage, it is true, often countenances such a
grammatical latitude, as the employment of the terms
"strongest and most vigorous," where "the least weakened," in strictness, should be used; and, it would
unquestionably be the very quintessence of pedan-
try, to cavil wantonly at such a slight departure
from what, upon a rigid construction alone, is improper. But, Darwin has here availed himself of
such latitude of expression, to hide a fallacy, fraught
with the most momentous consequences; and, therefore, a correct use of terms is demanded. Had Darwin
rigidly conformed to true principles of expression, he
would have said: The weakest and most degenerate

succumb to the hard conditions which constitute the Struggle for Existence; and the least weak and the least degenerate, and those which manage to hold their own, survive. Had he so expressed himself, no implication of advance in development would have arisen, as it does arise, when, in the face of the converse implication, arising from the fact of the Struggle for Existence, he uses the terms "strongest and most vigorous," in the stead of the terms, least degenerate, or least weak.

When Darwin says, that, in each generation, "the strongest and most vigorous" survive, and that they alone continue the line of descent for the given species, the presumption, arising in the mind of his reader (and the presumption which Darwin evidently designed should arise), is, that there is, therefore, advance in development. This presumption, as has already been shown, does not necessarily attend the fact of the selection of "the strongest and most vigorous." This presumption legitimately arises, only from such selection, and from conditions favorable to an advance in development, combined. The place, where the presumption has been generally employed, has been under domestication. There, the two conditions of the presumption, prevail. There are, generally, under domestication, both selection, and favorable conditions which have been observed generally to induce an advance in development.

Under nature, there is selection, but there are not favorable conditions; for, to work the selection there, there needs must be unfavorable conditions! In drawing the presumption, respecting animals under Man's care, especial note has been taken of the selection ; the favorable conditions remaining understood. Darwin has carried the idea of Selection, to organisms under nature ; and, availing himself of the circumstance, that the favorable conditions, have long been only tacitly understood, in drawing the presumption of advance in development, he has, in a field where favorable conditions do not obtain,—where unfavorable conditions confessedly prevail, aye, where the other condition of the presumption (namely, Selection) cannot obtain where favorable conditions exist,—illegitimately helped himself to the presumption of advance in development, which holds good, only where there are favorable conditions to imply such advance in development.   Under domestication, "the stronger and more vigorous," of any one generation, are usually stronger and more vigorous (where selection is exercised) than the individuals of the preceding generation.   Darwin, affects to believe, that all that is necessary, in order to prove advance under nature, is to show Selection; as that, generally, is all that seemingly needs to be done, under domestication.   But, the implication, which attends the fact of Selection, under domestication, does not attend the same fact under nature ; for, under domestication, there is an advance in development, which is implied by the favorable conditions under domestication: Whereas, the conditions under nature,—aye, the very conditions which, according to the argument needs must be very adverse, to work the Selection which is designed to prove the advance in development,—imply the converse, viz., that there is not such advance in development, but, rather, a retrograde movement, in even the elect, or the "stronger and more vigorous."

There is another fallacy in Darwin's use of the terms, "stronger and more vigorous;" independently of the consideration that, in view of the circumstances, they are grammatically incorrect. The assertion, that the "stronger and more vigorous" survive, may (when the sometime-mentioned latitude of expression is allowed) be true, in one sense; but is false, when viewed with reference to the inference designed to be drawn. In Darwin's statement of the *fact* of the Selection under nature, he uses the terms "stronger and more vigorous," as if he intended them as terms of comparison with their contemporaries only. In the *inference* which he draws, however, he employs them,—not as terms of comparison only with those individuals which have succumbed,—but as terms of comparison with the individuals of a preceding generation. When his readers read his statement, that "the stronger and more vigorous" survive, they yield assent to the proposition. Yes (they reason), they (the elect) are stronger and more vigorous than the weak ones with constitutions so impaired as to cause death. But, when the readers are asked to accept Darwin's alleged inference therefrom (*i. e.*, of advance in development), they are assumed (by Darwin) to have yielded assent to something entirely different. They assented to the implication, that the elect were stronger and more vigorous than certain of their contemporaries; and, now, in the inference forced upon them, they are coolly assumed

to have assented to an implication, that the elect were
stronger and more vigorous than their progenitors!
Verily, is it, that, by "words, words," alone, Darwin
passes "through the safe-gate into the temple of cer-
tainty." The touchstone to Darwin's fallacy, that Selection, *per se*, argues any advance in development,—
the failure to apply which has led to all the confusion,
—is the query: "Stronger and more vigorous? Compared with whom? Their contemporaries only? or
their contemporaries and predecessors?"

In Paris, under the Commune, when famine and
murder vied for the mastery, and in cities stricken with
the plague, "the stronger and more vigorous" survived
—But, "stronger and more vigorous," compared with
whom? Manifestly; compared, not with individuals
of the preceding generation, but with those only, placed
in the same straits with themselves.

According to Darwin's argument (?), the more adverse and unfavorable the conditions of life are, the
greater is the advance in development! because, as he
contends, the harder the conditions of life, the more
rigid and exclusive will be the Selection! Mephis-
topheles doubtless had in mind, this theory of Darwin,
when, in his advice to the student, he counseled him
to stick to "words," as a theory might well be built of
"words."

That the conditions, under nature, imply a retrograde movement in those even which are preserved
by Natural Selection; and, that, therefore, those conditions militate against Darwin's use of the terms
"stronger and more vigorous" to denote those se-
14

lected, cannot well be questioned by any one who reads Darwin's statements respecting Natural Extinction and Natural Selection. According to Darwin, all, even the elect, are amenable to the Struggle for Existence. Numbers are born into the world at a rate, Darwin says, which, if not met by Natural Extinction, would soon cover the world with the progeny of a single pair. They all join in the battle for life; and, although thousands succumb, they have during even their short lives, helped to sharpen the competition which "the stronger and more vigorous" have to endure; and have thus lent their aid to induce the deterioration of those selected to continue the line of descent. All have to struggle for their existence, from the hour of their birth to the moment of their death: according to Darwin. Natural Extinction carries off —not those whose constitutions are merely impaired, or those which are merely degenerate in structure, for multitudes of these do actually survive and procreate others endowed with their defects—but those only, whose impaired constitutions, or whose defective structures, are absolutely incompatible with prolonged existence. The adverse conditions, which occasion Natural Selection, manifestly do more than kill off the weakest. They also cause a degeneration, both of those which have barely escaped extinction, and of "the stronger and more vigorous." The "stronger and more vigorous" may, in view of the competition for means of subsistence, to which Darwin pictures them as being subjected, count themselves very fortunate, if they merely manage to hold their own. Holding their own, implies no advance in development; and the adverse conditions, shown by Darwin, imply that any move made by the "stronger and more vigorous," was in the direction of degeneration. Does not Darwin's statement of the fearful battle for life, imply, that, though possibly "stronger and more vigorous," they are generally, less fit, less strong, and less vigorous than the preceding generation?

Natural Selection, at the best, is nothing but a struggle or a protest against degeneration. The retreat of a man, with his face, however, towards the foe, typifies Natural Selection and the Struggle for Existence ; and any argument, designed to prove that the man was advancing upon his enemies, based upon the mere circumstance that his face was in the direction of advance, would be a perfect analogue of Darwin's argument from Natural Selection. The man's retrograde movement symbolizes the obvious effect of the adverse conditions under nature, which provoke the Struggle for Existence. The position of the man, confronting his foe while he retreats, symbolizes Natural Selection, or the survival of "the stronger and more vigorous." The mere survival of "the stronger and more vigorous" does not imply any advance in development. At the most, it can but imply a continuance, of those organisms, in the same state. Under the conditions of Natural Selection, and under the evidence which Darwin gives, of so many " rudimentary organs," and of so many "long-lost characters," the survival of "the stronger and more vigorous," proves only that the minimum of degeneration,

possible under the circumstances, obtains with these
elect; or, in other words, that the less degenerate and
the less injuriously modified individuals survive, whilst
the more degenerate and the more injuriously modified
individuals succumb.   Given, the absence of all knowledge of the nature of the conditions of life under
nature, the selection of "the stronger and more vigorous" implies merely, that these hold their own.   Given,
that knowledge of the conditions, which Darwin com-
municates to the reader, in his descriptions of the
Struggle for Existence, the selection of "the stronger
and more vigorous" implies that the "stronger and
more vigorous " merely yield the least, to the effect of
such adverse conditions.

Owing to the ingenious manner, in which Darwin
has availed himself of the presumption of advance in
development, from the fact of Selection, without form-
ulating such presumption in set and explicit terms; it
is open, to him, to deny that he has attempted to
prove that increments of development must generally
result from the selection of "the stronger and more
vigorous."   The main part of the strength with which
his theory of Natural Selection is credited, however, is
due to the belief, on the part of his readers, that the
selection of "the stronger and more vigorous" does
imply advance in development; and to the belief that
Darwin so contends.   Darwin, himself, unquestionably
counts throughout, for support to his theory, upon
this impression, so subtly conveyed by his handling
of the question.   It is true, that, with respect to the
variations, which, he confesses, are gratuitously assumed

to arise, "in the course of thousands of generations," he explicitly disclaims any intention to maintain that Natural Selection causes, or in any way produces their appearance, and alleges that Natural Selection confines its operation, solely to the preservation and accumulation of those variations after they have arisen.   But, this disclaimer he employs, solely in relation to these marked variations assumed to arise "in the course of thousands of generations;" and it ever seems, to the reader, not to apply to those very slight increments of development, which Darwin intimates, as strongly as he may, without explicit expression, to be the outcome of the mere selection of "the strongest and most vigorous."   The idea which, wittingly or unwittingly, has been conveyed by Darwin, and which has caused Natural Selection to be so widely reputed as a most potent factor of development, is, that, although the pronounced, tangible variations assumed to arise " in the course of thousands of generations," are not, in any way, produced by Natural Selection, but are merely preserved and accumulated by that factor; yet that Natural Selection does produce very slight, scarcely appreciable increments of development, by means of the survival exclusively of "the stronger and more vigorous."   Had Darwin's disclaimer, of any desire to maintain that Natural Selection induced the appearance of variations, been explicitly declared to cover these slight advances in development (which every one who reads Darwin's works, needs must conclude that he meant to represent as having been produced by the mere selection of " the stronger and more.vig-

14*

orous"), Natural Selection would never have enjoyed the reputation it has had, of being such a grand and important principle.

Second: Assuming, however, that the mere Selection, of "the stronger and more vigorous," does prove the appearance of slight increments of development, still his argument, that these may be so accumulated as to evolve higher species from ones lower in the scale, both begs the question at issue, and is negatived, in two several ways, by the very argument itself of Natural Selection. It begs the question, by tacitly assuming, that these slight increments of development are new developments, and that they may be accumulated indefinitely, or without any assignable limit; and, conversely, by assuming, that they are not the mere regain of developments, once lost by the given species, and that they are not capable, only of being accumulated to an extent, commensurate with the past degeneration of such species.

The argument itself of Natural Selection negatives this assumption,—viz., that these increments are new developments,—by postulating the necessary dependence, of Natural Selection, upon a hard Struggle for Existence which manifestly implies previous degeneration, in the organisms displaying the slight advances; and Natural Selection itself implies, that any such increments of development which may arise in "the stronger and more vigorous," are the mere regain, by means of the law of reversion, of what was before lost. For, the argument of Natural Selection absolutely requires, that the Struggle for Existence—which manifestly is a process of degeneration—should, in the order of time, precede Natural Selection; which is assumed to be a process of growth or of development. So, by the very terms of Darwin's argument, the strong presumption arises, that the increments of development—assumed to be the outcome of the selection of "the stronger and more vigorous"—are but the mere regain of what was lost by the degeneration so forcibly implied by the Struggle for Existence which preceded the action of Natural Selection.

But, the fact, of such degeneration, is not left to implication alone. Darwin shows explicitly, in his detail of a multitude of "rudimentary organs," and of "long-lost characters," that such degeneration actually did precede the action of Natural Selection.

It was open to Darwin, also to contend, that the Struggle for Existence implied advances in development, upon the principle that increase of activity often induces increase of growth in an organ. But, assuming such increase of structure, this is equally an instance of begging the question at issue. The presumption is, that such increase is but the regain of what was once lost. Any argument, of indefinite development, based upon such assumed increase of structure, would beg the question, by assuming, that the increase was a new development, in the given species. Darwin speaks of ducks which, by reason of their *habitat* having been removed to the highlands, have rudimentary, webbed feet. Place these ducks in an environment, where they may paddle, *ad lib.*, in the water; then argue from the re-development of the web in their feet, that, given such development within a year, these ducks may, within a million of years, develop into higher species and genera; and a perfect analogue will be had, of the argument from increase of structure following increased activity. The webbed feet are but the re-development, of what was once lost, by the species in question; and any argument, founded thereupon, designed to prove the possibility of indefinitely continued development, is manifestly a gross *petitio principii.*

Third: As we have seen, Darwin argues, that there must be slight advances in development, because, in each generation, Natural Selection picks out "the stronger and more vigorous" to continue the line of descent. Whatever semblance of strength is in this argument, we have shown to be due to the most transparent of fallacies. Conscious, probably, of the absurdity of such an argument, Darwin deemed it necessary to supplement this mode of getting the slight development, for Natural Selection to accumulate, with a gratuitous assumption.

He assumes, that there are pronounced variations which arise, under nature, seemingly in the same inexplicable and spontaneous manner in which he deems the improvements, under domestication, to present themselves. This is his assumption. His argument therefrom, runs to the effect; that, most probably the possession of such a variation gives to the individual possessing it, such an advantage in the struggle for existence, as to ensure its survival, and the transmission of such variation to its descendants; that such descendants, "in the course of thousands of generations," may develop another such variation; and, that, by the indefinitely continued accumulation of such variations, these individuals may develop into organisms as high as any in the scale of development.

Respecting his assumption, of the variations occurring "in the course of thousands of generations," he says:

"Can it be thought improbable (*sic*) seeing that variations useful to Man have undoubtedly occurred, that other variations useful, in some way, to each being, in the great and complex battle for life, should sometimes occur in the course of thousands (*sic*) of generations? If such variations do occur (*sic*) can we doubt (remembering that many more individuals· are born than can possibly survive), that individuals having an advantage, however slight, over others, would have the best chance of surviving and procreating their kind?"

Now, this is honest, frank, and ingenuous. He does not here,—as he does when treating of the survival of the merely "stronger and more vigorous"—endeavor to *prove*, by fallacious argument, that there are advances in development. But, he *assumes* that there are such advances in development;—the only appearance of an argument, in this connection, being his appeal to the circumstance that it cannot be alleged that the probabilities are against his assumption, inasmuch as such things occur under domestication. The probabilities, however, do obtain, against his argument; for, the conditions of life are different, being favorable to development in the one place, and unfavorable in the other. Having assumed these variations, he then proceeds in his endeavor to show, that Natural Selection may accumulate them, *ad infinitum.*

Exception to this assumption of variations occurring "in the course of thousands of generations," may be taken, only on the ground that it is gratuitous; and that (as with variations under domestication), he terms these variations "spontaneous," and gives no law by which their appearance is governed.

Fourth: Now, as to his theory, that Natural Selection may accumulate these assumed variations indefinitely: It begs the whole question; and begs it, too, in the face of a strong presumption, arising from the very requirements of the theory itself, and begs it, in the face of what Darwin has explicitly shown to be the actual effects of the operation of Natural Selection, the main factor of the theory.

The said presumption is the one, upon which we have already commented at length, namely, The presumption, of previous degeneration, arising from the unfavorable conditions under nature, which absolutely require to be unfavorable, upon Darwin's theory of Natural Selection, in order to bring about this very Selection.

The alleged, actual effects of the operation of Natural Selection, are, namely, the "rudimentary organs," and "long-lost characters," adduced, so frequently and abundantly, by Darwin himself.

Therefore, it is clear that Darwin's argument, from Natural Selection, is a *petitio principii.* Nay, more, the premises of such argument rebut its conclusion. For, the presumption, from Darwin's own argument, and from Darwin's own facts, is, that the variations, which he gratuitously assumes to occur under nature, are but the mere regain of developments, lost by the respective species in which they occur.

Given, the variations which he asks; assuming, even, that as many variations occur under nature, as are known to occur under domestication, and they avail Darwin nothing. The presumption is, that the species, in so varying, are but retrieving past degeneration.

Concede the efficiency of Natural Selection, in preserving and accumulating such variations, and it aids Darwin as little to attain the result he is so solicitous to achieve; for, if such variations are but the regain of lost characters, and are limited to the number and kind of such lost characters, how may Natural Selection continue long to accumulate, when the variations, which it is to accumulate, needs must give out, when all the lost characters are regained?

There is, really, no limit to the *potential* efficiency of Natural Selection. If the conditions of its operation would but hold out, it could perform all the wonders which Darwin ascribes to it. But they do not hold out. No more characters can be regained, and then accumulated by Natural Selection, than were lost. Darwin has proceeded upon the false assumption, that the gratuitously assumed variations under nature, are new developments. But this assumption of new growth or development is more than false; it is exquisitely absurd, inasmuch as the very argument itself, in which it appears, implies that it is false!

The question of the efficiency of Natural Selection is wholly immaterial. There is little doubt that, if this factor were not so " cabined, cribbed, and confined," it would be fully equal to the task of evolving a dragon from a mosquito. Natural Selection may be so efficient, potentially, that its capacity,—where suffered to display itself,—might be shown to be almost infinite. But, when the efficiency of Natural Selection, in accumulating variations, organs, or features, is circumscribed by the fact, that the variations, organs, or features, possible to be so accumulated, are restricted, in number and kind, to the number and kind previously lost by the respective, varying species; all speculation, as to what Natural Selection might or could do, if only it had sufficient variations, organs, or features to accumulate, will advance the theory of development, not a hair's breadth.

Darwin fancies, that, in the fearful struggle for existence which he describes as being continually waged, the possession of one of these slight variations, which are assumed to "occur in the course of thousands of generations," will give its owner such an advantage over its competitors, as will ensure its being classed with "the strongest and most vigorous," and as will therefore occasion its survival, by which it will be enabled to procreate its kind, and perpetuate the said variation in its descendants. This process, of the preservation of a varying individual, is assumed to repeat itself again and again, at intervals of a thousand generations or so; and the consequent aggregation of such variations is alleged to represent the assumed development of a lower into a higher species. But, unfortunately, the consistency of the beautiful and ingenious hypothesis, is marred, by the part thereof which prompts the reader to an estimate of the amount of degeneration wrought upon such a varying organism, by the fearful Struggle for Existence, in the interval, of the thousand generations, which preceded the mysterious appearance of such a variation. Given, the "Battle for Life" to have been continually waging, during such interval, as Darwin assumes it to have been; was the degeneration, effected during such period, greater or less, than the degree of subsequent development, represented by such occasional variation? and, is it likely, in view of the circumstances detailed, that such variation was *net* gain to the given species? are questions which obtrude themselves upon the reader, who is competent to discern, that subjective harmony, even, is wanting in Darwin's argument from Natural Selection.

This question, of *net* gain to the species is an eminently suggestive one. Fancy a person endeavoring to prove that a certain friend of his was growing rich, in trade; and doing it thus: He has a large stock of goods—Everybody seems to be in the same line of trade—Sharpest competition, between them, that you ever saw—There have been "panic times" ever since he started in the business, and the same lively competion—He has a large number of clerks and salesmen, whom he has to pay, whether there is business or not—He is under a heavy rent—The disadvantages, over which he triumphs, may be conceived, when I state, that only
15

once or twice in a month, does a customer stray along, to buy a dollar's worth of goods, and that the whole amount realized upon sales, during the year, by the whole trade, is only about twenty dollars—When such a customer makes his appearance, every one in the trade attempts to seize upon the poor man, and he stands the risk of being torn, limb from limb—My friend, however, is so bland, persistent, and persuasive that, during the whole time he has been in the business, he has secured every customer, despite all the exertions of his fellow-tradesmen, and borne him off triumphant—Such being the case, can you doubt that he, having such an advantage over the others (*sic*), has rapidly grown rich ?

His friend is thus proven (?) to have grown rich,—not by any calculation of his profits and losses,—but by an argument, based solely upon the advantages he possesses, over his competitors! The inducement to the argument, represents the friend and his fellow-tradesmen, suffering, most severely, from dullness of the times, from severe mutual competition, from heavy, current expenses, and from adverse conditions of almost every kind. Yet, notwithstanding the continual drain upon his friend's capital, our hypothetical friend lays stress, exclusively upon the circumstance, that once or twice, in a month or so, his friend alone, of all his guild, is able to secure a dollar's worth of sales; and he deduces the conclusion, that, because his friend is the most successful (or, to put it, as it should be, the least unfortunate) man in the business, the amount of his profits is to be estimated, simply and solely, by the measure in which he is more fortunate (or, rather, less unfortunate) than his fellows. It is manifest, however, that such measure of fortune, accruing from the occasional dollar which he receives, is not *net* profit, but the mere return, or regain (and that, but in a small degree), of the capital stock which has been fast melting away.

The analogy, we presume, is clear to all. This case is a fair analogue of Darwin's argument from Natural Selection. There was, originally, a certain amount of organic capital, in each species under nature. Darwin, in picturing the operation of Natural Selection, necessarily shows adverse conditions, whose obvious effect is a drain upon that capital. (Such effect is not merely obviously implied; but is shown in Darwin's "rudimentary organs," in his "long-lost characters," and in the wide scope which he ascribes to Reversion.) A favorable modification is assumed to occur "sometimes during the course of thousands of generations." This is the analogue of the tradesman's monthly sale of a dollar's worth of goods. Now, says Darwin, this assumed, favorable modification is a step in the advance of the given species towards a higher development. But, he has ignored the vital question as to whether it is *net* profit to the species in which the variation arises. It is, evidently, but the mere return of what has been lost. There has been,—according to the very argument which is used,—previous, organic expense, or loss; and this variation is but a partial return of the organic capital before expended. Before it was possible for him fairly to found any argument upon the profit or improvement, accruing to any animal or plant, he should have shown, that the organic capital, lost either a generation or two back, or thousands of generations back, had been all regained; and that the favorable variations assumed, are *net* profit, to the given species.   This, it is impossible for him to do.

We intend to show, in this work, by Darwin's own organic profit and loss account, contained in the books, entered up by himself, that there is not a single instance of profit (*i. e.* variation or improvement) adduced by him, which is *net* profit; and, conversely, that every positive variation or improvement, which he presents, is but *gross* profit, or mere regain of organic capital, once lost by the given species. We have heretofore shown, only, . that all of the variations are explicable upon this sup-position, and inexplicable, scientifically, upon any other. We shall, however, demonstrate that they are but the regain of capital once lost, under nature.   We shall demonstrate that each individual is ruined or impaired, in constitution and in fertility, in proportion as it falls short of the original, organic capital of its species. We shall show, that not a single individual has, by means of variation, ever made any *net* organic gain, relatively to the amount of organic capital with which its species once, originally started; but that, in proportion as it has retrieved what it once lost, is it normal in health, constitutional vigor, and fertility; and we shall point out the individuals, and the different species, which, either, have had but small losses under nature, or having had great losses, have, in a great measure, recovered them; and contrast their health, constitu-tional vigor and fertility, with the respective degrees,

of ruin, of those which still suffer under great losses
of organic capital, incurred under nature; or, of those
which, having lost but little under nature, have been
greatly degenerated by Man's Selection operating
solely for his benefit, instead of for the organisms'
good. This we shall do, not by mere speculation;
nor by the mere balancing of degrees of probability,
but by the crucial tests, Crossing and Close-Interbreeding, which are scales, or Biometers, adjustable,
respectively, degree for degree, to the several degrees
of ruin, and to the several degrees of accruing (gross)
profit, of all the individuals of every species.

CHAPTER VI.

THE SEVERAL PROCESSES OF FORMATION OF VARIETIES.

In the fourth Chapter, we alleged that there is but one, normal coördination of characters, in each species,—a coördination comprising all of the positive characters of the given species; and we asserted, and promised to prove, that the impaired coördination in individuals, consequent upon the struggle for existence under nature, is repaired and made perfect, in proportion to the regain of the long-lost characters of the species. The same principle was formulated, in the last chapter, wherein it was asserted that the regain of that portion of the organic capital, once lost by the respective species, is attended with physiological good.

Were reversion, under domestication, or the re-development of features once lost by an ancient progenitor, proportionately displayed under domestication, in all of the lost characters, the redemption of our promise, were a brief task. But, the characters suppressed, or reduced in the individuals, when taken from a state of nature, are not concurrently re-developed. Quite frequently, the re-development of a character, to the neglect of other characters, impairs the harmony and the coördination of the organization, to a greater degree, than existed before the animal or plant was

(170)

placed under domestication. The phenomena of divergence of character, or of disproportionate Reversion, whilst complicating the problem greatly, afford, however, proof stronger, and more conclusive, than would be available, were full and concurrent reversion, the unvarying feature, under domestication.

That physiological good, does, as a general rule attend the improvement of animals and plants under domestication, may be shown. Darwin says (p. 212, Vol. ii, *Animals and Plants, &c*):

"Domestication, as a general rule, increases the prolificness of animals and plants."

As we shall see, increase of prolificness, or of fertility, is the principal test of an improved, physiological state.

Instead of all the parts of the organization of an animal or plant being simultaneously and proportionately developed, under domestication, Man, when he has utility for his guide, preserves and accumulates those parts only, which he values, and which are useful to him, for some special purpose of his own. In species, where man's fancy, or amusement, comes into play, he develops but one of the varying parts, in each variety; sacrificing, and subordinating the other parts, in the same variety, to the end he has in view. In some species, Man looks to the improvement of one or two characters only, in the individuals. In other species, while he develops all of the characters, he does what is most injurious to the individual organisms; he suffers those characters to be developed, only, each in a different variety. Each individual of a species, Darwin, in his chapters on Analogous variation, shows to be capable of developing all of the positive characters of its species. But, the way varieties are formed, and formed so distinct, is, by Man's selection repressing this capacity in every direction, or in every character, and suffering it to be exercised in only the one character which Man assigns as the peculiar character of the variety, in which the individual has been placed. Darwin says, as has been before quoted,

" That we may infer, that, when any part, or organ, is either greatly increased in size, or wholly suppressed, * * the coördinating power of the organization will continually tend to bring all the parts again into harmony with each other."

If this be the tendency of the coördinating power of the organization, which it unquestionably is, it is manifest, that the system of man's formation of varieties, under domestication,—namely, of increasing, to a great size, the peculiarity of each variety, and of suppressing, or reducing, the other parts in the same variety,—is in derogation of this power, which "tends to bring all of the parts again into harmony with each other." The object of this chapter, is to see how, and how far, man has violated the normal, mutual relation of the parts. After having shown the many ways, in which he has varied the normal relation of the parts of a species, we shall proceed to show that Darwin is wrong, when he fancies, that man may mould an organism into any form he pleases, and yet not injure the individuals in a physiological sense. In this connection, he says (Vol. ii, p. 425):

"It is difficult to overrate our ignorance of the use·
of various parts of the organization."

The principal use of the various parts, is to preserve
the normal relation, or balance of the whole; and this
relation or balance may not be varied, *ad lib.*, by man,
without evil effects upon the physiology of the organ·
ism. Such evil effects we shall show to be registered,
in each individual; and to be susceptible of being read,
with perfect ease, by every fancier, breeder, horticulturist and agriculturist.

The principal reason, why proportionate re-development does not occur under domestication,—why all of
the characters do not, in each or in any individual, return concurrently to the original, perfect type,—why
all of the lost characters are not regained, in each individual,—is, not only because man does not desire to
develop all of the characters in each individual, but
because, also, the different individuals are subjected
to different conditions of life, which favor the development of special characters, in advance of the
development of others. Man avails himself of this
circumstance, and pushes the development of the first
character presenting itself (if it be a desirable character), to an extreme point. When an individual has one
character in the ascendant, man seizes it, and makes it
the peculiarity of a given variety, and suppresses the
development of all the other characters. Other individuals, with another character in an exceptionally-
advanced state of development, are made to constitute
another varietal type; and, the further the exclusive
development of the distinguishing mark of this type,

is carried, the more the individuals of this class, become disproportionately developed. Every deviation, among the individuals of a variety, "from the standard of excellence which the breeder has established in his own mind" (p. 237), is esteemed a degeneration; although such variation be of a positive character, and although it consist of an organ essentially necessary to secure the normal relation of the parts.

Thus, it is, generally, the case, that each variety possesses a character, which it is necessary that the other varieties should possess; and, each variety lacks all of the positive peculiarities, of the other varieties, which, for full physiological integrity, it is necessary that it should possess. In other words, the positive characters of a species, which it is essential should all be developed in each individual of that species, are, instead thereof, apportioned among different individuals, or different varieties. In other words, a multiplicity of divergent varieties in any species, necessarily implies the loss, in each variety, of the positive characters peculiar to the other varieties of the species. With many animals, absence of true proportion is occasioned, frequently, by blind conformity to certain standards, existing in the breeders' minds. Thus, when a breed acquires a reputation, or distinct character, all of its then existing points,—both those positive, and those negative, both, those parts, of intrinsic value, and those not,—are faithfully preserved; as if, the preservation intact, of the existing structure, were a *sine qua non* of its good quality, or of its purity of blood; and this occurs, even when some of its features are shockingly out of proportion, and when some are wholly suppressed.

Darwin says (p. 16, *Origin of Species*):

" Domesticated races * * often differ in an extreme degree, in some one part, * * when compared with one another."

(Page 31, *Origin of Species*): "One of the most remarkable features in our domesticated races, is, that we see, in them, adaptation, not indeed to the animal's or plant's own good, but to man's use or fancy."

(Page 33, *Origin of Species*): Darwin quotes Youatt, approvingly, as saying, that man, by Selection, as "with the magician's wand, * * may summon into life, whatever form and mould he pleases."

Simply varying the relations of the given number of parts belonging to a species, is not developing; and it shall be shown that, when the parts are not of the one, true ratio, there is evil inevitably entailed.

(Page 33, *Origin of Species*): Darwin says, that the very distinct varieties, observable under domestication, are "produced by the accumulation in one direction, during successive generations, of differences."

For breeders, and fanciers, to work upon, there are, at the start, under domestication, a certain number of characters in each species. In addition thereto, there are a number of characters, which were lost by a past generation, and which arise under the favorable conditions of domestication. From these characters, Man has formed the varieties of each species under domestication, by the following processes:

1. By the retention, of the individuals of a species,

at several stages of reversion, accounting merely for differences of size;

2. By continuing the process, of degeneration, commenced under nature, and retaining the individuals of the given species, at each stage of such degeneration, also accounting merely for difference of size;

3. By the re-development of the long-lost characters of the species, of which not a vestige remained; but, with an apportionment, or distribution of them, among different varieties ;

4. By the retention, of the individuals of several varieties, at each stage of the re-development of the lost characters allotted to their respective varieties, thus accounting for the sub-varieties of the third class ;

5. By the re-development of the rudimentary organs of the species, and their apportionment among different varieties;

6. By the retention of the individuals of several varieties, at each stage of the development of the rudimentary organs allotted to their respective varieties, thus accounting for the sub-varieties of the fifth class ;

7. By the extreme, and exclusive re-development (or selection), of one part only, in each variety, among those parts which have been only partially reduced, under nature ;

8. By the retention, of the individuals of several varieties, at each stage of the re-development of those parts, only partially reduced under nature ; thus accounting for the sub-varieties of the seventh class ;

9. By a process of degeneration, by which in several

varieties under domestication, Man effects the reduction or suppression of characters, which were not reduced or suppressed under nature ;

10. By the retention of the individuals, of several varieties, at each stage of such degeneration; thus accounting for the sub-varieties of the ninth class;

11. By the re-development of one only of the characters which have been lost, suppressed or reduced under nature;

12. By the retention of the individuals of several varieties, at each stage of the re-development of this one character which was lost, suppressed or reduced under nature, thus accounting for sub-varieties of the eleventh class.

Take a hundred rubber balls, of like size and character, and compress them all to half their size; then, in ten, or a dozen of the balls, relax the pressure, in a different part, in each ball; then, in others of the balls, relax, but slightly, the pressure, in each ball, in a part corresponding to the part with its pressure relaxed, in one of the balls of the first class; then, in other balls, relax the pressure all around, but in a different degree, in each ball; then, in other balls, instead of relaxing the pressure, much increase the pressure, upon a different part, in each ball; then, in other balls, instead of greatly increasing the pressure, in a different part, in each ball, increase the pressure, but increase it somewhat less, in a descending degree, in a part in each ball, corresponding to the same part in each of the balls of the preceding class; then, in other balls, increase the pressure, all around, in a degree varying with each ball,

16

instead of increasing it in parts only; then, in one ball, relax the pressure fully, in one part only; and then in other balls, relax the pressure in the same just-mentioned part, but relax it less and less, in a descending degree, in the several, remaining balls.

Having done this, conformably to direction, you will have varieties, of the, originally, one kind of ball, exactly analogous to varieties of a species under domestication. The compression, of the ball, represents degeneration; the elasticity, displayed upon relaxation of the pressure, corresponds to reversion. The disproportionate compression, and disproportionate relaxation, are respectively analogous to disproportionate Reversion, and to disproportionate degeneration, in organisms. The balls, in their original, normal state of expansion, represent the original, normal type of a species. As the restraint, upon the several balls, constraining them to a shape, not in harmony with the natural properties of their matter, is abnormal; so, the disproportionate development of varieties, is abnormal, as the retention, of their parts, at any stage short of full, complete reversion, is in derogation of the one, true ratio of their development. In the case of an organism, there is a crucial test, demonstrating most positively, that any constraint to a shape, short of the full development of all the positive features of the species, is injurious to physiological integrity.

The compression, of the ball, to half its size, does not exactly represent the degeneration in species, under nature. For the compression, above mentioned, is impliedly equal, all around; whereas, degeneration is not equally effective, upon all the characters of a species. It reduces some very slightly; much reduces others; and wholly suppresses still others; according to the conditions of life, to which the several races, under nature, were subjected.

The several processes, of formation of varieties under domestication, are nearly all exemplified in the case of the Pigeon. This species, under domestication, is pre-eminently conspicuous among those whose varieties are greatly divergent in character.

"In practice," says Darwin (p. 125, *Origin of Species*), "a fancier is, for instance, struck by a Pigeon having a slightly shorter beak; another fancier is struck by a Pigeon having a rather larger beak; and on the acknowledged principle that 'fanciers do not and will not admire a medium standard, but like extremes,' they both go on choosing and breeding from birds with longer and longer beaks, or with shorter and shorter beaks."

"Compare," says he (p. 22, *Origin of Species*), "the English Carrier, and the shortfaced tumbler, and see the wonderful difference, in their beaks, entailing corresponding differences in their skulls."

"The Carrier is also remarkable" (p. 22, *Origin of Species*), "from the wonderful development about the head"—from "greatly elongated eyelids, very large external orifices to the nostrils, and a wide gape of mouth. The shortfaced tumbler has a beak, in outline, like that of a finch. * * The Runt is a bird of great size, with long massive beak and large feet; some of the sub-breeds of Runts have very long necks, others very long wings and tails, others simply short tails. The Barb is allied to the Carrier, but instead of a very long beak, has a very short and very broad one. The Pouter has a much elongated body, wings, and legs, and an enormously developed crop. * * The Turbit has a very short and conical beak, with a line of reversed feathers down the breast, and it has the habit of continually expanding, slightly, the upper part of the œsophagus. The Jacobin has the feathers so much reversed along the back of the neck, that they form a hood, and it has proportionally to its size, much elongated wing and tail feathers. The Trumpeter and Laugher, as their names express, utter a very different coo, from the other breeds. The Fantail has thirty or even forty tail feathers, instead of twelve or fourteen, the normal number in all members of the great pigeon family; and these feathers are kept expanded, and are carried so erect, that in good birds, the head and tail touch; the oil gland is quite aborted."

A certain number of characters belong to the species, Pigeon. Those characters, which were, under nature, lost, and which are re-developed, under domestication, are distributed among different varieties and these characters, and the others, simply have their proportions, and their number, varied in the different varieties. In some varieties, some of these characters are wholly suppressed, or greatly reduced. All of the positive characters should be developed, fully and proportionately, in each individual. Each variety, obviously, then, falls short of the true type, viz., the sum of all the features. It is our task to show, that, inasmuch as each variety so falls short, evil is entailed upon it. This is done in the succeeding chapter.

(Page 262, Vol. i.) The fancier, says Darwin:

"Endeavors to exaggerate every peculiarity in his

breeds.   A great authority says, 'Fanciers do not, and will not admire, a medium standard, that is, half and half, which is neither here nor there, but admire extremes.' "

"Domesticated races differ much, in some one organ, from the other races of the same species," * * though "the remaining parts of the organization will always be found in some degree different" (p. 150, *Origin of Species*).

Varieties, under domestication, "show adaptation to his (man's) wants and pleasure" (p. 14, Vol. i, *Animals and Plants, &c*).

"Domesticated races of animals, and cultivated races of plants, often exhibit an abnormal character, as compared with natural species; for, they have been modified, not for their own benefit, but for that of man" (p. 14, Vol. i).

Each individual Pigeon varies a little, in several ways, from even the others of the same variety, or sub-variety.   Each differs, slightly, from the others of the same variety, and, greatly, from others of the other varieties, in the length, size, or number, of the wing-feathers; in the length, size, or number of the tail feathers; in the length, number, or size of the primary wing-feathers; in the number, length, or breadth of the ribs; in the size, and form of the body; in the number, and size of the scutellæ; in the size of the eye, and eyelids; in the size, length, and thickness of the feet and legs; in the length, and size, and breadth of the tongue and beak; in the size, and shape of the lower jaw; in the amount of wattle; in the heaviness of the coating of feathers; in the size,

16*

and shape of the sternum, and of the scapula; and in every detail of the internal organs, of the skeleton, and of external adornment.

The mode, in which Man gets such distinct varieties, is by refusing to re-develop all of the characters, concurrently; and, by pushing the re-development of one, two, or but a few characters only, in any one variety.

Under the heading of "Tendency in Man to carry the practice of Selection to an extreme point" (p. 290, Vol. ii), Darwin says:

"It is an important principle that, in the process of selection, man almost invariably wishes to go to an extreme point (!) Thus, in useful qualities, there is no limit to his desire to breed certain horses and dogs as fleet as possible, and others as strong as possible; certain kinds of sheep, for extreme fineness, and others, for extreme length of wool; and he wishes to produce fruit, grain, tubers, and other useful parts of plants, as large and excellent as possible. With animals, bred for amusement, the same principle is even more powerful; for fashion, as we see even in our dress, always runs to extremes (!) This view has been expressly admitted by fanciers. Instances were given in the chapter on the Pigeon, but here is another: Mr. Eaton, after describing a comparatively new variety, namely, the Archangel, remarks, 'What fanciers intend doing with this bird, I am at a loss to know, whether they intend to breed it down to the Tumbler's head and beak, or carry it out to the Carrier's head and beak; leaving it as they found it, is not progressing.' Ferguson, speaking of Fowls, says, 'their peculiarities, whatever they may be, must necessarily be fully developed; a little peculiarity forms naught but ugliness, seeing it violates the existing laws of symmetry.' So, Mr. Brent, in discovering the merits of the sub-varieties of the Belgian canary-bird, remarks, 'Fanciers always go to extremes; they do not admire indefinite properties.'"

He continues:

"This principle, which necessarily leads to divergence of character, explains the present state of various domesticated races. We can thus see, how it is that race-horses and dray-horses; greyhounds and mastiffs; which are opposed to each other in every character, —how varieties so distinct as Cochin-China fowls, and bantams; or Carrier Pigeons with very long beaks, and Tumblers with excessively short beaks; have been derived from the same stock. As each breed is slowly improved, the inferior varieties are first neglected, and finally lost. * * * Selection, whether methodical or unconscious, always tending toward an extreme point, together with the neglect, and slow extinction, of the intermediate and less valued forms, is the key which unlocks the mystery how man has produced such wonderful results * * * Continued divergence of character depends on, and is, indeed, a clear proof, as previously remarked, of the same parts continuing to vary in the same direction."

Instead of the pressure of degeneration being relieved in every part, in every individual, it is relieved, and reversion allowed to operate, solely in one part, or in a few parts, in each variety of the species. With the Pigeon, and with some other animals, all, or almost all of the characters of the species are regained; but they are suffered to be developed, not in each individual, or variety, but in different individuals or varieties. Then, many characters are reduced or suppressed, either directly by man, or owing to disuse. This disuse would not reduce the characters, were a reasonable degree of selection, or of care, exercised by man. But, the reduction, or suppression, is thus suffered by man, because:

"Man," as Darwin says (p. 492, Vol. ii), "does not regard modifications in the more important organs * * * as long as they are compatible with health and life. What does the breeder care about slight changes in the molar teeth of his pigs, or for an additional molar tooth in the Dog; or for any change in the intestinal canal or other internal organ?" (Darwin does not say this invidiously, but approvingly). "The breeder cares for the flesh of his cattle, being well marbled with fat, and for an accumulation of fat, within the abdomen of his sheep, and this he has effected. What would the floriculturist care for any change in the structure of the ovarium, or of the ovules? * * * When he has produced any modification in an important part, it has generally been unintentionally, in correlation with some other part, as when he has given ridges and protuberances to the skulls of fowls by attending to the form of the comb."

Every character, which goes to make up any species, even the hair, feathers, hoofs, horns, teeth, tail, and ears is, by man, in some variety, exalted into undue prominence, or wholly, or partially suppressed; and thus a line of divergence from the other varieties of the given species, is thereby established. As Darwin says, If the fancier:

"Simply" (p. 506, Vol. ii) "admired, for instance, short-beaked, more than long-beaked birds, he would, when he had to reduce the number (of birds) generally kill the latter; and there can be no doubt that he would thus, in course of time, sensibly modify his stock."

A priori, it is not likely that nature suffers tamely this moulding, of a species, into any form which the utility, fancy, fashion, or caprice of man may dictate.   There is a penalty visited upon each individual organism, commensurate with the degree of its departure from the sum of all the positive features of its species. The most outrageous liberties are taken with animal and plant forms ; and, when the penalty presents itself in the shape of the evil effects of close-interbreeding, man, blind as a mole, can not discern the relation between these evil effects, and the disproportionate development which he has occasioned ; but, needs must relegate the phenomena to his favorite category of the inexplicable; or, what is more asinine, he lumps all of the degrees of such effects together, and dubs them a "great law of nature !"

Among all the animals, under domestication, which have been degenerated, in character, by man, the pig is pre-eminently conspicuous.   The more improved (?) the pig becomes, the more are its legs reduced.   In the "best bred" pigs, the legs are so small as to be absolutely incompatible with locomotion, and they are incompetent to the very support of the animal.   When it is required to remove such individuals, from place to place, it is necessary to carry them.   It is, also, often as much as the existence of the individual is worth, to stand it upon its legs.   The snout is likewise reduced; being, sometimes, no longer than the nose of a human individual.   The tusks are well nigh suppressed ; the front of its head is rendered short and concave.   Its coat of bristles is suppressed.   Its hair is much re-

duced.   Its tail is infinitesimal in character; and the
whole plan of the organization of the animal, seems to
have been resolved into a mere barrel of fat.   Darwin,
in an ecstacy of admiration, at the signal triumph
achieved, in these animals, by means of selection,
terms them, "wonderfully improved." He says (p.
283, Vol. ii):

"Our wonderfully improved pigs could never have
been formed, if they had been forced to search for
their own food."

He says (p. 360, Vol. ii):

"Nathusius has shown, that, with the improved
races of the pig, the shortened legs and snout, the
form of the auricular condyles, of the occiput, and the
position of the jaws, with the upper canine teeth pro-
jecting in a most anomalous manner in front of the
lower canines, may be attributed to these parts not
having been fully exercised.   For, the highly cultivated races do not travel in search of food, nor root up
the ground with their ringed muzzles."

"Again," he says (236, Vol. ii), "hear what an excellent judge of pigs, says: 'The legs should be no longer
than just to prevent the animal's belly from trailing on
the ground.   The leg is the least profitable (!) portion
of the hog, and we therefore require no more of it than
is absolutely necessary for the support of the rest.'
Let any one compare the wild boar with any improved breed, and he will see how effectually the legs
have been shortened."

With horses, sheep, and cows, all of the characters
of the respective species, are generally re-developed,
in each variety; although in all of the varieties, the
perfect proportion of the characters is, in a greater or
less degree, absent.

With Plants, there is a great reduction and suppression of many characters. Under domestication, the floriculturist and agriculturist aim at the exclusive development of those parts which they value. Other characters of the species, are, either, left greatly reduced, are suffered to become wholly suppressed, or are systematically suppressed by man.

Darwin says (p. 509, Vol. ii):

"The best proof of what selection has effected, is, perhaps, afforded by the fact that, whatever part or quality, in any animal, and more especially, in any plant, is most valued by man, that part, or quality differs most in the several races. This result is well seen, by comparing the amount of difference between the fruits produced by the varieties of the same fruit tree; between the flowers of the varieties in one flower garden; between the seeds, roots, or leaves of our culinary and agricultural plants, in comparison with the other, and not valued, parts of the same plants."

Thus, if it is the fruit which is the desired feature, the plant will have that character so developed as to approximate perfection; whilst the flowers (including the petals, stamens, pistils, ovaries, ovules) and the leaves, the seed, the roots, the bark, the chemical elements, and the many other characters, will not only be neglected, but will be greatly reduced or suppressed; entailing thus, a development of the most disproportionate kind. With different plants of the same species, and even of the same variety, the neglected parts will vary, to some extent, in the degree of their development, owing to the varying conditions of life to which they are subjected; for, as Darwin says

(p. 304, Vol. ii), in speaking of the action of the conditions:

"Even the seeds, nurtured in the same capsule, are not subjected to absolutely uniform conditions, as they draw their nourishment from different points."

And again (p. 337, Vol. ii):

"Slight variations of many kinds * * * are retained as long as plants are grown in certain soils, of which Sageret gives, from his own experience, some instances."

These conditions, entailing slight changes, or slight advances in re-development, in the neglected parts, it may be well carefully to note; as they resolve the puzzling (to Darwin) phenomena of the Self-Impotence, and of the Crossing of plants.

Darwin says:

"The Relative position of flowers, with respect to the axis, and of seeds in the capsules," has some effect, in "inducing variability."

"With cultivated plants," he says, "it is far from rare, to find the petals, stamens, and pistils represented by rudiments."

Again, he says:

"The chemical qualities, odors, and tissues of plants are often modified by a change which seems to us slight. The Hemlock is said not to yield conicine, in Scotland. The root of the Aconitum *napellus* becomes innocuous, in frigid countries. The medicinal properties of the Digitalis are easily affected," &c., &c.

"With all improved Plants, * * they (floriculturists and agriculturists) examine the seedlings, and destroy those which depart from the proper type."

By this " proper type," is meant, a type in which the valued character of the individuals is improved, in a special way, and in which the parts not valued are degenerated in a particular way. It has required a great deal of care, and of selection, to fix the individuals of a variety, to a certain persistency of type. All of the characters evince an inclination to improve, *i. e.*, to revert; and, if this disposition is not kept down by vigorous weeding out of the " sports," as they are called, the individuals might, it is true, improve in those of their characters which are little developed; but that is not what the agriculturist, or horticulturist, wants. He desires to keep the variety uniform, so as to make it recognizable ; and he effects this, by requiring the individuals of the variety, to adhere strictly to the standard he has formed. Man is jealous, frequently, even of an improvement, in the part he values ; fearing lest he may not be able to fix the additional improvement, and make a variety; and, apprehensive that the plant may take upon itself to improve, also, in the other characters which he does not desire to have developed. Thus, if a " Bullock's heart " variety of the Cabbage, should present individuals, with an improvement obviously superior to the " Bullock's heart " leaf, those individuals would be remorselessly destroyed ; for, improvement is not so much an object, as a class of individuals which will perpetuate their exact kind. Again, if grain be, for instance, slightly cylindrical in character, the individual grains, adhering rigidly to the prescribed type, will be valued, and alone preserved. Those departing

17

from the regular shape, or form, will be mercilessly
proscribed ; and, if the leaves, or other portions of the
plant (the flowers, for instance), should attempt to improve, and to revert to the original type, subsisting before
the degeneration, under nature, occurred ; the agriculturist would be almost transfixed with horror, at such
audacity.   He adheres most religiously, to the belief
that plants were made for his use ; but the trouble is,
that he, on the whole, defeats such use, by the manner
in which he uses the bounty vouchsafed him.

Darwin says (p. 242, Vol. ii) :

"The finest shades of difference, in wheat, have
been discriminated, and selected with * * *
much care."

The seeds only, in this species, are attended to.
The leaves, flowers, &c., are all disproportionately
developed.   In fact, the further the exclusive improvement of the seed is carried, the more the true, normal
relation of the parts, is violated.   Darwin may well
assert that "Sterility is the bane of horticulture," when
all plants are cultivated upon a vicious system, entailing a most abnormal coördination of the parts of the
species."

"Compare," says Darwin (p. 34, *Origin of Species*),
"the diversity of Flowers, in the different varieties of
the same species, in the flower-garden; the diversity
of leaves, pods, or tubers, or whatever part is valued,
in comparison with the flowers of the same varieties;
and the diversity of the fruit of the same species in the
orchard, in comparison with the leaves and flowers of
the same set of varieties.   See how different the leaves
of the Cabbage are, and how extremely alike the

flowers; how much the fruit of the different kinds of gooseberries differ in size, color, and hairiness; and yet, the flowers present very slight differences. It is not that the varieties which differ largely, in some one point, do not differ at all in other points. * * * The laws of correlation of growth, the importance of which should not be overlooked, will ensure some differences, but the leaves, the flowers, or the fruit will produce races differing from each other, chiefly in these characters."

(It is these slight differences which, when united in mongrel offspring, effect the good which is occasioned by Crossing.)

The above cases represent the formation of varieties, by the development of one character only, of the species; and, by the retention of such character, at each stage of reversion. Each part, itself, is composed of several characters; and the different development of these characters, constitute varieties formed of the various developments of the one part. Thus, the leaves in different varieties of a species, may be of many different sizes, and of many different shapes (the same being modifications of the one normal shape), or, they may be more or less fleshy, and variously reticulated; or, they may be of several degrees of smoothness, or of several degrees of hairiness. The stems also may be variedly herbaceous, or variedly woody. The branches also may be more or less drooping, or more or less erect. In the flowers of each, or of several varieties, the stamens, pistils, calyx, corolla, anthers, ovules, ovaries, seed vessels, &c., may be of a different ratio with each other; or, some of these characters may even be greatly reduced or wholly suppressed, represented by mere rudiments, or having not a vestige left. The capacity for reversion, in the parts not valued, is not encouraged, but, rather, suppressed, by every possible means.

"No one supposes," says Darwin (p. 48, *Origin of Species*), "that all the individuals of the same species, are cast in the same actual mould."

No one supposes that they are actually cast in the same mould ; but, he who would understand the developments, arising under domestication, must hold that there is but one, *normal* mould for all the individuals of the same species, and that all of the varieties and races, under domestication, and under nature, are but various modifications of such original, true mould. All of the individuals of a species, are, originally, from the same mould. The mould, however, has been bent and distorted (by the adverse conditions of nature, and by man's misguided policy of selection), into every conceivable, diminished shape, and size. Those individuals only, which answer, in their structure, to the true mould of their species, are , physiologically perfect. The true, normal mould is capable of covering all the positive differences of the varieties, and of the individuals of the same species. Given, the modification which, in any individual, the true mould of its species has undergone; and, the evil effects which constitute the penalty for such departure from such mould, will be observed to be in proportion. In proportion also, as the individuals return to the size, and shape of the original mould, will the evil, attendant upon their modification of such mould, abate. It is evident, upon Darwin's own showing of the manner in which varieties of a species are formed, that each variety, when not distinguished from the others of the same species, merely by a negative character, has in it an element, which, if joined to another variety, would measurably advance the development, of such other variety, towards the original type or mould of the given species; and, that the combination of all the positive characters of many and widely distinct varieties of a species, in a single, or in each, individual, would realize the true mould, which is the sum of all the positive developments, possible in such species.

17*

CHAPTER VII.

The principle of Reversion implies, that all the positive characters, of any given species, were originally, fully and proportionately developed, in each member of such species, and that such type alone is perfect, physiologically, as well as anatomically. Hence, it follows, that any modification of such type, must be injurious. It also follows, that the physiological state, of individuals, previous to their developing variations under domestication, should be a defective one, owing to the then absence or reduction, in them, of the characters, which they subsequently develop, and which are assumed to be essentially necessary to their physiological as well as structural integrity. It equally follows that, in proportion as such individuals regain these lost or reduced characters, should there be an abatement of the physiological evil occasioned by such loss or reduction; and it follows that, when all the positive variation possible for an individual of a given species, has been effected, there should exist a perfect, physiological condition in such individual.

To this, it may be answered, that such results are

(194)

obvious, theoretically; but, in default of positive proof thereof, it is all mere speculation.   At the same time, it will be admitted that, if such required proof is adduced, the principle of one, normal type, to each species, and the principle that all positive variations are but the regain of lost or reduced characters, are demonstratively proven.

Such proof is available.   The phenomena of Crossing, and of Close-Interbreeding, conclusively, aye, demonstratively, show, that an organism is vitiated by the reduction, suppression, or absence of any character or characters of its species.   They show, that any ratio, between the characters of which an individual is composed, other than that ratio which subsists, when all of the positive features of the species are fully and proportionately developed, impairs the normal coördination of the parts.   They show, there can be perfect coördination of parts in an individual, only when all the positive characters of its species are present and fully developed.   They show that, in each species, all of the positive features, which it is possible for such species to develop, are wonderfully united, and have such delicate and intimate relations, that it is impossible to vary the proportions of such parts, without detriment to the organism, as a whole.   They show, that such reciprocal dependence of all the characters, of a species, on each other, precludes the possibility of any organism being modified in any part, without entailing a breach of the laws of organization. They show, that the laws, of the whole organism, fail to operate fully, perfectly, or normally, when any of the characters, of its species, is modified or absent. They show, that the further that degeneration, under nature, or that degeneration under domestication, has been carried, the more is the physiological integrity of the individuals, in question, impaired, on account of the loss, in such individuals, of characters of their respective species, or on account of the establishment of an abnormal ratio of the characters of their respective species. They show, that the further that positive Reversion is carried, or the more that characters are regained, and the nearer the original, perfect type of the given species, is approximated, the greater is the repair of this lost, physiological integrity. They show, that, only when reversion has been fully effected,— when all of the lost characters, of the respective species, have been regained,—and when the sum of all the positive features, of the given species, is realized in the individual, can there be full, physiological perfection.

The state of the individuals which vary, is shown to be a deficient, physiological condition, previous to their development of positive variations. That this is due to their then, deficient, structural condition, is attested by the circumstance that in proportion as they return to their full structural integrity,—that is, in proportion as they vary positively, or re-develop the characters assumed to have been originally lost,—do the physiological evils abate, and cease altogether when the full amount of positive variation possible for that species, has been effected. The connection of the evil effects with the deficient, structural condition of the individuals, is also proven by the fact, that, if the variation under domestication be of a negative character,—that is, if any character be reduced or suppressed,—the evils are observed to be proportionally augmented.

As then, the loss or reduction of any character entails physiological evil, the deficient, physiological condition of individuals, previous to their development of positive variations under domestication, proves that such individuals have had characters lost or reduced, under Nature; and, as the development of positive variations under domestication, abates the physiological evils (when such variations are proportionately developed), it follows that such variations are but the regain of those lost or reduced characters.

That evil is caused by a departure from the perfect type of the species, is shown by the phenomena of close-interbreeding. That good is occasioned,—or, rather, that the evils of a departure from the perfect type, are retrieved,—by a return to such normal type of the given species, is shown by the phenomena of Crossing.

Darwin asserts, reiterates again and again, and seemingly never tires of adducing facts to show, that good results from crossing distinct varieties of the same species, and that evil follows from interbreeding individuals of the same variety. Why these effects should flow, he does not know. But, such results, while confessedly wholly inexplicable upon Darwin's hypothesis, are, *a priori*, to be expected upon the theory of Reversion.

By crossing, each parent variety supplies, in the

mongrel offspring, a character or characters which the other parent variety lacks. The offspring of a cross, then, possesses two characters, at least, where either of its parents possessed one; and, thereby, either a full, or a measurable return to the original, perfect type, comprising all of the characters of the species, is effected. If a return to the sum of all the characters of the species, should result in physiological good, then a cross does but fulfill the requirements of the theory of Reversion, when the effects of a cross are (what Darwin has established, as unexplained facts merely), viz., increased fertility, and increased constitutional vigor.

If, on the other hand, an individual, wanting in any character, or lacking the full development of any character of its species, is, upon the theory of Reversion, to be esteemed physiologically defective, inasmuch as it falls short of the full, possible development of its species; then, it is to be expected that, when such individual is interbred with another, similarly defective, the evil entailed by such incomplete, or disproportionate development, will, in the offspring, be intensified, and become more manifest. As a fact, such is the case.

The evil effects of Close-Interbreeding, Darwin confesses, are wholly inexplicable upon any theory that he can devise. Yet, the theory of Reversion gives them a rational, full and conclusive explanation.

Not only are these results of crossing, and of close-interbreeding, wholly unintelligible to Darwin, but he shows, that there is a graduated scale of such results, both in crossing and in close-interbreeding; and, these almost infinite variations in quantity of effect, he is alike at a loss to explain.

Now, the reader will see that, if it can be shown that, in Close-Interbreeding, such graduated scale of effects, ranges from the maximum, in those individuals most degenerated or most disproportionately developed, down to zero, in those individuals with all the characters of their respective species fully and proportionately developed, the theory, that there can be but one, perfect form, for each species, and that any modification of such form is deleterious, will be conclusively proven.

If, conversely, it can be shown, that the graduated scale, of good effects, in Crossing, ranges from the maximum, in those individuals which have mutually much to contribute to the offspring, which their mates respectively lack, down to zero in those individuals which cannot mutually contribute to the offspring, a character or characters which their mates respectively lack, such theory, of a perfect, normally immutable type, for each species, will be proven to demonstration.

The phenomena of Crossing, and of Close-Interbreeding, not only prove the theory of Reversion, but they directly disprove Darwinism. They not only tell a tale, the converse of that which Darwin would have his disciples to believe; but they are grossly and irreconcilably at variance with his theory. They show, demonstratively, that varieties are not "incipient species," and that varieties may not, by any possibility, diverge into distinct species. They show, demon-

stratively, that the divergence of character, by which
he affects to believe, varieties are evolved into distinct species, is not normally possible; for, they
show, that the actual divergence of character shown,
is at the expense of the animals' and plants' vigor
of constitution, and of their fertility; and that, instead of such divergent varieties diverging into distinct species, they diverge inevitably to sterility and
to death! They show that the exclusive possession,
of any positive character, by any variety of a species
(which is necessarily implied by divergence of character), is to the detriment of the individuals of the other
varieties of the same species. They show, that the
possession of any negative feature, or the reduction,
suppression, or absence of any character, or a different
ratio of the development of the characters, from that
of the original type, is injurious. They show, that
there cannot be more than one variety, of any species,
consistent with physiological integrity; and that Darwin's divergent varieties are but injurious modifications of such normal variety which is the sum of all
the possible characters of the given species.   .

The phenomena of Crossing, and the phenomena
especially of Close-Interbreeding, have long been the
occasion of a spirited controversy between two schools
(as they may be called), intent, the one on affirming,
and the other on denying, the fact that the alleged
effects do flow.

The question, particularly, whether evil effects result from Close-Interbreeding, became of moment,
with them, not because of its intrinsic importance,

but by reason of the implications, it was fancied, its determination carried with it. Those who were of a "liberal" cast of thought, wished, by establishing the negative, to prove that the inhibition of religion against marriages of consanguinity, is wholly arbitrary, and that it has no justification, upon natural grounds. The other school are, for obvious reasons, bent· upon showing that such intermarriages may not be contracted, with impunity.

On the one side, the almost universal aversion to such marriages, is adduced. The lowest and most degenerate tribes of men are pointed out as holding it in the most abhorrence. Nor does their evidence end here. The lower animals and plants contribute testimony which is seemingly well nigh overwhelming. The sterility of well-bred pigs, and of the high fancy breeds of pigeons and of fowls, when interbred, are noted; aye, so peculiar are the evil results, in many instances, that it is generally remarked, that the very improvements, which man effects in Pigs, Pigeons, Fowls, and Plants, seem only to aggravate the evil results of Interbreeding. The many instances, of Self-Impotent Plants, also furnish evidence so pronounced, that it would seem that the voice of cavil should be hushed.

On the other hand, those who contend that evil does not result from marriages of consanguinity, advance facts which are equally impossible to be gain-·said. They argue, that, although the aversion to interbreeding is general, the fact that the prohibition obtained with the least force among the most civilized nations of antiquity, and the fact that it is observed

18

most religiously by the most degenerate tribes of Africa, show that it is a mere superstition, lingering traces only of which prevail, and prevailed of old, among the most cultured nations. Egypt, they say, even in the zenith of her civilization, observed the prohibition not at all; and, they contend, that the prejudice has ever been least, in the regions around the Caucasus, where the proportionate development of Man implies intellect above the average. The history of the Ptolemies, whose frequent intermarriages between brother and sister, during a period of 300 years, are attested by history, affords, they contend, conclusive proof that evil does not result. The history of Cleopatra, the last sovereign of that dynasty, though not the last descendant, was certainly not, they urge, that of a person, in whom any mental or physical degeneracy was observable; although, they concede, with delicate irony, that her moral comportment may have, to some extent, betokened the evil.

Nor is it to Man only, they say, that they must look for evidence to sustain their position. Horses, sheep, and cattle have been bred, *inter se*, in the closest relationship, for generation and generation following generation; yet, no evil resulted; but, on the contrary, the animals displayed marked improvement. Many special instances are given, where the horse has long resisted breeding, in-and-in, between the nearest relations. The Leicester sheep have been bred in-and-in, over sixty years, without the introduction of a single new ram into the flock. With Cattle, the bull, "Comet," is a well known instance of very close interbreeding.

Its pedigree, and that of its descendants, are frequently quoted. Another equally remarkable case, is that of

"The famous bull, Favorite (who was himself the offspring of a half brother and sister from Foljambe"), which "was matched with his own daughter, grand-daughter, and great-granddaughter; so that the produce of this last union, or the great-granddaughter, had fifteen-sixteenths, or 93.75 per cent. of the blood of Favorite, in her veins. This cow was matched with the bull Wellington, having 62.5 per cent. of Favorite blood in his veins, and produced Clarissa: Clarissa was matched with the bull Lancaster, having 68.75 per cent. of the same blood, and she yielded valuable off-spring" (Darwin's *Animals and Plants, &c.*, Vol. ii, p. 146).

These instances, they hold, show conclusively, that evil effects do not result from close-interbreeding, or from marriages of consanguinity; that, there is some-thing wrong, or suspicious, about the cases, implying that evil does follow; and, that, to sum up the whole question, the prohibition against marriages of near relations, is but another device of priestcraft to hold the ignorant in bondage.

The further these schools advance their accumu-lations of facts, the worse confounded, seemingly, grows the problem; and, the cream of the joke lies in this, that each side taunts the other, with the imputa-tion, that those of the other school have no practical knowledge of the subject, or they would not deny, what is established by the experience of all breeders. The retort to this, by either, is, the confrontation, of their opponents, with facts, respectively, showing no evil, and showing great evil; and the cynical query, how the others avoid the inference from such phenomena?

Those, to whom it never has occurred, to consider whether interbreeding may not be merely the *occasion* of the evils entailed, and not the *cause*, have long been puzzled to know, to which side, the balance of the evidence inclines. If disciplined in scientific habits of thought, they find,—when assured as to which side has the preponderance of testimony,—that such assurance aids not at all to extricate them from their quandary. For, what is, then, to be done with the residual facts,—the well attested phenomena, advanced in support of the argument on the other side? There will still remain, to plague the man who has settled, in his own mind, that the weight of the evidence is on a particular side, a perplexing array of facts, which are as far from being resolved scientifically, as they are impossible to be gainsaid. If the conclusion achieved be, that interbreeding does cause evil, how deal with the many instances showing, that close interbreeding may be carried on, in the closest degree of relationship, for generation upon generation; and which refuse to be moulded into even seeming accordance with such conclusion? And, if the other opinion be adopted, there equally remains a number of similarly stubborn facts, which refuse to conform to any such award.

There was, once, a man named Buckle. This man commenced to write what he termed a "History of Civilization in England." Happily, for civilization in England, he, his demise made, before the work was half finished. He plumed himself upon being an inductive philosopher (it was lucky that he did, as his readers would have never suspected it); and represented his mode of discovery of sociological, ethnological, and other truths, to be a process peculiarly positive and scientific. The process was this: He relied solely upon statistics: When a problem presented itself, he carefully added up such of the figures, in said statistics, which to him appeared to refer to that side, of the question, which he fancied to be the truth. He also added the figures on the opposing side: He compared them: If the sum on the side, first mentioned, preponderated; the question was, then, scientifically and positively resolved. All cavil at the result, could be naught but the emanation of an ignorant and superstitious mind, fatally bent upon being perverse.

To give the man his due, in candor it must be stated, that, if the sum, of those figures, in the statistics, which pertained to. the side, from which his prejudices leaned, was greater than the sum of those on the side he favored, he yielded his preconceived opinion, and deferred, with grace, to the statistics; for, from them, it was scientific heresy, to hold, there could be any appeal. Thus, the "liberal" tone of his mind would have occasioned a predilection for the side which contended, that no evil results from close interbreeding; as the ascertainment of such to be a fact, would show that the religious command, to abstain from consanguineous marriages, was a senseless prohibition. If, however, he had added up his little sums, and had found the testimony of experience to be (to
18*

the extent, only, of one, two, or half a dozen instances),
preponderant in favor of the view, that evil does result;
he would have declared, upon the infallible authority
of those statistics, that evil always does result from
close interbreeding, or from consanguineous marriages; and this, despite his laudable desire to curtail
the tyranny which priestcraft exercises over the vulgar,
—principally, by withholding from them, all statistics!

Darwin is a disciple of Buckle (in the second
volume of his "*Animals and Plants under Domestication*," the former, in a plaintive tone, regrets that Mr.
Buckle's rigid processes of discovery precluded his
acceptance of the evidence, showing Inheritance, because the results had not been formulated in statistics,
and were, therefore, not susceptible of addition, and of
comparison, by sums). Following out Buckle's process, and prompted thereto by an ulterior aim to which
we shall later advert, Darwin affects to believe that, in
the solution of the question of interbreeding, where
there is such an amount of conflicting evidence, it
merely behooves him, to ascertain the weight of the
different testimony, and then to determine for the side,
which he finds preponderant. The weight of the
testimony appears to be overwhelming, in favor of the
view, that evils do flow from interbreeding. Therefore, he concludes, that evil inevitably follows, and is
always eventually caused by the mating of relations.
The exceptional phenomena are allowed to care for
themselves. As he postulated "an innate tendency,"
to stop all inquiry into the cause of variations, so he
here lumps all of the phenomena of crossing and of

close-interbreeding, and ascribes them to "a great law of nature,"—a mode of explanation which obviously is naught but a rendering of his ignorance into the semblance of knowledge.   He remarks (p. 327, *Origin of Species*) :

"How ignorant we are, on the precise causes of sterility;" and, he says (on p. 109, *Origin of Species*), "that close interbreeding is a general law of nature, utterly ignorant though we be of the meaning of the law."

Thus he states his "great law of nature" (p. 109, *Origin of Species*):

"I have collected so large a body of facts, showing, in accordance with the universal testimony of breeders, that, with animals and plants, a cross between different varieties, or between individuals of the same variety, but of another strain, gives vigor and fertility to the offspring; and, on the other hand, that close-inter-breeding diminishes vigor and fertility; that these facts alone incline me to believe that it is a general law of nature (*utterly ignorant though we be of the meaning of the law*) that no organic being fertilizes itself for an eternity of generations; but that a cross with another individual is occasionally,—perhaps, at very long intervals,—indispensable."

If it be "a general law of nature," that evil should flow from close-interbreeding, and that good should result from crossing, why do not the same degree of evil, and the same degree of good, result, respec-tively, from crossing, and from close-interbreeding, in different individuals, when there is a like degree of relationship, or a like distinction between the animals or plants coupled?   We should at least, expect a like degree of good, and a like degree of evil, when there is a like degree of relationship, or of distinction, in individuals of the same species. . Why do the evil effects of close-interbreeding, recur, at different periods, with different individuals of the same species? Why is close interbreeding of such doubtful, and varying effect? Why is it .so problematical, in any given degree of interbreeding, whether evil, or good, will result? Why is it, that good frequently results, from this process, when by " a general law of nature," as Darwin has it, evil is essentially inherent in such a process? He himself says, again and again, that close-interbreeding is that process, upon which breeders mainly rely, to effect improvement in their breeds. He also shows, that different species of animals and plants, are differently affected, by the same degree of interbreeding; and that different animals and different plants, of the very same species, are also differently affected. The effects of the same degree of inter-breeding, are also shown to be different, in different varieties; different, in individuals of the same variety; different, in individuals of the same herd or flock; different, in individuals of the same family; aye, different in flowers on the same plant; different, in flowers on the same bough or branch; and different, in flowers on the same twig!

The good, from the same degree of crossing, like-wise, differs, in the same way. Why this inconstancy? Why this variability, in the effects which follow, if there be "a great law of nature?"

Why is it, if the evil effects are due to interbreeding,

per se, that, with the same degree of interbreeding, with different individuals of the very same species, fertility graduates from zero to perfect fertility?

Why is it, that, with horses, sheep, and cattle, very little evil effects are observable? and, that, with some individuals of those species, no evil whatever follows, however long continued, and close the interbreeding may be?

Why is it, on the contrary, that with pigeons, fowls, and pigs, the greatest evil is the outcome of any degree of interbreeding, even when there is no relationship of blood? Why is it, that, with a short-beaked tumbler, for instance, interbreeding is not possible, without great evil resulting, even when the individual is interbred with another of the same variety, which is removed from it, in blood, for thousands of generations, and which was reared in a distant country?

Why is it, that, with cattle, sheep, and horses, varying degrees of evil are observable, in different individuals of the same species, and in different individuals of the same breed, from the same degree of close-interbreeding; and that, in some individuals, there are no evil effects? Why is it, that, with pigeons, fowls, and pigs, varying degrees of evil are observable in different individuals of the same species, and in different individuals of the same variety, from the same degree of interbreeding?

Why is it, that with pigeons, fowls and pigs, the more highly improved the varieties are, the greater are the evil effects; and, the less improved that the varieties are, the less are the evil effects? Why is it, that the highly cultivated pig is susceptible of the greatest evil effects; and that the least-cared for pig,—the one which is forced to root around, for its living,—displays little, or no evil effects, from the same degree of close-interbreeding? Why is it, that the more widely divergent the varieties of a species are, the greater are the evil effects from interbreeding? and why is it that the increase of good, from crossing, is the greatest with them?

Why is it, that the most well-bred animals, of the horse, sheep, and cow species, are the ones which need the least crossing, to ward off lessened fertility, when it is the finest bred animals among the pig, pigeon, and fowl species, which require it the most?

Why is it, that the more that varieties realize Darwin's divergence of character (which, according to his view, is to convert them into distinct species), the greater is the need, that they be crossed in order to avert the sterility and delicacy of constitution which, he asserts, always accompany such divergence of character?

Why,—to urge the most significant of questions, the answer to which involves a full refutation of Darwinism,—are the individuals of a divergent variety, which Darwin deems an "incipient species," sterile, or partially so, when interbred together; and, why are they of greatly increased fertility, when crossed with individuals of other divergent varieties of the same species; when the individuals of a species, are generally fertile with each other, and absolutely sterile (or produce absolutely sterile hybrids), when crossed with individuals of another species?

Possibly, it is below the dignity of "a great law of nature," to resolve such trivial details.

In some cases, there are no such effects as are alleged by Darwin. In the other cases, there is such an infinite variety, in the quantity of the effects, that the mind instinctively spurns such a makeshift of ignorance, as is Darwin's "law of nature," ascribing the good which results from Crossing, to Crossing, *per se*, and the evils resulting from interbreeding, to interbreeding, *per se*.

The objections here urged against his "law of nature," are not mere objections; they are disproofs. For, the facts, adverted to, are not only left unexplained by his doctrine, but are wholly subversive of it.

The confusion, prevailing upon the 'subject, has been only augmented, made worse confounded, by • Darwin's senseless generalization. The subject, too, is one, a correct understanding of which, is absolutely necessary to correct principles of breeding. There is, probably, no necessity, more imperatively felt, than that of a knowledge of the cause of the effects of crossing, and of close-interbreeding. Darwin has committed himself to a general proposition which, a very slight consideration of the facts, should have shown him, to be both unsustainable, and absurd. There are published, at the present time, by the veriest and most unlearned of tyros, in the veterinary art, works on breeding, in which the "law of nature," which Darwin propounds, is contemptuously rejected, as plainly incompetent to cover the facts; and, in which, is intimated the existence of some other, and true law, which, while rendering explicable all the many variations in the quantity of the effects, and the frequent absence of all such effects, will show close-interbreeding to be but a mere condition.

Infinitely varied as are the facts of crossing, and of close-interbreeding, they are susceptible of easy and simple resolution, when the fact is recognized, that want of integrity of structure, in the individuals of any species, entails, in proportion, a want of physiological integrity; and, that, when such want of integrity of structure is repaired (as it is in crossing, through each parent contributing to the offspring, a positive character which the other parent lacks), a proportionate return to physiological integrity, is secured.

Upon this principle, every one, without exception, of the various perturbations, to which the reproductive elements are observed to be subject, becomes perfectly explicable, and susceptible of both qualitative and quantitative prevision. This explanation accords, most rigorously, with each and every one of Darwin's tens of thousands of facts,—whether of sexual, or of asexual reproduction. Each one, of the thousands of individuals of each species, will, when questioned, by means of this rule, respond, and give the degree of its departure from the original, perfect type of its species. The evil effects of close-interbreeding, are faithful indications of the degree of such departure; and, the increase of good from crossing, is an indication of the degree of return, which has been made towards such type. By this rule, moreover, the different data,—

esteemed so mutually incompatible,—of those who concur in, and of those who demur to Darwin's conception, are shown to be in perfect harmony with each other. All the discord is harmony, when understood. The variations in the quantity of the results of crossing and of close-interbreeding, are a mighty maze, but not without a plan. Each degree of effect, answers, faithfully, to a corresponding degree of the cause assigned; and, where the cause is observed to be absent, there the effects are seen not to prevail.

The theory of reversion,—or theory of the necessity of the proportionate development of all the characters of a species,—explains, in the simplest manner possible, all and each of the many different variations in the quantity of the effects of crossing, and close-interbreeding; and explains the irregular recurrence of such effects. By it, scientists, and every breeder, fancier, horticulturist, and agriculturist, are enabled to solve the question, why there exists such a gradation, even within the same species, between those individuals evincing the greatest evil effects, and those displaying the least, or none at all; by having disclosed to them, in the cause, a corresponding gradation, between those individuals, lacking a large number of characters, or having them disproportionately developed to the greatest degree, and those individuals possessing all, or nearly all of the characters of their species, fully and proportionately developed.

It is in the similar departure, of each of the parents interbred, from the true mould, or original type of their species, that we find the cause of all the disorder

19

manifested in the general organization, and of all the disorder in the reproductive system. The power of propagation, in the parents, and the constitutional vigor of the offspring, are lessened, in proportion to the amount of departure from the sum of all the characters; and are increased, in proportion as the individuals return to that type. It is not relationship, which causes the evil. Relationship simply implies similarity of structure, in the parents. The evils of lessened fertility, and of lessened constitutional vigor, are displayed, when the parents are similarly disproportionately developed, similarly wanting, or similarly defective, in features of their species.

The loss, or reduction, of any characters, is deleterious to either parent: When the parents pair, the evil, consequent upon such loss or reduction, is aggravated, or intensified. Thus, there are one hundred and fifty different varieties of the pigeon. The members of each divergent variety, necessarily lack the positive peculiarities of the other varieties. If, then, two of the same variety interbreed, the evil, entailed by the absence of the positive peculiarities of the other varieties, is intensified.

Full health of the whole, or full functional activity of the whole organism, subsists, not in the development of some parts, or of some organs alone, but solely in the full development of them all. Perfect fertility, or perfect, constitutional vigor, consists only with the sum of all the positive features of the species. The capacity of the reproductive elements, is dependent upon the full representation, therein, of all the parts. Where, then, some of the parts are not present, the reproductive capacity is impaired; and, if there be a certain number of characters wanting, absolute sterility sets in. Harmonious play and movement of all the parts, as in a mechanism, is requisite. There must, as a *sine qua non* of physiological integrity, or of normal coördination, be perfect exactness,—the closest fitting in of each part. "All must full or not coherent be," And all must rise (*i. e.*, revert), in due degree. If "'Tis but a part we see, and not the whole," the organism is *thrown out of gear* (to use a Yankeeism).

An individual, of any species, can exist in a perfectly healthy, normal state, only as a whole;—that whole, which comprises all the positive features of its species; and, it is a fundamental and egregious error, to suppose that,—as with pigeons and fowls, under domestication,—the characters of the respective species may be divided among many different varieties, consistently with physiological perfection. It is an error, also, to suppose, that the characters which, in the well-bred (?) pig, are reduced or suppressed, may be so reduced or suppressed, without evil being entailed. It is an error, also, to suppose that the true ratio of the development of the characters, respectively, of the horse, sheep, and cattle, may be varied in the individuals of those species, without detriment to their fertility and constitutional vigor.

Either, immediately, as with fancy pigeons, with fancy fowls, and with highly cultivated pigs; or, in course of time, as with well-bred horses, cattle, and sheep,—dependent, always, upon the degree of disproportionate development of the individuals,—will the individuals, when interbred, dwindle, grow feeble, become of lessened fertility, and eventually grow sterile.

If a great number of characters, of the respective species, be reduced, or suppressed, the evil will ensue immediately, with any individual bred with another of the same variety; although there subsist between the two, no degree of relationship. If the number of characters so lost or reduced, be a degree less, the evil will, either, be less, from the same degree of interbreeding; or be the same, from interbreeding with a distant relative. If, still less, be the loss or reduction, the evil will, either, be less from the last mentioned degree of interbreeding; or, be the same, from interbreeding with a relative, a degree nearer. If, less, again, be the disproportionate development, the evil will, either, be less, in the last named degree of relationship; or, be the same, only, with a nearer relative (say), a cousin. If, less, still, the evil will, either, be less, with the cousin; or, be the same, if the interbreeding, with a cousin, be continued for more than one generation; or, be the same, from an intermarriage of father and daughter, or of mother and son. If the reduction, or suppression, of characters, be small, the evil will, either, be less from the interbreeding of a son and mother, or of a father and daughter; or, be the same, if such interbreeding be continued for more than one generation; or, be the same, if the intermarriage be between brother and sister. If the organisms approximate the full and proportionate development of all the characters of their species, the evil will, either, be less, from the. intermarriage of brother and sister; or, be the same, if the interbreeding be carried on for more than one generation. If the approach to the original type of the species be nearer, the interbreeding of brother and sister, may be carried on, for many generations; but, the effects of the slight disproportionate development, will begin to tell, after some period of such long-continued close-interbreeding.

If there be no reduction or suppression of any of the characters of the species, and no disproportionate development whatsoever, the original type is then realized, and interbreeding may be carried on, *ad infinitum*, in any degree of relationship, however close, without any evil effects; provided, of course, the individuals, in question, always retain their full integrity, and, that each of those individuals with which any such interbreeds, is alike the sum of all the positive features of the species.

The above descending scale of effects obtains, of course, only where the law of inheritance fully operates, where like produces like, and where relationship actually occasions, what it generally implies, viz., similarity of defects. The effect is due, to each parent lacking like points of structure, and to the aggravation, or augmentation of such evil, in the offspring.

The evils, from close-interbreeding, grow less and less as the integrity of the organism is repaired or regained; or, they grow greater and greater, in proportion as the animal or plant recedes from the original type of its species.

The close-interbreeding, of those which answer to the original type of their respective species, is attended with no evil whatever.

Darwin attributes every imperfection, existing in the offspring of parents related in blood, to the fact of consanguinity alone; which is manifestly absurd. For, even if there be no consanguinity, or relationship between the parents, but there be similarity of defects, the result is the same; and, if there be consanguinity, and no structural defects, there will be no evil entailed. Consanguinity, *per se,* adds not a jot nor a tittle to the evil effects.

Mere relationship has not any influence, in producing the evil effects. Given, full and proportionate development, the *same blood* is in no wise injurious. There is nothing necessarily pernicious, in a marriage of consanguinity. It occasions evil, generally, merely because, it is far more likely for parents, which are descendants of the same near ancestor, to have similar defects, than it is, for those not bound together by any tie of blood. The nearer the connection, between the individuals paired, the greater is the probability of evil in the offspring; but, solely because, such blood relationship generally implies, that the defects which every individual has, more or less, will be similar, in the pair so related, and thus augmented in the offspring. The more remote is the connection between the couple, the less, the other things equal, will be the probability of evil; for, remoteness of connection generally implies dissimilarity of development. If the connection be very remote, there is even some probability, that good, instead of evil, will result from pairing; for, it is likely, that though the parents may, perhaps, be equally defective, their defects may lie, in each, in a different portion of the structure, from what they do in the other; and, thus such, or some of the defects, in either, may then be supplied, in the offspring, by corresponding, positive developments, in the other.

There is evil wrought upon the aggregate of every organism, in proportion to the amount of characters which are reduced or suppressed. The breeding of one such individual, with another, defective in exactly the same characters, aggravates the evil. The reason, and the sole reason, why relationship enters as an element into the problem, is because the ratio of the development of the characters, is similarly incomplete. To produce evil, the ratio of development of the characters must, in the animals interbred, be a like, false ratio. If a true ratio, no evil follows; if a false ratio, but not a like ratio, good instead of evil may flow; for, the deficiencies in the ratio of each, are likely, then, to be supplied by positive quantities in the ratio of the other.

Two cousins may be seemingly free from all defect; but, nevertheless, may possess, and most probably will possess, a similarly disproportionate development. Lessened fertility, and loss of constitutional vigor, in their offspring, will then be displayed, through the evil of the disproportionate development, above assumed, being intensified by the progeny's having transmitted to it the accumulated evil.

On the other hand, two cousins may marry, who are equally disproportionately developed, and as much so as were the pair last assumed; and no evil be observed to result. The reason will be; the relationship does not, in such instance, carry with it similarity of defect. Although equally disproportionately developed, they are not similarly so. Relationship, even when there are defects, does not always or necessarily imply similarity of defect, in form or structure. One of the two cousins, may,—where the bond of his relationship with his cousin, was his maternal grandmother,—have inherited his structure from, either, his paternal grandfather, or paternal grandmother, or from his maternal grandfather; or, where his parent, who was of kin to his cousin, was his mother, he may have inherited his structure wholly or in great degree, from his father. If he derived a structure from either of these, or from all conjointly, or from some only; and, if his maternal grandmother had thus no influence in determining his features of growth; it is manifest, that the circumstance of his wife being his cousin, could not occasion any evil in his offspring.

To ascribe the difference, in the quantity of effects from the same degree of interbreeding, to unlikeness, *per se*, or to likeness, *per se*, is absurd. Such an explanation is little more than a mere restatement of the phenomena; or, rather, a restatement of some only of the phenomena. For, such an hypothesis fails to cover many facts,—facts which are not merely left unresolved, but which conclusively negative such an idea.

Herbert Spencer attributes the differences in the effects to likeness, and to unlikeness, *per se ;* and, it is amusing to note the pretentiously philosophical manner in which he gives back to his readers, as an explanation, *the very facts which he essayed to explain for them !*

Individuals, realizing the perfect type, will be absolutely alike; yet, they are the very individuals which are exempt from any evil, from any degree of close-interbreeding; whereas, if they interbreed with individuals unlike themselves, their offspring will be of lessened fertility, and of lessened vigor; because, such unlike individuals will necessarily be defective in some character, in order to be unlike those of the perfect type.

It is not mere unlikeness; it is unlikeness of defect, which abates, or precludes the evil effects; and it is not mere likeness, but likeness of defects, which causes or, rather, aggravates, the evil. Where two animals are deficient in the same endowments of their species, there is no or little chance of repairing those portions of the organism's balance; but, rather, an almost inevitable necessity of augmenting those faults, in the offspring. When, however, they are dissimilarly defective, there is a strong probability, that the faults of either will be remedied, in the offspring, by positive, corresponding features in the other. Defects in each, or some defects in each, will be supplied by an excellence which the other derives, perhaps, from an ancestor, not common to the former.

Darwin says (p. 84, Vol. ii):

"Certain individuals are prepotent, in transmitting

their likeness.   *   *   *   It would appear that, in certain families, some one ancestor, and, after him, others in the same family, must have had great power in transmitting their likeness through the male line; for we cannot otherwise understand how the same features should so often be transmitted after marriages with various females, as has been the case with the Austrian Emperors, and, as, according to Niebuhr, formerly occurred in certain Roman families, with the mental qualities.   The famous bull, Favorite, is believed to have had a prepotent influence on the short-horn race. It has also been observed with the English race-horse, that certain mares have generally transmitted their own characters, whilst other mares, of equally pure blood, have allowed the character of the sire to prevail."

When an individual, with a positive character, strongly developed, mates with another, with the same character less developed, or indifferently well developed, or somewhat reduced, the former will be prepotent, in such character, over the other; because the character mentioned, will, other things equal—for instance, if the same character, in the less potent parent, be not so much reduced, or so wholly suppressed, as to diminish, in the offspring, the size of the character— be transmitted to such offspring.   The reason why, in these cases, the smaller development, of the character, in the less potent parent, does not obtain to diminish the size of the character, as it exists in the prepotent parent, is because, there still remains, in the less potent parent, the power of reversion in such character, which concurs with the same character, in the prepotent parent, to keep it up to the high state of development.

This is borne out by observation; for, as a general rule, when an individual is prepotent, the features which evidence the prepotency, are characters which are positively and strongly developed. This is the case with the likeness of the Austrian Emperors, with the likeness of the Stuarts and others, which, were displayed by strongly-marked facial features.

The line of Judah, it may here be remarked, would never have continued so long as it has, in despite of interbreeding, had not the Jews been broad-faced, and of strong facial features, implying proportionate development in other respects. The extermination of the Puritan race is not wholly due to the cause so generally assigned by physicians. The "hatchet-face" of the Yankee, and the corresponding development of the rest of his frame, are answerable for much of the sterility which has awakened inquiry into the said "social evil." The matrons of New England have been sinned against most vilely, in this regard, by ignorant and presumptuous sciolists. The race is fast being run out; but its women, at least, should not be suffered to pass away, unrelieved of a load of unmerited obloquy.

Mental characters obey the same rule of prepotency; as they are ever dependent upon structural conformations—upon particular coördinations of cerebral tissue. If, however, characters, in any individual, are positively developed in structure, but through disuse, or other cause, have become rudimentary in function, any individual, of corresponding, negative characters, with whom the former mates, may be prepotent.

Another rule, which may be observed to obtain, in determining prepotency, is, that, if any given ratio (whether of a positive, or of a negative cast) of the development of the characters, of the species, has been long maintained, either through interbreeding, or through the long-continued, fortuitous mating of individuals similar in development, the product of such a line will generally be prepotent, even when mated with individuals, with characters whose usual effect would be to alter or amend such ratio.

With respect to the prepotency of sex, adverted to above by Darwin: While such prepotency is frequently explicable, upon the above principles, it is also amenable, frequently, to another rule. Many characters are correlated, either directly or indirectly, with both primary and secondary sexual characters. Both the sperm, and the germ, undergo, before fecundation occurs, an independent, though very small development, just appreciable by the microscope. If the congression of the two transpires, when the spermatozoön, for instance, has advanced, but little, in its development, and after the ovum has run much or all of its course of little, independent development, the female element will have, not only the power of impressing its special, sexual coördination upon the foetus, but will often, perhaps, have also the power to influence the development of the characters, common to both sexes, but which are correlated, in some respects, with the female's primary or secondary, sexual parts. As this physiological law is operative, in so many ways which are determined by an equal variety of degrees of the respective development of either, and of both, of the sexual elements, it is proper to reserve the full treatment of the question until the phenomena of generation engage our attention.

A case, illustrative of the rule, that prepotency is due, frequently, to the long maintenance of a given ratio of development, is to be found in the following remark of Darwin (p. 89, Vol. ii, *Animals and Plants, &c.*):

"A purely bred form of either sex, in all cases in which prepotency does not run more strongly in one sex than the other, will transmit its character, with prepotent force over a mongrelized and already variable form."

There is another reason for this phenomenon, besides the fact, that the prepotent form has long been persistent in its peculiar type. The reason is an obvious one, upon the theory of reversion. To Darwin, this, with all of the other facts on breeding, is inexplicable. Having vitiated his theory at the start, by leaving the question of the cause of variation, or improvements, unresolved, it is incompetent to the explanation of any of the phenomena.

In the "mongrelized and already variable form," all of the characters of its species, or the major portion of them, are striving to revert to the original, full development, proper to the perfect type. No one, of the characters, is predominant; or, if there be one or more advanced in development, it is very little in the ascendant. When crossed with "a purely bred form," which has (especially when it belongs to a widely divergent variety), one character, of its species, most decidedly developed, this "purely bred form" becomes prepo-

20

tent, in the offspring; because its pronounced peculiarity, concurs solely with the corresponding character
in "the mongrelized and variable form," and aids its
development alone, and not that of the other characters.   The consequence is, that the offspring resembles
more the purely bred form.   It could not well do
otherwise.   If it resembled the mongrel form, the influence of the strongly marked character in the "purely
bred form," would be left unaccounted for; whereas,
when the result is as is seen, in the prepotency of the
"purely bred form," all of the influences of the several
characters, in either form, are manifest.   This prepotency is explained, simply, as the resultant, of the accession of one very dominant force, to a like, but lesser
force which is one of many equal forces.

Darwin says (p. 92, Vol. ii, *Animals and Plants, &c.*):

"On the whole, the subject of prepotency is extremely intricate.   *   *   *   It is, therefore, not surprising that every one hitherto has been baffled in
drawing up general rules on the subject of prepotency."

If the improvements, and positive variations observable, had been recognized, as the mere regain of impaired
integrity; neither he, nor others, would have been so
baffled.   Darwin's error has lain, in ignoring physiology; and, in confining himself, exclusively, to anatomical tests,—to mere diversities in structure, without
ascertaining whether those diversities had any effect
upon the general system of functions.   Anatomy and
physiology are correlative sciences, each being the
complement of the other; and neither may be well

studied, or understood, without the other. It is a fact, beyond all question, that Darwin, so far from striving to resolve the physiological phases of his problem, is systematically bent upon rendering them worse confounded. It is possible, that he is moved to such a course, by an uneasy consciousness that their explanation would confound all of his speculations. ·Be that as it may, however, there is no doubt, whatever,—for, it is by him explicitly avowed,—that his design, in adducing the facts of physiology, is to show that they cannot be explained, and, then, from the impossibility of accounting for them, to deduce the conclusion, that the insuperable objection to his theory, the sterility of hybrids, is an argument which cannot be relied upon as conclusive, as the whole subject of fertility and sterility is incomprehensible. This flimsy device will be completely unraveled in the succeeding chapters of this work.

Two Classes of Evil Effects occasioned by Close-Interbreeding:

There are two classes, of the evil effects, which are occasioned by close-interbreeding.

The one class, comprises the effects wrought upon a part, or parts, in the offspring, by the mere augmentation of the structural defects, in such part or parts, in the parents.

The influence, however, which the reduction, or suppression of any part, exerts, does not stop with the said reduction or suppression of such characters ; but, entails evil upon the aggregate,—upon the organization, as a whole, and upon the reproductive elements.

The evils entailed upon the aggregate, upon the organization as a whole, and upon the reproductive capacity, constitute the second of the two classes.

In all organisms, there is, normally, a reciprocal balance of all the organs, and parts, of the respective species. The maintenance of this balance, constitutes full physiological perfection ; and, when any part or parts are wanting, or reduced, this balance is impaired; and an evil effect is wrought, which is over and above the mere deficiency in the parts. The evils, entailed upon the aggregate, are loss of fertility, and of constitutional vigor.

The deficiency, in parts, sometimes works no appreciable functional derangement, in such parts, or in the adjoining parts ; although a deficiency, whether working functional derangement or not, in the part, always effects some functional derangement, in the aggregate. But again, quite frequently, the slightest possible loss of tissue, will occasion deleterious effects upon the parts involved, of the most serious character; while, the effect upon the aggregate, or upon the coördinating force of the whole, is infinitesimal, as in blindness. If cousins married, who, in the structure of the eye, were slightly deficient, but not so deficient as to produce, in them, any inconvenience, or consciousness of their defect, their offspring would, possibly, then, have said defects augmented, and be wholly, or partially blind. If such couple were proportionately developed in other respects, the evil upon the aggregate, would never be appreciably displayed, in any degree of close-interbreeding, however long-continued. The degree, in which the offspring's fertility and constitutional vigor would be affected, would be proportionate, simply, to the small amount of tissue, which was wanting in the structure of the eye,—which effect would be, practically, *nil*, even if the offspring and their descendants interbred, brother and sister, for thousands of generations.

A long catalogue could be given, of all sorts of evils, in parts, which are augmented in close-interbreeding; but, whose effect is, of itself, little upon the coördination of the whole; viz., cerebral affections, apoplexy, epilepsy, insanity, gout, consumption, asthma, stone in the bladder, amaurosis, hypermetropia or morbid long sight, myopia or short sight; and, in horses, for instance, ring-bones, curbs, splints, spavin, founder, roaring, or broken and thick wind, melarosis and blindness.

Contradistinguished from these effects upon the parts themselves, are the effects upon the aggregate; which Darwin cannot explain. They are lessened fertility, sterility, loss of constitutional vigor, and a general breaking up of the whole constitution.

A man may have all of the specific diseases, to which flesh is heir; yet, if he be otherwise proportionately developed, in all the characters of his species, he, and his descendants, may go on, for many generations, interbreeding as close as did the Ptolemies, and remain of undiminished fertility. The impairment of the balance, would be in proportion only to the amount of tissue destroyed, in the parts so affected, and not to the degree of the diseases' ordinary, baneful influence.

20*

This proportion, too, would not be a direct one; for, if the diseases involved many parts, their symmetrical effect would measurably poise the balance which, action in one part alone, would have more disturbed.

A man, however, very disproportionately developed, may be free from all specific diseases; yet, if he breed with even the most distant of traceable relatives, he probably will, either, be sterile, or give birth to off-spring which will be sterile; and he, and his offspring, will be of much weakened constitution. The well-bred (?) pig, with the regulation reduction of legs, of snout, of front of the head, of tusks, and with bristles suppressed, may be free from all particular diseases, yet it will most probably be sterile with even distant relatives, and even with others of the same breed; whereas, the pig that roams the woods for a living, and has the characters, above mentioned, proportionately developed, instead of having them reduced; may have every disease, peculiar or common to pigs, yet it will be very prolific, in any degree of close-interbreeding.

Darwin cannot understand why this is so. He can appreciate, how there is evil from the mere augmenta-tion of morbid tendencies; or, how there is evil in par-ticular parts from the aggravation of the parents' defects in those parts; but, he is at a complete loss, to under-stand how, or why, the effects upon the aggregate, and upon the reproductive system, are wrought. His idea, that he may vary an animal or plant, *ad lib.*, and mould it, to any form he pleases, precludes his arriving at the truth, namely, that normal coördination consists solely with the development of all the parts of the given species; that full capacity of the reproductive element requires a full representation therein, of all the forces of all the parts of the species; and, that, when any of the parts fail to contribute their quota, of force, to such reproductive element, the capacity of such is lessened, and impaired, in proportion.

He says (p. 144, Vol. ii, *Animals and Plants, &c*) :

" That evil directly follows from any degree of close-interbreeding, has been denied by many persons; but, rarely, by any particular breeder ; and never, as far as I know, by one who has largely bred animals which propagate their kind quickly. Many physiologists attribute the evil, exclusively, to the combination, and consequent increase of morbid tendencies, common to both parents; that this is an active source of mischief, there can be no doubt. It is, unfortunately, too notorious, that men, and various domestic animals, endowed with a wretched constitution, and with a strong hereditary disposition to disease, if not actually ill, are fully capable of procreating their kind. *Close-interbreeding, on the other hand, induces sterility; and this indicates something quite distinct (!) from the augmentation of morbid tendencies common to both parents.* The evidence, immediately to be given, convinces me that it is a great law of nature" ("Law of nature" was an excellent good term, before it was ill sorted ; therefore, scientists had need look to it), " that all organic beings profit from an occasional cross with individuals, not closely related to them in blood; and, that, on the other hand, long-continued close-interbreeding is injurious. Various general considerations have had much influence in leading me to this conclusion ; but the reader will probably rely more on special facts and opinions. The authority of experienced observers, even when they do not advance the grounds of their belief, is of some little value. Now, almost all men who have bred many kinds of animals, and have written on the subject, such as Sir J. Sebright, Andrew Knight, &c., have expressed the strongest conviction, on the impossibility of long-continued close-interbreeding. Those who have compiled works on agriculture, and have associated much with breeders, such as the sagacious Youatt, Low, &c., have strongly declared their opinion to the same effect. Prosper Lucas, trusting largely to French authorities, has come to a similar conclusion. The distinguished German agriculturist, Hermann von Nathusius, who has written the most able treatise, on this subject, which I have met with, concurs."

It is thus seen, that Darwin, while rightly conjecturing the cause of the evil effects upon the parts of the organism, is puzzled, respecting the cause of the effects wrought upon the aggregate—effects which are evidenced in loss of fertility and of constitutional vigor.

The experienced breeders and writers, of whom he speaks, are unquestionably right, in their conclusion that, as a fact, such effects do most frequently result. But, they do not all refer them to "a great law of nature," or to any other such "innate tendency," or similar, metaphysical entity; and, then complacently imagine that they have explained (!) them. Fancy the perfect howl of derision, which would be set up, by the mutual admiration society of English philosophers, were a person, suspected of being tinctured with orthodoxy, to attempt to shirk the solution of a body of facts, by referring them to "a great law of nature!" Breeders, whilst recognizing the truth of the facts, advanced by Darwin, are not so obtuse, as to disregard the significance of the important circumstance, that the effects of the same degree of close-interbreeding, vary widely, not only with individuals of different species, but also with individuals of the same species, and even of the same variety, and of the same breed, both in the quantity of the evil, and in the period of its recurrence. It is a consideration, of these circumstances, which moves many, even of the unlearned, to scorn such an unphilosophical mode of induction (or deduction, for it is hard to tell what it is), as Darwin essays, when he postulates, or deduces, "a great law of nature!" It would afford inexhaustible amusement, to know what Darwin's major premise is, if his "great law of nature" be a conclusion. It must be, in the similitude of this: Phenomena, which are scientifically inexplicable, are due to a "great law of nature;" the phenomena of close-interbreeding, are scientifically inexplicable; Ergo: the phenomena of close-interbreeding are due to "a great law of nature." If his law be an induction: the mere intimation, to such effect, should suffice to start Bacon from his grave, to deplore the time, the event shows that he wasted, in warning his disciples against the error of incomplete induction.

Breeders see, that, with such variations in the quantity of effect, attendant upon close-interbreeding, the process itself cannot be the cause, but must be the occasion only. What the cause is, they are at a loss to say. But, they can well see, that in-and-in breeding is not the cause.

A scientist, however, who may,—as Darwin has

done, with full impunity, and with the hearty con-
currence of the scientific world,—deduce a law of indefinite progress, from what the very terms of his
problem show, to be but instances of regain of developments previously lost; who founds his theory
upon an "innate tendency," or upon ignorance; and,
who, throughout all of his works, makes his ignorance
enact the role of positive factors, may well, and con-
fidently, count upon the implicit reception of any
absurdity which he may see fit to devise, to hide the
inconsistencies of his hypothesis.

All of the exceptions, here taken, to Darwin's "law
of nature," as applying to close-interbreeding, obtain,
mutatis mutandis, with equal force, when urged against
the other phase of his "law," which applies to Crossing.   The same variations in the quantity of the effects, from the same degree of crossing, are observable.

When each, of two individuals paired, has much to
contribute, to the offspring, which the other lacks, the
good, resulting from such cross, is great.   Where each
has but little to contribute, which the other lacks, the
good resulting is small.   If but one of the parents has
any characters to contribute to the offspring, which the
other lacks, the increase of good, in the offspring, will
be such only, relatively to the parent whose deficiencies
were supplied, and which had naught to give, but what
the other parent also gave.   When good results to the
offspring, relatively to both parents, as it generally does;
it is because, defective parts in either, are supplied,
by positive parts in the other,—through each of the

parents having something to bestow, where existed defects in the coördination of the other.

If proof of this principle be required, observe all of
the cases of crossing; note the amount of structure,
which is possessed by either parent, and which is
wanting in the other; mark the advance towards
structural integrity, made upon the parents, by the offspring; and, then observe the constant relation, subsisting between the gain, to the offspring, in fertility,
and in constitutional vigor, and the advance, made
by such offspring, in mere, structural development.

Note the great improvement, in fertility, and in constitutional vigor, resulting from crossing two widely
divergent varieties, of. pigeons, which have, each, an
important; and strongly pronounced character, which
the other does not possess.   Note, on the other hand,
the comparatively little increase in fertility, and in
vigor, which follows from crossing two well-bred
varieties of the horse, of the sheep, or of the cow
species, which are distinguished from each other, by
but some slight differences in the ratio of the development of their characters.

In order to demonstrate, that the good effects, occasioned by crossing, are due to the increased return,
made by the offspring, to the structure of the original
type, which possessed all of the characters of the
given species, it is not necessary to invent any metaphysical entity; to seek refuge behind any " great law
of nature," fashioned for the nonce; nor to appeal to
any gratuitous supposition, which is, besides, incompetent to explain the many differences in the quantity of

the effects. The reason alleged, is founded on the observed results of breeding, as detailed by Darwin; is in the strictest accordance with every variation in the results; is a reason, not merely deduced from the law of reversion, but supported and confirmed by daily experience; and is the only reason, or explanation, which covers all of the phenomena.

To Darwin, the good, resulting from crossing, is as insoluble, as are the phenomena of close-interbreeding; or (to use a simile of his own, respecting the cause of variations), as insoluble as the problem "of free will and predestination." The phenomena of crossing, are also, by him, relegated to the mysterious operation of the same "great law of nature," to which he refers the phenomena of close-interbreeding. Controversialists, speculating upon the problem of free-will and predestination, might acquire from Darwin, light to guide them through their theological mazes. If he, Darwin, may, within the realm of nature, resolve a body of conflicting phenomena, by ascribing them to "a great law of nature;" may not a theologian, with equal (aye, immeasurably greater), propriety, resolve his transcendental difficulties, by ascribing all the points for which he contends, in the controversy respecting Free will, to "a great supernatural law!!"

He says (p. 213, Vol. ii, *Animals and Plants, &c.*):

"Abundant evidence has been given, that crossing adds to the size, vigor, and fertility of the offspring. This holds good, even when there has been no previous close-interbreeding. It applies to individuals, of the same variety, but belonging to different families, to distinct varieties, and partially even to species. In the latter case, though size is often gained, fertility is lost."

Even if Darwin had perceived, that the contribution, to the offspring, by either parent, of a character which answered to the part deficient in the other parent, could furnish an explanation of the good resulting from crossing; such a solution upon the hypothesis of evolution, would not be so satisfactory, as it is upon the theory of Reversion. For, upon the theory of Reversion, the characters, supplied to the offspring, are characters which were once lost, the regain of which, is needed to secure perfection; whereas, upon the theory of evolution, there is no explanation, of why the mere addition of characters, should bring with it, increased fertility: seeing, that species, with a small number of characters, are generally as fertile, and sometimes more so, than species, with a development greatly more complex. Neither would there be any assignable reason, upon Darwin's theory, why, where there was, in each parent, a positive peculiarity, and a defective character, the defective character should not be prepotent over the positive character, and evil result, in the offspring, through the defects in either, sinking the corresponding, positive developments in the other parent.

The reason, why good, instead of evil, results, when two individuals, dissimilarly defective, are crossed, is, because, in the defective points of each, the power of reversion exists, ever ready to assert itself, under conditions in anywise favorable; and, this capacity joins

21

with the other parent's positive characters which correspond, to effect the development of such characters in the offspring, and a return, full or measurable, as the case may be, to the perfect type.   If this power of reversion were not present, there would be no reason, why the defective points of each parent should not, in the offspring, be prepotent, over the positive peculiarities of the other; instead of, as is the fact, the positive peculiarities of the one, supplying the deficiencies of the other.   It is true, that, under certain unfavorable conditions, militating against the operation of reversion, the defects in each or in one, may be, to some degree, prepotent over the positive features in the other.   Such a phenomenon, however, is rare.   When such is the case, however, there is always to be observed an abatement, or absence, of the good, ordinarily resulting from crossing.   This explains the few cases, where, as Darwin shows (with reluctance, because they contravene his law), no good, and even evil, result from a cross.

Crossing undoes, either wholly, or in a measure, the injury attendant upon a departure from the original type;—restores, in a degree, to the offspring the vigor and fertility which defects in development, had, in the parents, destroyed or impaired.   It is by the conjunction, in the offspring, of the positive characters in which either parent differs from the other, that the good is effected.   It is not the mere addition of structural parts, but the consequent, improved physiology, which secures the benefit from a cross.

Darwin says (p. 142, Vol. ii, *Animals and Plants, &c.*):

"The gain in constitutional vigor, derived from an occasional cross, between individuals of the same variety, but belonging to distinct families, or between distinct varieties, has not been so largely, or so frequently discussed as have the evil effects of close interbreeding. But the former point (the gain in constitutional vigor, which is derived from crossing) is the more important of the two, inasmuch as the evidence is more decisive. The evil results from close-interbreeding, are difficult to detect, for they accumulate slowly and differ much in degree, whilst the good effects which almost invariably follow a cross, are from the first manifest."

In the following Chapters, we shall trace in detail, the truth of the principle of Reversion in its application to Crossing and Close-Interbreeding; and show that, however widely the several species may differ in the results of the several modes of Selection to which they have been subjected, they all establish and confirm, most positively, the theory that the evil results, of Close-Interbreeding, are due to the absence, in the individuals, of characters proper to their respective species; that the good results, from Crossing, are due to each of the parents' contributing, to the offspring, a character or characters which. are absent in the other parent; that there is but one normal type, for each species, which is the sum of all the positive characters of such species; that no positive variation is possible, in any species, after the members thereof, have regained all the characters which the species once lost; that any modification, or departure from the perfect type of a species, is attended by physiological evil which is merely aggravated by Close-Interbreeding;

and that any return to such type, whether effected by direct Reversion, by Crossing, or by Grafting, is attended by a physiological regain, or abatement of the evils entailed by the loss or reduction of characters.

The space available would not suffice for all the proofs on hand; so, it has been deemed advisable, merely, to furnish evidence respecting one or more of those species which principally illustrate either of the four more pronounced modes of Selection.

Pigeons and Fowls constitute the subject of one Chapter, because they both represent the mode of Selection by which lost characters, of a species, are indeed all regained, but regained only to be apportioned among distinct varieties, and not developed, all, in each variety.

Pigs form the subject of another Chapter, because they represent that mode of Selection, pursued by breeders, by which characters, of a species, instead of being developed, are reduced and suppressed.

Horses, Sheep, and Cows constitute the subject of another Chapter, because they represent the mode of Selection by which the lost and reduced characters, of a species, are (comparatively speaking) all concurrently regained and re-developed in each individual or variety, and a very close approximation to the full and proportionate development of all the parts, of a species, effected.

Plants form the subject of another Chapter, because they illustrate the effects flowing from that mode of Selection which develops to a great, or to the extreme point, one only of the characters of a species; and, principally, because they show that Reversion explains the seemingly-inexplicable results of Crossing, of Close-Interbreeding, and of Self-Fertilization, even when there prevail such infinite variations in the quantity and quality of those results, as are known to obtain with Plants.

Numberless other evidences,—showing that any departure from the type of the sum of all the positive characters of the species, is fraught with proportional evil upon the aggregate, as well as upon the parts involved, and showing that any (proportionate) return to the perfect type (however effected), issues in an abatement of such evil,—could be furnished from Darwin's own notes of the breeding of Dogs, Rabbits, Bees and, in fact, of all the domestic animals. The reader, however, will doubtless concur in the opinion that, after the testimony adduced in relation to the Crossing, Close-Interbreeding, and Self-Fertilization, respectively, of Plants, Pigeons, Fowls, Pigs, Horses, Sheep, and Cows, all further proofs, in support of the theory of Reversion, and in Refutation of Darwinism, may justly be dispensed with.

21*

CHAPTER VIII.

The Crossing and the Close-Interbreeding of Pigeons and of Fowls.

Each of the species, Pigeon and Fowl, affords a crucial instance of the truth of that theory of interbreeding, which is deducible from the assumption of reversion.

It has already been shown in Chapter vi, on The Processes of Formation of Varieties, that, with Pigeons and Fowls, all or most of the characters, respectively lost or reduced by those species, have been regained, not concurrently, but each character, in a different variety. Man, it has been shown, there looks to the development of only one of such lost or reduced characters, in each variety. In the Fantail, the character, which such name connotes, is alone regained, and its development pushed to an extreme point; whilst the rest of the long-lost or reduced parts are suffered to remain respectively reduced, and suppressed. In the Pouter variety of the Pigeon, the individuals "show" such "adaptation to his (man's) wants and pleasures," and "have been" so "modified not for their own benefit, but for that of man," that the individuals of this variety (for instance), lack all, or nearly all, of the positive peculiarities of the other one hundred and forty-nine varieties of the said species.

(242)

Not only is the principle illustrated, in these two species, the Pigeon and Fowl, of a distribution, among several and distinct varieties, of the characters regained; but, the effects of all the other processes of the formation of varieties, are also observable, in varieties of these two species. Disproportionate development, with the varieties of these species, is effected, not merely by failure to develop all of the characters, concurrently, in each individual, but also by direct degeneration,—by the direct suppression or reduction of fea- · tures which had escaped the ordeal of the Struggle for Existence.

Such species should, *ex hypothesi*, be notable for evil effects when their individuals are bred in-and-in. If, for instance, the individuals of the Fantail variety which is below referred to, lack not only the full development of the peculiar character of their variety, but lack also, all of the positive peculiarities of all the other varieties of their species,—which they needs must,—it is manifest, that interbreeding will, by the physiological effects, wrought upon such individuals, decide positively, one way or the other, whether evil flows, from the departure of the individuals from the type of the sum of all the positive features of their species.

If the individuals of a variety, not only lack all the positive peculiarities of the other varieties, but are distinguished from the others by a negative, instead of a positive, feature, the evil effects of close-interbreeding should, *a priori*, be the greater.

Darwin says (p. 237, Vol. ii, *Animals and Plants, &c.*):

"A great winner of prizes at the Pigeon shows, in de- ·

scribing the shortfaced Almond Tumbler, says, 'There
are many first-rate fanciers who are particularly partial
to what is called the goldfinch beak which is very beautiful; others say, take a full-sized round cherry, then
take a barley-corn, and judiciously placing and thrust-
ing it into the cherry, form as it were your beak; and
that is not all, for it will form a good head and beak,
provided, as I said before, it is judiciously done; others
take an oat; but as I think the goldfinch beak the hand-
somest, I would advise the inexperienced fancier to get
the head of a goldfinch, and keep it by him for his
observation.'   Wonderfully different as is the beak of
the rock-pigeon and goldfinch, undoubtedly, as far as
external shape and proportions are concerned, the end
has been nearly gained."

When it is remembered, that, not merely is the beak,
in this variety, moulded according to the fashion,
caprice, and fancy of man, in violation of the true proportion which is essential to physiological integrity;
that, not merely does it lack, from eighteen to twenty-
eight (of the forty) tail-feathers, of the Fantail variety, together with its power of erection of the same;
that, not merely does it lack "the wonderful development of the head," "the greatly elongated eyelids," the
"very large external orifice to the nostrils," and "the
wide gape of mouth," of the Carrier; that, not merely,
also, does it lack the "great size," "long, massive
beak," "large feet," the "very long neck," and the
"very long wings, and tail" of the Runt; that, not
merely does it lack the "much elongated body and
legs," and "the enormously developed crop," of the
Pouter; that, not merely does it lack the "line of
reversed feathers, down the breast," of the Turbit;

that, not merely does it lack "the feathers, so much reversed, along the back of the neck that they form a hood," of the Jacobin ; and, that, not merely does it lack the power of utterance of the coo, alone retained by the Trumpeter and Laugher; but, that it also lacks, to a greater or less degree, development in the size, and shape of the body; in the number, and size of the scutellæ ; in the size of the eyes, and eyelids ; in the length, and breadth of the tongue ; in the amount of wattle ; in its coating of feathers ; in the size, and shape of its sternum, and of its scapulæ ; in the number, and size of its vertebræ, and in many details of its skeleton, and of other internal and external organs ; it is apparent, that here, in this variety, and in the other divergent varieties of the species, which are, *mutatis mutandis*, likewise, disproportionately developed, the greatest evils are to be expected from close-interbreeding, and the greatest increase of good, from crossing distinct varieties.

The Fowl has its characters, similarly distributed, among its different varieties, and similar, evil effects are, therefore, to be expected to result from close-interbreeding.

It is also to be expected, that, when two varieties, of the Pigeon or of the Fowl, are crossed, good will result; owing to the fact, that some of the characters which one variety lacks, will be supplied by the characters which the other possesses.

The results anticipated, *ex hypothesi*, are fully borne out, by the facts recorded by Darwin. (It is scarcely necessary to reiterate again, that the facts are inexplicable by him; for, they are all inexplicable, by him. The sum of his insight into the phenomena he has collated, is, that " the stronger and more vigorous survive." If enlightenment should be sought, by a breeder, upon any one of the million of facts contained in "*Animals and Plants under Domestication*," Darwin would answer, that, upon that subject, " our ignorance is profound;" but, the breeder would be assured, that, of his descent from a monkey, there was neither ignorance, nor doubt.)

The following quotation, from Darwin, establishes, conclusively, the point maintained. Not only is the absence, in any given variety, of the peculiarities of the other varieties, prolific of evil; but, the further the development of the peculiarity of the given variety, is pushed, the greater becomes the evil; because, such development, by making such character more and more predominant, augments the disproportion, and vitiates the true ratio of development of the characters of the species. It is, also, to be remarked, that, where the degeneration of any character is desirable, with fanciers, the evil, wrought by close-interbreeding upon such part, will not be esteemed an evil, because it subserves the object designed by the fancier. The evils, however, which are wrought upon the aggregate, and which display themselves in lessened fertility and in delicacy of constitution, are, all other things equal, the greater in such a case.

"*With Pigeons*," says Darwin (p. 150, Vol. ii, *Animals and Plants, &c.*), "*breeders are* UNANIMOUS, as previously stated, *that it is absolutely indispensable,*

*notwithstanding the trouble and expense thus caused,
occasionally to cross their much-prized birds* with individuals of another strain, ·but belonging, of course,
to the same variety. It deserves notice, that when
large size is one of the desired characters, as with
Pouters, the evil effects of close-interbreeding are
much sooner perceived, than when small birds, such
as shortfaced tumblers, are valued. *The extreme delicacy of the high fancy breeds*, such as these Tumblers,
and improved English Carriers, *is remarkable, they are
liable to many diseases, and often die in the egg, or
in the first moult; and, their eggs have genexally to be
hatched under foster mothers.* Although these highly
prized birds have invariably been subjected to much
close-interbreeding, yet *their delicacy of constitution
cannot, perhaps, be thus fully explained.* Mr. Yarnall
informed me, that Sir J. Sebright continued close-
interbreeding some owl-pigeons, until from their extreme sterility, he as nearly as possible, lost the
whole family. Mr. Brent tried to raise a breed of
Trumpeters, by crossing a common pigeon, and re-
crossing the daughter, granddaughter, and great-granddaughter, with the same male trumpeter, until he obtained a bird with fifteen-sixteenths of Trumpeters'
blood; but then the experiment failed, for 'breeding so
close, stopped reproduction.' The experienced Neu-
meister also asserts, that the offspring from dovecotes,
and various other breeds, are 'generally very fertile,
and very hardy birds;' so again MM. Boitard and
Corbié, after forty-five years of experience, recommend
persons, to cross their breeds for amusement; for, if
they fail to make interesting birds, they will succeed,
under an economical point of view, 'as it is found that
mongrels are more fertile than pigeons of pure race.'"

"Pigeons of pure race" lack many of the characters
of their species. "Mongrels" possess two characters,

and frequently more, where either of their parents possessed one; hence, the greater fertility of the mongrels.
The reason that dovecotes, trumpeters, and common
pigeons, "and various other breeds," are, compared
with the "high fancy breeds," "generally very fertile
and hardy birds," is because, whilst in the "high fancy
breeds," one character, or more, is pushed to an extreme point, the development of the characters, in
the dovecotes, &c., is nearer to the true proportion.
Although many of the characters are reduced, they
are reduced, in these breeds, in something like proportion.

The extreme delicacy, and sterility, of the "high
fancy breeds," of pigeons and fowls, should be borne in
mind, by the reader; for, as will be seen, these traits
conclusively negative Darwin's conception, that these
divergent varieties may diverge into distinct species.

Darwin speaks, above, of the mongrels from a cross,
not being "interesting" birds. The reason they are
esteemed, "not interesting," to the breeder, is, because
they have the characters of the species, approximating
concurrent, and proportionate development; whereas,
no pigeons are "interesting," to men happily termed
"fanciers," unless they have one, or a few characters,
pushed to the extreme of development, and out of all
proportion to the others. The "interesting" birds,
have to pay for their charms, by the "delicacy of constitution," and the "sterility," which are so "remarkable."

"EVIDENCE OF THE EVIL EFFECTS OF CLOSE-INTER-
BREEDING," says Darwin (p. 145, Vol. ii, *Animals and*

Plants, &c.), " CAN MOST READILY BE ACQUIRED IN THE CASE OF ANIMALS SUCH AS FOWLS, PIGEONS, &c. * * Now, I have inquired of very many breeders of these birds, and *I have hitherto not met with a single man who was not thoroughly convinced, that an occasional cross with another strain of the same sub-variety, was not absolutely necessary.* Most breeders of highly improved, or fancy birds, value their own strain, and are most unwilling, at the risk, in their opinion, of deterioration, to make a cross. The purchase of a first-rate bird, of another strain, is expensive, and exchanges are troublesome ; yet all breeders, as far as I can hear, excepting those who keep large stocks, at different places, for the sake of crossing, *are driven, after a time, to take this step."*

The reason, why " evidence of the evil effects of close-interbreeding, can most readily be acquired, in the case of animals, such as Pigeons, Fowls, &c.," is insoluble by Darwin. He simply records the fact, without attempting to explain it. The real reason, is, because the varieties of these species are divergent in character ; and divergence necessarily implies disproportionate development. For, it takes many positive characters to make many divergent varieties, and such characters, instead of forming peculiarities of several classes within the same species, are all, according to the theory of reversion, needed in each individual of the species. Consequently, it is to be expected, that, when these characters, instead of being concurrently developed, in each individual, are apportioned among different varieties, and when the true integrity of the species, is thus impaired, some evil or injury must follow ; and, as Pigeons and Fowls are the species, wherein the true

22

proportion of their respective characters, has been thus most outraged, it is, to them, one should look, for the greatest evil effects from interbreeding individuals, similar in the defects of their development.

Each one of the varieties, respectively, of the Pigeon, and of the Fowl, lacks all of the positive characters which form the distinguishing marks of the other varieties of the same species. As, therefore, the absence, in any variety, or individual, of any character of its species, must, *ex hypothesi*, be deleterious to its physiological integrity, there is little room for marvel at the evil results of the close-interbreeding of these animals.

There is as little occasion, to wonder at the good which, Darwin alleges, results from crossing two varieties of any one of these species. For, as he elsewhere says, they "differ in an extreme degree, in some one part, when compared with one another" (p. 16, *Origin of Species*). When two such varieties are crossed, the offspring acquires some character, or characters, which either of its parents lacked, and so much the nearer is the approximation, in the offspring, to the original, perfect type ; hence, the good resulting.

These two species, the Pigeon, and the Fowl, are the species, upon the divergence of character in whose varieties, Darwin mainly relies, to show that varieties are "incipient species," or distinct species, in the process of formation. Yet, in the very exposition of his hypothesis of such divergence, he reveals a state of facts, which signally confutes such a view. For, he clearly shows, by his remarks (which are frequently reiterated) concerning the evil results of interbreeding the highly improved or fancy birds, and concerning the absolute necessity of crossing them with individuals of the other varieties, that this very divergence of character, is in derogation of the fertility and constitutional vigor of the individuals of the divergent varieties;—aye, incompatible, when carried to any great extent, with their very existence; for, he says (p. 270, Vol i, *Animals and Plants, &c.*), that:

" *The young of all highly improved fancy breeds, are extremely liable to disease and death!*"

This shows conclusively, that the further that this process of divergence (upon which he counts to evolve the varieties of any species, into distinct species), is carried, the nearer, step by step, do the varieties, so divergent, approximate complete sterility and extinction!

On the other hand, it is shown, by his remarks, already quoted, and by those quoted below, *that the only means, by which such divergent varieties may regain their fertility, and retrieve their shattered constitutions,* is, by *undoing the very process which, he would have his readers believe, evolves them into distinct species!*

Even though the phenomena of close-interbreeding, and of crossing, did not conclusively imply, that the sum of all the positive characters of the respective species, was the only, perfect type; what would be the strength of an argument, favoring the evolution of species, by means of divergence of character, when the individuals of each of the varieties, assumed to be so diverging into distinct species, meets with completely shattered constitutions, and with sterility, before they have half accomplished such process of divergence!

Not only do the phenomena of close-interbreeding, constitute an insuperable bar to any such result as evolution, into distinct species, by means of this divergence; but, the man is likewise blocked, in the other direction, by the fact of the sterility of hybrids!

If the proofs of reversion, the phenomena of close-interbreeding, the phenomena of crossing, and the fact of the sterility of hybrids, do not constitute the elements of a complete demonstration; then a demonstration is impossible, without the domain of mathematics.

Again, he says (p. 150, Vol. ii, *Animals and Plants, &c.*):

"*With all highly bred animals*" (he here obviously speaks of the animals which are divergent in character; for, he elsewhere says, "*with animals not divergent in character*, such as cattle and sheep, *interbreeding may be long carried on without any decrease in fertility or vigor*"), "*with all highly bred animals, there is more or less difficulty, in getting them to procreate quickly, and all suffer much from delicacy of constitution;* but, I do not pretend that these effects ought to be wholly attributed to close-interbreeding."

Strictly speaking, no evil is to be attributed to close-interbreeding. It is disproportionate development which causes the evil: Close-interbreeding but aggravates such evil. The "difficulty," of which he speaks, "in getting highly-bred animals to procreate," and their "delicacy of constitution," are in proportion to divergence of character, or rather to defects in structure which such divergence ordinarily implies. Each highly-bred, divergent variety obviously lacks all of the positive peculiarities of the other varieties of its species. It generally lacks even more characters, than these. The more varieties, with positive peculiarities, there are, within a species, the greater, generally, is the number of characters which each such variety lacks. Therefore, the evils of close-interbreeding tell sooner, and are the most disastrous, with the most divergent varieties.

Those who do not discern the method, in Darwin's seeming candor, may express surprise, that this constant relation,—traceable between lessened fertility, and the absence or reduction, in the individuals, of characters which belong to the given species,—should not have suggested itself to Darwin. But, it is manifest, that, if he saw this relation, it must have occurred to him, that it was to the interest of his strained hypothesis, that it should not appear; for, it forcibly, and necessarily implies, that all of the characters, possible to be developed in any individual, belong to each and every individual of that species; and, that divergent varieties subsist, in derogation of their full vigor and fertility.

But, why,—it may be urged,—is it, that Darwin states the facts, which thus tell against his hypothesis, so fully and so clearly? The reason is, that the possibility of such relation being perceived, was, to his mind, very remote; whereas, there stood, like Fate, confronting his hypothesis, the objection of the sterility of hybrids, which was an inevitable and well-

22*

known difficulty in his way; and which, he saw, could be dodged, only by recording all of the complicated and seemingly inconsistent and inexplicable phenomena of the crossing and close-interbreeding of individuals of the same species, and, then, candidly (?) putting it to his readers, Whether any reliance could be placed upon the obvious inference from the sterility of hybrids, when the whole subject of sterility and fertility, both within the same species, and with different species, was in such an inextricable maze!

‘ This accounts for his suicidal course, in adducing so plentifully, and so strongly, phenomena which show, that evil attends, degree for degree, departure from the one, normal type of any species. This expedient is (to borrow an expression, once used by George Henry Lewes, in another connection), “facile, but futile.” For, the maze, in which the phenomena mentioned are involved, is not inextricable; the idea of reversion, and of proportionate development, being the thread, which resolves all of the confusion into the most beautiful harmony.

But, his device is equally futile, even upon the supposition, that the facts adduced, are not explicable. Explicable or not, both classes of phenomena confound all of his speculations. For, as the obvious inference, from the sterility of hybrids (even when such phenomenon is unexplained), is the negation of Darwin's theory; so, the obvious inference, from the sterility which attends divergence of character, is (even when such phenomenon is unresolved), in diametrical opposition to such theory. To take, then, these two obvious inferences, and with each, gratuitously to attempt to cancel the other, is to perform a feat, never before surpassed by the most dextrous of intellectual jugglers.

Darwin says (p. 143, Vol. ii):

"It should, however, be clearly understood, that the advantage of close-interbreeding, as far as the retention of characters is concerned, is indisputable, and often outweighs the evil of a slight loss of constitutional vigor."

The expression "as far as the retention of characters is concerned," shows, that he means, that when a breeder is developing one lost or reduced, character alone, in a variety, in order to secure the dominance of that character, and the suppression or reduction of the other characters, it is necessary and desirable, to breed it closely with individuals possessing the same abnormal, or monstrous structure. He frequently reiterates an injunction of his, to breed from the "best" animals; when it is apparent, to every one who entertains the idea of reversion, even for an instant, that, with varieties in whose species there are many other varieties with positive peculiarities, those individuals, which are intimated to be the "best," are the ones in which disproportionate development invites the greatest evils, from close-interbreeding;—and, they are the ones which are really the more degenerate, the further the development of the special excellence of each, is pushed, because the proportion of the characters is thus marred.

With varieties, such as those of the Pigeon, and of

the Fowl, which, to the fancier, have their criterion of
excellence, in the abnormally great development of one
character alone, to the exclusion of the development of
many other characters of that species, barrenness, and
delicacy of constitution, are always prolific sources of
trouble; and this trouble is always in proportion to the
degree of "improvement," which the individuals of
such divergent varieties attain.   Of this, the "high
fancy breeds" of the Pigeon and of the Fowl, are
notable instances;—the very "improvement" of such
breeds, is productive of the evils which usually accompany close-interbreeding.

Darwin, in the following remarks, ventures very close
to the true law of development, and to the true reason
of the evils, concomitant on interbreeding.   The Bantam
is wanting, in several characters of the Fowl species;
and, of course, evil is attendant upon their absence.
The true light seems just to glimmer, for an instant,
upon Darwin's mental horizon:

"The Sebright Bantam is much less prolific" (p. 127,
Vol. ii, *Animals and Plants, &c.*), "than any other breed
of fowl, and is descended from a cross between two
very distinct breeds, recrossed by a third sub-variety.
But, it would be extremely rash to infer, that the loss
of fertility was in any manner connected with its crossed
origin, for it may, with more probability, be attributed
either to long-continued close-interbreeding, or *to
an innate tendency (!) to sterility, correlated with the
absence (!) of hackles, and sickle tail-feathers.*"

It is strange, that, when Darwin can perceive such a
relation between the sterility of the Bantam, and the
absence of certain of the characters of its species, he

does not also discern the relation, which is observable, in every individual of every species, between its sterility, or the degree of its lessened fertility, and that amount of the characters of its species, which it lacks.   It is equally strange, that such partial guess at the truth, has not led him further, and revealed to him, that the full and concurrent development of all the parts of a species, is essential to physiological integrity, and to full procreative power.   It is, however, requiring too much to expect a theorist to develop such a "lead," when the absolute requirement of his hypothesis, is, that many of the characters of each species should be distributed, or apportioned, among several varieties.

One type alone, of each species, is normal.   Nature errs not from her end, by the existence of a multiplicity of types (*i. e.* varieties), in a species.   For, for each and every deviation from the one type, a penalty, commensurate with such departure, is visited upon the individual.   Nature, then, does not deviate from the type prescribed; for every fact, in the whole of her realm, attests most clearly, that physiological integrity can be retained, only by strict conformity to the mould enjoined.

"Turning now to Birds," says Darwin (p. 154, Vol. ii, *Animals and Plants, &c.*), "*In the case of the Fowl, a whole array of authorities could be given against too close-interbreeding.*   Sir J. Sebright positively asserts that he made many trials, and that his fowls became * * * small in the body, and bad breeders.   He produced the famous Sebright Bantams, by complicated crosses, and by breeding in-and-in; and since his time, there has been much close-interbreeding with these Bantams. I have seen Silver Bantams, directly descended from his stock, which had become almost as barren as hybrids; for, not a single chicken had been, that year, hatched from two full nests of eggs."

The proofs, which we advance, of the truth of the theory of Reversion, are, viz., the fact, that, with all of the individuals, which are most wanting in the characters of their respective species, there is the greatest evil, from close-interbreeding; and, the fact, that, with all of the individual animals or plants which most approximate full and proportionate development, there is the least degree of such evil. But, taking a single instance, there is none which presents such a delicate, crucial test of the truth of the theory of reversion, as the following remarkable case. The animal, mentioned below, advances, in but the slightest appreciable degree, to the perfect type of its species; yet, Darwin, who is wholly ignorant of the cause of the effect which he records, has remarked the physiological gain, which accompanies the slight, structural regain.

He says (p. 154, Vol. ii, *Animals and Plants, &c.*):

"I have noticed, as a general rule, that even the slightest deviation from feminine character, in the tail of the male Sebright (Fowl)—say, *the elongation, by only a half an inch, of the two principal tail-feathers (!)—brings with it improved probability of increased fertility !*"

In a note, to page 155, Vol. ii, *Animals and Plants, &c.*, Darwin says:

"See also the 'Poultry Book,' by Tegetmeier, 1866,

p. 135, with respect to the extent to which cock-fighters found that they could venture to breed in-and-in, viz., occasionally, a hen with her own son; 'but they were cautious not to repeat the in-and-in breeding.'"

Again he says, on the same page :

"Mr. Wright states that Mr. Clark, 'whose fighting-cocks were so notorious, continued to breed from his own kind, till they lost their disposition to fight, but stood to be cut up, without making any resistance, and were so reduced in size, as to be under those weights required for the best prizes; but on obtaining a cross from Mr. Leighton, they again resumed their former carriage and weight.' It should be borne in mind, that game-cocks, before they fought, were always weighed, so that nothing was left to the imagination, about any reduction or increase in weight. Mr. Clark does not seem to have bred from brothers and sisters, which is the most injurious kind of union. * * I may add that Mr. Eyton, of Eyton, the well-known ornithologist, who is a large breeder of Gray Dorkings, informs me, that *they certainly diminish in size, and become less prolific, unless a cross with another strain is occasionally obtained.* So it is with Malays, according to Mr. Hewitt, as far as size is concerned."

"We thus see," Darwin continues, "that THERE IS ALMOST COMPLETE UNANIMITY, *with poultry breeders, that* when Fowls are kept at the same place, *evil quickly follows from interbreeding carried on to any extent*, which would be disregarded in the case of most quadrupeds. On the óther hand, it is a generally received opinion that *cross-bred chickens are the hardiest, and most easily reared.* Mr. Tegetmeier, who has carefully attended to poultry of all breeds, says that Dorking hens allowed to run with Houdan, or Crevecœur cocks, 'produce, in the early spring, chickens, that for size, hardihood, early maturity, and fitness for the market, surpass those of any pure breed that we have ever raised.'"

The reason, why these great evils prevail among Fowls, is, because each individual, either, lacks many of the following characters, or has them, in a greater or less degree, reduced; viz.: the beak, the comb, the spurs, sickle tail-feathers, head, neck, wings, legs, feet, wattle, hackles, ear-lobes, wing-feathers, vertebræ, coating of feathers, crest of feathers, &c. All of the breeds are but various modifications of the sum of all the characters, fully developed. It is apparent, then, that, generally, each of the breeds possesses some positive character or characters, which the other breeds lack. What he says, therefore, respecting the physiological advantages to be derived from crossing the breed, is exactly what is to be expected by one whom the conception of reversion has led to believe, that perfection resides, only in that individual in which no positive character, of its species, is wanting.

He says (p. 280, Vol. i, *Animals and Plants, &c.*), Fanciers "admit, and even overrate, the effects of crossing the various breeds" of fowls. On page 287, Vol. i, *Animals and Plants, &c.*, he again notes the fertility of the offspring of crossed breeds.

On page 229, Vol. ii, *Animals and Plants, &c.*, he again says:

"Domesticated varieties, such as those of the Dog, Fowl, Pigeon, several Fruit trees, and culinary vegetables, which differ from each other, in external characters, more than many species, are perfectly fertile, when crossed, or even fertile in excess, whilst closely allied species are almost invariably in some degree sterile."

Each variety, of the Fowl, and of the Pigeon, is not only defective in the mere ratio of the development of its characters, but it also lacks many characters. Such disproportion entails the evils of close-inter-breeding. Each variety possesses a feature which, if joined with that of another variety, will insure a step towards the original type. This conjunction of the characters of two varieties, in one individual, is effected by crossing; and, as a consequence, there is a beneficial effect.

Each variety moves along a separate, divergent line, towards the true mould of the species. This advance, however, produces more evil, than if all the characters were suffered to lie proportionately reduced; because the true ratio of the development of the characters, is greatly prejudiced by this exclusive development of one character. Only by the union of all the divergent lines of growth, may physiological perfection be attained; and, when two such divergent lines are united, in one individual, the evil is measurably lessened.

As he has asserted, that it is difficult to get highly-bred animals to procreate, so he says again, that (p. 271, Vol. ii, *Animals and Plants, &c.*): "*Highly-bred animals are liable to degeneration.*" As has been more than once asserted, a multiplicity of divergent varieties, in any species, implies the absence, in each, of what constitutes the peculiarities of the other varieties. It is the disturbance of the balance of the characters,

23

occasioned by pushing these peculiarities to an "extreme point," which causes the pronounced degeneration of the highly-bred animals.

With respect to Pigeons, which are more divergent in character, than even the Fowl, he says (p. 27, *Origin of Species*):

"The hybrids, or mongrels, from between all the domestic breeds of Pigeons, are perfectly fertile. I can state this from my own observation purposely made, on the most distinct breeds. Now, it is difficult, perhaps impossible, to bring forward one case of the hybrid offspring of two animals clearly distinct, being themselves perfectly fertile."

In the chapter on "The Sterility of Hybrids," it will be seen how strongly this militates against his theory.

"Pigeons" (p. 29, *Origin of Species*) "were much valued by Abner Khan in India, about the year 1600; never less than 20,000 Pigeons were taken with the court. 'The monarchs of Iran and Turan sent him some very rare birds;' and, continues the courtly historian, 'His Majesty, by crossing the breeds, which method was never before practiced, has improved them astonishingly.'"

It is obvious, that, if the gain in sterility and constitutional vigor, resulting from crossing, be due to each parent contributing, to the formation of the offspring, a character or characters which the other parent lacks, the gain must be in proportion to the number of features so contributed ; and, that the more distinct the crossed breeds are, the greater should be the good which flows. Darwin states, as matter of fact,—the

cause of which is wholly undreamt of in his philosophy,—that such is the case.

Says he, p. 236, Vol. i, *Animals and Plants, &c.*:

"MM. Boitard and Corbié affirm, after their great
experience, that, with crossed pigeons, *the more distinct
the breeds, the more productive are their mongrel offspring.*" (!)

The above quotation furnishes the key to the whole
mystery of the good resulting from crossing. Apply
this rule, to all of the many millions of animals of every
species, and it will be found, that the increased good
from crossing, is in proportion to the amount of positive characters, of the given species, which have been
supplied, to fill a want, existing in either parent.

Darwin says:

"Varieties, however much they differ from each
other in external appearance, cross with perfect facility,
and yield perfectly fertile offspring" (p. 326, *Origin of
Species*).

Aye; and, as he states above, the more that they
differ, the greater is the increase of fertility, when
crossed.

"The perfect fertility of so many domestic varieties,
differing widely from each other in appearance, for instance, as those of the Pigeon, or those of the cabbage,
is a remarkable fact; more especially, when we reflect how many species there are, which, though resembling each other most closely, are utterly sterile
when crossed" (p. 327, *Origin of Species*).

Now, would any suspect, from the bland manner in
which this last observation is made, that the obvious
and admitted significance of the fact of the sterility of

species when crossed, militated most strongly against
Darwin's theory?   He is aware, as he shows by explicit statements made elsewhere to that effect, that
such is the necessary import of the fact.   Yet, here,
instead of using a deprecating tone, in stating the fact,
he records it, as though, if not strongly confirming his
theory, it was in no manner,—apparent or real,—in
opposition to his views of development.   He resorts,
throughout his works, most frequently, to this happy
device, of obviating the adverse impression which the
facts are calculated to awaken in the minds of his
readers.   This is a sample of the child-like and bland
comportment, from which has enured to him, a reputation for candor.   He is never candid, save when the
facts are so well-known, that the absence of their mention, would recoil with hundred-fold force against his
theory; or, where the facts are designed to subserve
some ulterior aim he has in view.   There are many
facts, which come naturally within the scope of his
work, which are, by him, quietly ignored.   The fact of
the sterility of crossed species, or of their hybrids, had
to be stated; for, it would have been fully recognized
as fatal to his theory, if urged first by an opponent.   As
its mention was inevitable, he does the next best thing
to omitting it; he recites it, in a tone which seemingly
goes very far to divest it of its dangerous effect upon
his theory.

That it is possible, to combine the features of all the
different varieties of a species, in one individual, is
shown by the experiment of Darwin, recorded below.
That, which has hitherto precluded the conception of

a perfect type for a species, has been the notion, that such a type would involve the union of all the varietal *types;* whereas, it is not the *types* which need to be united,—but the positive characters, those which are peculiar, and those which are common to the several varieties.

"All the domesticated races" (of the Pigeon), says Darwin (p. 235, Vol. i, *Animals and Plants, &c.*), "pair readily.together, and what is equally important, their mongrel offspring are perfectly fertile. To ascertain this fact, I have made many experiments which are given in the note below; and recently Mr. Tegetmeier has made similar experiments, with the same result."

NOTE:—"I have drawn out a long table of the various crosses, made by fanciers, between the several domestic breeds, but I do not think it worth publishing. I have myself made, for this special purpose, many crosses, and all were perfectly fertile: I have united, in one bird, five of the most distinct races, and with patience, I might have united them all (!) The case of five distinct breeds being blended together, with unimpaired fertility, is important, because Gärtner has shown, that it is a very general, though not as he thought, universal rule, that complex crosses between several species are excessively sterile."

Again he says (p. 236, Vol. i, *Animals and Plants, &c.*):

"When we consider the great differences between such races as pouters, carriers, runts, fantails, turbits, tumblers, &c., the fact of their perfect, or even increased fertility, when inter-crossed in the most complicated manner, becomes a strong argument in favor of their having all descended from a single species."

Aye; and, when we consider that "increased fer-
23*

tility" attends, degree for degree, the union, in any individual, of the peculiar characters of any two or more
of these varieties, it becomes a strong argument in
favor of there being but one normal type for the
species Pigeon; and, becomes a strong argument, also,
in favor of the view,—so strongly confirmed by the
phenomena of close-interbreeding,—that any modifications of that type, such as are implied by the many
great and positive differences between such varieties,
work evil to the constitutions, and to the reproductive
systems of the individuals. When Darwin had united,
in one bird, five distinct varieties, he had, before his
eyes, the closest approximation to the perfect type of
the Pigeon, which he had ever beheld. Had he ex-
perimented further, with that bird, he would have
found that its offspring could withstand, what no other
Pigeons could possibly suffer, viz., long-continued
close-interbreeding, for generation after generation, in
the nearest degree of relationship, and without any, or
with very little, evil effects wrought upon the constitution, or reproductive system.

Again, on pages 247–8, he cites as a "fact," that:

"All the races, though differing in many important
points of structure, produce perfectly fertile offspring;
whilst, all the hybrids which have been produced
between even closely allied species, in the Pigeon
family, are sterile."

It is, because the races do differ "in many important points of structure," that their mongrels are
"perfectly fertile." Physiology demands, that all of
those "many important points of structure," be com-

bined in each individual; as a *sine qua non* of full, functional integrity. The same good does not follow, from crossing species (such as the common pigeon, and the dove), because, as is obvious, there is not, in such a case, an advance to a common, perfect type; and, because, in a hybrid, the characters of the two species, are mixed together, in a manner, which precludes the actual coördination from being impressed, in miniature, upon the reproductive tissue; as is done, where the characters of the individual, belong to one and the same species.

With respect to this question, as it concerns the Fowl, he says :

" In considering whether the domestic breeds (Fowl) are descended from one species, namely, G. *bankiva*, or from several, we must not overlook, though we must not exaggerate, the influence of the test of fertility. Most of our domestic breeds have been so often crossed, and the mongrels are so largely kept, that it is almost certain, that, if any degree of infertility had existed among them, it would have been detected. On the other hand, the four well-known species of Gallus, when crossed with each other, or when crossed, with the exception of G. *bankiva*, with the domesticated Fowl, produce infertile hybrids. * * The argument of fertility must go for something."

The address, with which this delicate subject is here handled, would move the envy of Oily Gammon. Every one knows, and Darwin clearly understands, that an unanswerable objection to his theory, is the sterility of hybrids, which imposes an effectual bar to his confounding the species. Yet, with tact inimitable, he

requests his readers not to overlook (*sic*) the facts
upon which the said objection is based! and gravely
assures them that "the argument of fertility must go for
something." Solicitous, however, lest his injunction,
not to overlook the question of fertility, should be
too fully complied with, he, with an air, exquisitely
judicial, guards them, carefully, from running upon
Charybdis, by warning them, that they "must not exaggerate the influence of the test of fertility." The
state of mind, which is occasioned, in his readers, by
this dexterous treatment of a witching point, is such,
that they wholly waive the impression, by them first
entertained; suffer vague doubts, respecting the validity
of the objection, to enter their minds; modestly distrust their own capacity to gauge the question; and,
end by fancying, that they owe a debt of gratitude to
Darwin, for kindly arresting them, when they were on
the very verge of metaphysics—which, an English-
man ever affects to regard, as his *bête noir*.

"The argument of fertility" does "go for something." What it "goes for," is, that the varieties are
not "incipient" species; and, that they are physiologically incompetent to become distinct species: for, the
individuals composing these divergent varieties lose
their fertility, when bred among themselves, and approximate perfect fertility, only when crossed with individuals of a separate variety; whereas, species are
notable, for having their respective individuals fertile,
inter se, and sterile, when crossed with individuals of
other species. Verily, "the argument of *fertility* must
go for something;" but, it is refreshing, here to see

Darwin coolly advance such a proposition, when he is desirous of having the argument of *sterility* go for nothing.

"It is a singular fact," says Darwin, p. 305, Vol. i, "that the males, in certain sub-breeds (of Fowls), have lost their, secondary masculine characters; and, from their close resemblance in plumage to the females, are often called 'hennies.' There is much diversity of opinion, whether these males are, in any degree, sterile; that they, sometimes, are partially sterile, seems clear, but this may have been caused by too close-interbreeding."

The mere absence of the said characters explains the sterility, partial or total. Each degree, of loss or of reduction of characters, entails lessened fertility, until that amount of modification is reached, which is the maximum compatible with any reproduction; then total sterility sets in.

"An experienced writer remarks," says Darwin, p. 155, Vol. ii, "that the same amateur (in Fowls), as is well-known, seldom long maintains the superiority of his birds; and this, he adds, undoubtedly is due to all his stock 'being of the same blood;' hence, it is indispensable, that he should occasionally procure a bird of another strain. But, this is not necessary, with those who keep a stock of fowls, at different stations. Thus, Mr. Bollance, who has bred Malays, for thirty years, and has won more prizes with these birds, than any other fancier, in England, says, the breeding in-and-in does not necessarily cause deterioration; 'but all depends upon how this is managed. My plan has been, to keep about five or six distinct runs, and to rear about two hundred or three hundred chickens each year, and select the best birds from each run for cross-

ing.   I thus secure sufficient crossing to prevent deterioration.'"

It is plain, that, when Mr. Bollance says, that "breeding in-and-in does not necessarily cause deterioration,"
he shows, that he knows whereof he speaks, better than
does Darwin.   It is clear, that Mr. Bollance would not
have formulated any "general law of nature," for a
factor so infinitely variable in the quantity of its results, as is close-interbreeding.

The reason, why the evils of interbreeding, are
lessened by keeping the animals at different places,
is, because the different conditions, prevailing. at such
different places, entail slight differences in the growth
of the individuals.   Such slight structural differences
suffice to stave off the evils attendant upon close-interbreeding.   Different organs of the body, are differently
affected,—either favorably or unfavorably,—in different
places.   This may be due to the differences in the food,
in the air, in the water, or in the amount of exercise
required for the legs and wings.   These conditions act
directly, upon the organs or parts obviously involved.
But, differences of growth, are entailed in other parts
of the organization, by correlation with the parts,
immediately affected.

Thus, two individuals, derived from the same strain
or family, will have their likeness to each other lessened, by being subjected to different conditions.   When
they interbreed, therefore, there is not the same amount
of increased evil, that there would have been, had they
been reared under exactly similar circumstances; for,
there is not close similarity of defects; but each, proba-

bly, has, to contribute to the offspring, a little of positive structure in which the other is deficient.

The slight differences, which distinguish individuals in the same herd, or flock, will, in some cases, where such differences are positive, and where the degeneration, reduction, or suppression of the several characters, is not too far gone, suffice to avert the evils of interbreeding. They may avert them, for a time; or, make the evils manifest themselves, only when there is the closest interbreeding; or, after many generations of such close-interbreeding.

Darwin commends certain processes of selection by man, which involve the loss, to individuals, of characters of their species, and he also notes the evils of lessened fertility, and of lessened constitutional vigor, which follow the loss or reduction of any characters; yet, with the two terms of an obvious relation, thus clearly present to him, and while he even formulates such relation, he is conveniently obtuse to the fact, that it bears most conclusively against his theory. Thus, in the quotations given below, he approvingly quotes the reduction and the suppression of characters; and then remarks the deterioration, attendant upon such "serious defects in structure," and upon such violation of "the mutual relations of the parts." Yet, notwithstanding all, he pursues the uneven tenor of his hypothesis,—namely, that divergence of character will produce distinct species,—seemingly serenely oblivious of having mentioned anything which, in the least, militated against his views.

He says (p. 241, Vol. ii, *Animals and Plants, &c.*):

"It was ordered that the Polish cock should have no comb or wattles, and now a bird thus furnished, would be at once disqualified."

It will be remembered, that he has previously stated, that the absence of secondary, masculine characters, occasioned partial or perfect sterility.

He then states the induction (alluded to above), which, if he had any scientific acumen at all, should convince him, that he may not normally, or with impunity, mould organisms into any form he lists; but, that all of the characters of the species, are absolutely essential to physiological integrity.

"When man," says he (p. 273, Vol. ii, *Animals and Plants, &c.*) "attempts to breed an animal with some serious defect in structure, or in the mutual relation of the parts, he will either partially, or completely fail or encounter much difficulty, and this is, in fact, a form of natural selection. We have seen, that the attempt was once made, in Yorkshire, to breed cattle with enormous buttocks, but the cows perished so often, that the attempt had to be given up. In some short-faced Tumblers, Mr. Eyton says, 'I am convinced that better head and beak birds have perished in the shell, than were ever hatched.'"

The "better head and beak birds" to which he refers, means those with the smallest beaks and heads. The violation of "the mutual relation of the parts," does not end with this deterioration, in size, of the head and beak, but extends, by correlation with those characters, to the legs and feet; and is aggravated by the reduction, in such birds, of many other features.

"In order," he says (p. 283, Vol. ii, *Animals and Plants, &c.*), "that selection should produce any result, it is manifest that the crossing of distinct races, must be prevented.   *   *   Although free crossing is a danger on the one side, which every one can see, too close-interbreeding is a hidden danger, on the other side."

In other words, crossing "must be prevented," because such a process would prejudice the special excellence of the breed, and imperil the predominance of the one part valued, by the development of the other parts.   "Serious defects in parts," and "in the mutual relation of the parts," are what constitute the excellence of the birds, in fanciers' eyes; for the pronounced and exclusive development of some one peculiarity is what makes each variety so unique and valuable.

On the other hand, "too close-interbreeding is a hidden danger," because it is the Nemesis attending, the suppression of those other parts, which are suppressed in order to throw the given peculiarity into prominence.

To put the whole philosophy of Darwin's double warning, in a nutshell: All the characters are necessary to be developed, in each individual; but, if the fancier desires individuals, with one character only well-developed, and with the other characters reduced or suppressed, he must take care not to cross, for that will be aiding the development of the characters which it is desirable should be suppressed; and on the other hand, he must look out for the evils which are visited upon the individuals, for having those other parts reduced, or suppressed.

24

Another close miss is made, below, at the true law.

"Facts teach us," says he (p. 282, Vol. ii, *Animals and Plants, &c.*), "a valuable lesson; namely, that we ought to be extremely cautious in judging what characters are of importance, in a state of nature, to animals and plants."

This question is solved, to a nicety, by the process of close-interbreeding. If great evil flows from such a process, there are many characters wanting, which are of importance: If no evils flow from any interbreeding, however close or however prolonged, all of the characters of importance are present in the individual: All of the positive characters of the given species, are in a physiological view, of importance; both, in a state of nature, and in a state of domestication.

It is manifest, that, if the theory of reversion, or proportionate development be true, it must be impossible for any of these divergent varieties to transmit its type for any great length of time, in an unbroken line of descent. Such is the fact. The long-continued interbreeding of animals, lacking so many of the characters of their species, would necessarily occasion debilitated constitutions incompatible with existence, and also occasion complete sterility. The history of the different breeds, respectively, of the Pigeon, of the Fowl, and of the Pig, reveals that such has been the case; that it is, and has ever been, necessary, frequently to replenish the stock of such breeds, by means of crossing, and by accessions, or the new selection of such varieties, from the races under nature, or from the less divergent, and therefore the more proportionately developed varieties.

Darwin notices, that mention has been made, at intervals during the last three hundred years, of several varieties of the Pigeon, like those at present prevailing; and he tacitly assumes, that those varieties have been propagated, for that length of time, and that existing varieties are the pure, lineal descendants of those varieties. Now, the existing varieties cannot be traced, to any great period back. They are independently produced from the wild, or rock-Pigeon (*Columba livia*). It was impossible, for our fancy varieties, to have survived for the assumed length of time, without an immense amount of crossing. For, individuals, so disproportionately developed, as are those of the high fancy breeds, must inevitably die out, unless such violation of the true mutual relation of their parts, is retrieved by crossing, continually resorted to. The individuals are incapable of close-interbreeding, without injury; and, the further their divergence in character is carried, the more their eventual extinction is hastened. The only way that they may be able to survive, is at the cost of their distinguishing type, namely by crossing. When they have been crossed, interbreeding may be carried on for awhile; after which, to stave off extinction and sterility, they are compelled to take on other characters than those which distinguish their variety, and they suffer, thereby, both the decrease of their special excellence, and a relative abatement of its predominance. In this way only, may varieties, which lack any of the positive characters of their species, and

which have the development of one character alone
carried to an extreme point, be saved from extinction.
The following is the cycle, around which such abnormal
types must swing: They diverge, in character; meet,
in consequence, the plainest threat of absolute sterility
and death from interbreeding; they then forsake their
types, for the nonce, to retrieve, by crossing, the characters they need, to secure physiological repair; and
then diverge, anew, to repeat again the same round.

Such a round, however, has not long been pursued,
in the past. These divergent varieties have died out,
from the evil effects which such an abnormal ratio of
development of their characters has entailed. The
seeming, long continuance of high fancy breeds of
Pigeons, for instance, is due, not to those breeds having perpetuated their kind, for such length of time;
but, to such breeds, having been recruited, from time
to time, by accessions from the wild pigeon stock
which, though degenerate, is yet of greater physiological value, owing to the proportion of the characters
being better preserved, than it is in those breeds
wherein one or more characters are given an undue
ascendancy. It is impossible for any breed or variety,
long to exist and preserve its type, when it lacks many
of the characters of its species. Forms, and groups of
forms, have disappeared from the earth. These forms,
after having arisen, have spread and continued abundant for an era, and have eventually declined and
become extinct. It is not necessary, to invoke cataclysms, with which to account for species having been
swept from the face of the earth. Certain sets of con-

ditions are necessary for the full development of the characters of the several species. These conditions change. With the change in the conditions, comes the modification or suppression of certain of the characters. Such modification of structure, entails lessened fertility, and, eventually, absolute sterility. The Madeira beetles, for instance, which, Darwin says, have been compelled, by the prevalence of high winds, to reduce their wings to a rudimentary condition, are passing through a course of extinction. Such reduction creates lessened fertility, and lessened constitutional vigor. The accumulated action of interbreeding, will, in time, carry them off. Doubtless, other changes, in the conditions of life, will ensue, and will, by causing further modification of their form, hasten the sterility, which will end the species.

Evolutionists argue, that there is a harmony, in these adaptations, between the organism and its environment; that is, for instance, between the reduction of these beetles' wings and the high winds of their *habitat*. Whatever that harmony may be; there is no harmony, but an absolute incongruity, between the modified structure and a perfect, physiological state. There is, in one sense, a harmony subsisting between the fox who has gnawed off his leg, and the trap which closed upon Reynard's crural appendage. For, if the relation were not that of a trap and a dismembered fox, there soon would be no Reynard. But, perfect harmony, assuredly, cannot be here predicated. Vital, or Life harmony (as it might be termed), there doubtless is; but anatomical and physiological har-

24*

mony, there, incontestably, is not.   All of the instances
of adaptation, shown by Darwin, are, when they involve
a decrease of structure, instances which imply an advance towards sterility, and consequent extinction.
Where the adaptations cited, show increase of structure, the adaptations are possible, only because they
are the regain of structural integrity, previously lost.
It has been urged, that it is gratuitous, to allege that an
animal is in any way inferior, after having lost a character, through adaptation to changed conditions of
life.   The answer to this is: We do not call imperfection what we merely fancy such, but prove it to
be imperfection, by the facts of close-interbreeding,
which demonstrate, that physiological evils, viz., lessened fertility, and lessened constitutional vigor, are
wrought upon the organism, in proportion, degree for
degree, with such alleged imperfection.

With varieties, under domestication, this process of
extinction, by means of the evils resulting from the
interbreeding of forms wanting in characters of their
species, is, with Pigeons, Fowls, and Pigs, hastened
by Man, through his effecting the reduction of so
many characters, in each variety, and through his
altering the ratio of the development of the characters
which remain.   Such varieties cannot long survive, if
they retain always their peculiarity of form.   Darwin
speaks of high fancy varieties of the Pigeon, being
known, for hundreds of years ; and, obviously desires
it to be inferred, that such varieties may so long breed
their kind.   This they cannot do.   Of these varieties,
he himself says ; that they "seem both to have origi-

nated and disappeared," and to have appeared again, "within this same period," of two hundred and odd years. He also refers to, and records the many breeds which "have become extinct" (p. 508, Vol. ii, *Animals and Plants, &c*). .

The reason, that these fancy varieties continue their breed the length of time that they do, is, because, first, the differences, between the individuals of each variety, serve, in a measure, to stave off the evil effects for a time; secondly, because these varieties frequently cross; and, thirdly, because these varieties change their forms, from time to time, by means of the action of reversion in some of their characters, and of the influence of Man's Selection.

Darwin says (p. 262, Vol. ii, *Animals and Plants, &c.*) :

"Fashions do, to a certain extent, change; first, one point of structure, and then another, is attended to." And again he says, "The fancy ebbs and flows."

This fashion and fancy are quite frequently controlled and directed, unconsciously to man, by the fact that health and breeding capacity are to be found, only in those individuals which depart in some point from the defective, varietal type. Man, therefore, in picking out the strong individuals and the good breeders, unwittingly changes the form of the variety.

With improved breeds of horses, of sheep, and of cattle, there is a probability of their being able to continue their line, for many centuries, because they generally approximate the full and proportionate development of their respective species.

CHAPTER IX.

The Crossing and the Close-Interbreeding of Pigs.

Of the smaller animals, the Pigeon, and the Fowl, as we have seen, show adaptation to man's use or fancy, at the greatest expense to their structural integrity. The results are, great disproportionate development and, as a necessary consequence of this, the greatest degree of the evils which are occasioned by close-interbreeding. In all of the larger animals, except the Pig, adaptation to man's use, has harmonized, to a greater or less degree, with the development, in each individual, of all the characters of its species.

With the Pig, as has just been remarked, it is otherwise. This species is the most disproportionately developed, of all the larger animals, under domestication. The disproportionate development, however, is due to a different occasion, from that which has entailed the abnormal structures of varieties of the Fowl, and of the Pigeon. In these species, under domestication, the false ratio of the development of their characters, is due, principally, to man's selecting, as the peculiarity of each variety, one only of the characters which were reduced or suppressed, under nature; and to his pushing the development of that character, to an extreme point. Thus, while all of the characters of the species,

(280)

Pigeon, for instance, are developed, under domestication, they are not all developed, in each individual; but, many of them are apportioned among different varieties.

With the Pig, however, there has been, under domestication, *direct* reduction and suppression of many of its characters. The same characters, have, in the main, been reduced or suppressed, in all of the improved (?) varieties of this species. Darwin, speaking of breeding in general, and of the divergence, which is so notably exemplified in the case of the pigeon, says (p. 290, Vol. ii, *Animals and Plants, &c.*):

"Selection, whether methodical or unconscious, always tending towards an extreme point, together with the neglect and slow extinction of the intermediate and less valued forms, is the key which unlocks the mystery how man has produced such wonderful results. In a few instances, selection, guided by utility, for a single purpose, has led to convergence of character. All the improved and different races of the Pig, as Nathusius has well shown, closely approach each other in character, in their shortened legs, and muzzles, their almost hairless, large, rounded bodies, and small tusks."

The only differences between the several breeds of Pigs, are the degrees to which this reduction and suppression has been carried; and the degrees in which those characters which have been retained, have been developed.

In all of the highly improved breeds, the legs, the tusks, the bristles, the hairy covering, the skin, the front of the head, the jaws, and the tail, have, as has already been shown, been well-nigh eradicated, leaving them to serve as the merest appendages to a trunk, which, the more to vitiate the true ratio of the features of the species, has been monstrously developed.

It is manifest, then, that it is to the Pig, of all the larger animals, to which recourse should be had, for evidence of the theory, that the evil effects of interbreeding, are due to a departure from the mould, which comprises the full development of all the characters of the given species.

If there was ever a species, under domestication, with "serious defects in structure, or in the mutual relation of the parts," it is the Pig, as it presents itself, when "highly-bred."

Similarly: If there was ever a species, under domestication, which displayed marked evil effects from interbreeding, it is the Pig. To no other species, under man's care, does Darwin's remark, that, "Highly-bred animals are eminently liable to degeneration," so appropriately apply. For, it has been frequently remarked, by breeders, unconscious of the cause of the phenomenon they note, that the more improved the Pig, the more susceptible does it appear to be to the evils of lessened fertility, and delicacy of constitution.

Conformable to the presumption, raised by the great reduction in the characters of the Pig, is the following remark of Darwin:

"WITH PIGS," says he (p. 151, Vol. ii, *Animals and Plants, &c.*), "THERE IS MORE UNANIMITY *amongst breeders, on the evil effects of close-interbreeding, than, perhaps, with any other large animal.*"

The evil effects of interbreeding, in the case of the Pig, are a matter of general notoriety. In all of the discussions, on the subject of in-and-in breeding, no case meets with such continual mention. Those, who endeavor to gainsay the fact, that evil is generally attendant upon close-interbreeding, signally and miserably fail to invalidate the fact, that "well-bred" Pigs die out altogether, after having been bred in-and-in, for only a few generations. No one considers the fact, at all questionable; though a few verge close upon the truth, when they demur to the force of the circumstance; and allege that, somehow or other, man's treatment of the animals, has occasioned the evil effects. How the course of breeding, to which the Pigs are subjected, has to do with the phenomenon, they are at a loss to say.

The theory of proportionate development, discloses the mystery. The suppression of certain characters,— which, though of no direct use to the breeder, are yet of incalculable, physiological importance to the animal,—has been the aim and object, in the development of all the breeds. Being thus abnormally developed, physiological, evil effects result, as matters of course.

It is apparent, that the evils, of interbreeding, will never be corrected, whilst scientists prescribe to breeders, such a mode of selection, as the following:

"Again," says Darwin (p. 236, Vol. ii, *Animals and Plants, &c.*), "hear what an excellent judge of Pigs, says, 'The legs should be no longer, than just to prevent the animal's belly from trailing on the ground. The leg is the least profitable portion of the hog, and we therefore require no more of it, than is absolutely necessary for the support of the rest.' Let any one compare the wild boar with any improved breed, and he will see how effectually the legs have been shortened."

Let any one compare, also, the fertility and strength of constitution, of the wild boar, or of any other pig which runs wild and has its several characters developed by exercise, or by correlation with organs which have been developed by exercise, with the little breeding capacity, and the weakness of any, so-called, improved breed, and he will see how effectually has the improved breed been punished for its departure from the true proportions of the original type.

Darwin says:

"Our wonderfully (!) improved Pigs could never have been formed, if they had been forced to search for their own food" (p. 283, Vol. ii, *Animals and Plants, &c*).

No; nor would they be so susceptible to the evil effects, which have been brought upon them, through outraging the proportion which is so necessary to physiological integrity. Had they been suffered to search for their own food, their legs would have grown to a size, proportionate to that of their body; and their hair, bristles, tail, head, tusks, and snout, would also have been adequately developed, through correlation with the legs.

But, as Darwin says (p. 492, Vol. ii):

"Man does not regard modifications in the more important organs   *   *   as long as they are compatible with life. What does the breeder care about any slight change in the molar teeth of Pigs   *   * ?"

Man thus contemptuously intimates his indifference to the development of characters which do not subserve his purposes; yet, when grave evil waits upon such neglect, Man shuts his eyes to the clear connection between the two, and lulls his scientific instincts, by pompously referring the strange phenomena to a "great law of nature!"

That the cause assigned by the theory of Reversion, for the lessened fertility, and for the delicacy of constitution of Pigs, is a true one, is placed beyond all doubt, by the fact, before alluded to, viz., that, with those individuals of the species, under nature, and with those individuals of which little or no care is taken, there is very little evil entailed; and, that little is developed, only after many generations of the closest interbreeding. The reason lies in the circumstance, that, in the individuals under nature, and in those individuals which are little cared for, those characters are developed, which man either directly, or indirectly suppresses when he superintends the breeding of the animals. With Pigeons and Fowls, as has been seen, the farther, also, that man carries his care of the animals, the greater are the evils of close-interbreeding. But the cases are not exactly analogous. With Pigeons and Fowls, the reason why physiological degeneration attends the highly bred breeds, is generally because, in each such variety, the major portion of the characters become relatively reduced, by the exclusive development of the peculiarity, of the breed,—which peculiarity is ever being carried to an "extreme point." With the Pig, however, the reduction, in many of the characters, is not only relative

25

to the advanced, exclusive improvement of other characters, but is an absolute reduction. The more the
trunk is developed, the further, absolutely, are the legs,
tusks, hair, bristles, &c., reduced. Therefore, the greater
the improvement, the greater the evils of close-interbreeding. For, the point is made, by breeders, to carry
the reduction of the legs, tusks, hair, snout, &c., as far
as is compatible with the continued existence of the
animal.

Although the characters, mentioned as reduced, are
reduced in all of the highly improved individuals and
breeds, yet the very capacity to discriminate between
the different breeds, and between different individuals
of the same breed, shows, that the characters have not
all been reduced in the same degrees. The reduction,
in one character, has not, in one breed, or in one individual, been so great, as it has been in another breed,
or other individual ; and, where one individual, or
breed, is much reduced in one character, and little reduced in another character, the converse may obtain,
in other breeds, or in the other individuals. So, it is
clear, that some gain, to offspring, in physiological
integrity is possible, when two breeds, or distant individuals, are crossed.

Where individuals fail to breed, owing to their disproportionate development, the impotence is not absolute. Those very individuals will be quite prolific, when
paired with individuals of dissimilar development. The
reason is, a certain number and proportion of characters are required, in the parent, for reproduction. If
an individual falls short of the required number and

proportion, it will be sterile, with others, of a like structure; because, from them, the characters wanting, obviously cannot be supplied. But, when such individual is bred with another, dissimilarly developed, he will be fertile ; because this other has positive differences which go to make up, in the reproductive elements, the requisite number of characters required for any degree of fertility. Thus, it is clear, that two individuals of different breeds, each of which is perfectly sterile with others of its own breed, may be highly fertile with each other.

The keeping, of stock, at different localities, has been noticed, by Darwin, to have a tendency to eradicate the evils of interbreeding. The reason is, at different localities, there is different air, different food, there may be different occasions for exercise of the legs and of other parts; and the effect on the development of any one part, by means of such agencies, involves a certain degree of effect upon the development of other parts, by correlation. This is the mystery of the lessened evil effects, attendant upon the same degree of interbreeding, when the individuals have been kept at different stations. The mere difference, of the ground, in one yard, where fowls, or Pigs are kept, being undulating, to a degree, just perceptible to the eye ; and of the ground, in the other yard, being of a dead level, would occasion some decrease in the evil effects of breeding two relations, kept at the different places. The little increase, in exercise, required by the nature of the ground, in the first instance, would strengthen different parts and muscles of the legs and feet; thence, by correlation, the head, and all of its appendages, would be developed; and thence, also, by correlation, the hind portion of the body, and its appendages, would be favorably influenced.

Darwin's theory denies him all knowledge of these principles. The facts, however, which are inexplicable to him, and which most forcibly suggest such principles, he gives:

"Mr. Druce," he says (p. 151, Vol. ii, *Animals and Plants, &c.*), "a great and successful breeder of the Improved Oxfordshires (a crossed race), writes, 'without a change of boars, of a different tribe, but of the same breed, constitution cannot be preserved.' Mr. Fisher Hobbes, the raiser of the celebrated Improved Essex breed, divided his stock into three separate families, by which means he maintained the breed for more than twenty years (!) 'by judicious selection from the three distinct families.' Lord Western was the importer of a Neapolitan boar and sow. From this pair, he bred in-and-in, until the breed was in danger of becoming extinct, 'a sure result (as Mr. Sidney remarks) of in-and-in breeding.'"

These pigs, to which he refers, would not have withstood the interbreeding, which they did, before threatening to become extinct, had they been of the type of the well-bred (?) English pigs. They were Neapolitan pigs, and had not the characters of legs, &c., so much reduced, as the fashion, prevailing in England, requires.

Darwin continues:

" Lord Western then crossed his Neapolitan Pigs with the old Essex, and made the first great step towards the improved Essex breed. Here is a more interesting case. Mr. J. Wright, well known as a breeder, crossed the same boar with the daughter, grand-daughter, and great-granddaughter, and so on, for seven generations. The result was, that, in many instances, the offspring failed to breed; in others, they produced few that lived; and, of the latter, many were idiotic, without sense even to suck, and when attempting to move, could not walk straight. Now, it deserves especial notice, that the two best sows produced by this long course of interbreeding, were sent to other boars, and they bore several litters of healthy pigs. The best sow, in external appearance, produced during the whole seven generations, was one in the last stage of descent; but the litter consisted of this one sow. She would not breed to her sire; yet bred, at the first trial, to a stranger in blood, so that, in Mr. Wright's case, long-continued and extremely close-interbreeding did not affect the general form or merit of the young; but, with many of these, the general constitution, and mental powers, and especially the reproductive functions, were seriously affected."

With respect to this last remark of his, it may be asked : How is it possible, in his eyes, for close-inter-breeding to affect, unfavorably, the general form of the young, when the very degeneration in form, which is occasioned by interbreeding, is what he, and other breeders of Pigs, esteem an improvement ? Interbreeding intensifies any evil in parts. So, when a well-bred Pig has its legs, tusks, &c., further reduced by such a process, Darwin looks upon such an effect, as an improvement which but enhances the value of the animal. The same simple remark he makes, when speaking of Pigeons. As before noticed, he, with charming simplicity, notes that the evil effects produced upon the form, is far more noticeable in the case
25*

of long-beaked Tumblers, than it is with short-beaked
Carriers.   Of course it is; for, the aim of the breeder,
with the Tumblers, is to reduce the beak; and, when
this purpose is subserved by interbreeding, the breeder,
of course, cannot see, that any evil is produced.

To show, that these "innate-tendency"-and-" great-
law-of-nature" breeders and philosophers actually
fancy, that they may, *ad lib.*, normally mould the form
of an animal, as clay in the hands of the potter, the
following suffices (page 236, Vol. ii, *Animals and
Plants, &c.*):

"The eye has its fashion at different periods; at one
time the eye high and outstanding from the head, and
at another the sleepy eye sunk into the head."

The sleepy eye, sunk into the head, is both a structural, and a physiological defect. When, then, interbreeding were to intensify such defect, Darwin would
naively note, that he could not see that interbreeding
injuriously affected the form of the animal.   The question, in all such cases of evil effect upon the form, is,
with Darwin, resolved into the inquiry, What is the
fashion?

When a sow has not been bred in the strictest conformity to the English standard for the porcine form,—
which demands the greatest reduction, of all the characters (save the fat), that is consistent with the Pig's
existence,—it is possible for such sow to reproduce a
Pig.   But, it is rather hard to expect the sow,—when
a lump of fat only, has left the impress of its force,
upon her reproductive element,—to effect such a differentiation of parts, as is required for the formation of

offspring. "Bricks without straw," were a facile operation, by comparison. It is, without doubt, true, that, were the sow as well disciplined in habits of thought, as have been those of her brethren who have "trod the boards;" and, were she to devote her accomplishments to the study of Herbert Spencer's "First Principle," she might (were no aberration of her cerebral or reproductive system, to follow therefrom) learn the trick (even were she the mould of form so dear to an English pork-breeder's heart) of how to evolve, by a necessary law, a homogeneity of fat, into that heterogeneity of adipose tissue, yclept a Pig. Herbert Spencer is immeasurably more astute than is Darwin, in his exposition of the processes of evolution. When improvements occur, Darwin, with a simplicity, born of little knowledge of the cavils in which some people unkindly indulge, ascribes them to "innate tendency," to "spontaneous variability;" a course, which at once discloses, that such terms are but the counters for ignorance. Not so Herbert ·Spencer. Herbert Spencer explains the improvements, by referring them to a law which lies on the uttermost verge of the domain of the Knowable; which he terms "the instability of the homogeneous," by which a "differentiation" ever results, from "a state of homogeneity," into "a state of heterogeneity." The beauty of this explanation lies in the circumstance, that his disciples, by the time that they have acquired a faint glimmering of the meaning of his terms, are so completely exhausted, that they have not even a grain of cerebral phosphorus left, with which to gauge the

utility of information, so happily conveyed. If English-
men valued their reputation among posterity, they
would make a holocaust of Spencer's works; for, to
have such a tissue of charlatanry represent, as it is
said to do, the highest phase of English thought, is the
most disgraceful commentary upon the intellectual life
of a nation, ever recorded in history.   By this, it is not
meant to intimate that the intellect of Spencer, is on a
level with his works.   To insinuate anything of the
kind, would be as unfair, as it would be to estimate
the understanding of a politician, from the impolitic
and inane measures which party exigencies, and am-
bition for preferment, had counseled him to advocate.
Herbert Spencer has merely availed himself of the prevailing mode of thought, and of the intellectual weak-
nesses of the English people, to insure his personal
fame.   No man could play so deftly upon the prejudices of the heterodox, and make them digest such
absurdities as he has propounded; and not be a man
of an order of intellect, somewhat above the average.
It seems, even, here and there throughout his works,
that he has, in a vein of cynical humor, endeavored,
to see how far he might carry an experiment, upon
English credulity, without detection.   A case in point,
is where he animadverts, in the most unmeasured terms,
against the illegitimate and unphilosophical mode of
referring any phenomena to "innate tendencies," or
other "metaphysical entities;" whereas, his whole
system is built upon such proscribed references; and
these "metaphysical entities" do yeoman's duty, upon
well-nigh every page of his works.   His principal cue,

in the elaboration of his synthesis, seems to have been, that man, however heterodox he may be, is not,—cannot be,—content with disbelief alone; he needs a complimentary belief, and is ever ready to believe anything and everything (however absurd) which harmonizes with his disbelief. Very, very few have ever read Spencer's works; yet every man of "liberal" ideas, swears by them.

To return to the sow: Darwin says (p. 151, Vol. ii, *Animals and Plants, &c.*):

"Nathusius gives an analagous, and even more striking case; he imported, from England, a pregnant sow, of the large Yorkshire breed, and bred the product closely in-and-in, for three generations; the result was unfavorable, as the young were weak in constitution, with impaired fertility. One of the latest sows, which he esteemed a good animal, produced, when paired with her own uncle (who was known to be productive with sows of other breeds), a litter of six, and a second time, a litter of only five weak, young pigs. He then paired this sow with a boar of a small, black breed, which he had likewise imported, and which boar, when matched with sows of his own breed, produced from seven to nine young; now, the sow, of the large breed, which was so unproductive when paired with her own uncle, yielded to the small black boar, in the first litter, twenty-one, and in the second litter, eighteen young pigs; so that, in one year, she produced thirty-nine fine, young animals."

The reason was: from the boar, of her own kind, she received a male, sexual element, impressed with the force of the few characters only, which she herself had; while, from the strange boar, which most probably

differed positively, from her, in several characters, she
received an element which augmented the power of
reproduction, by adding, to what she gave to the formation of the offspring, the force of characters which she
had not.

The effects of interbreeding, upon the fertility of
Pigs, must not be estimated by the amount of fertility in this animal, as compared with the amount
of fertility, in other species.   The evil effects are to be
estimated, by comparison only, with the maximum
amount of fertility, for the given species.   Thus, even
when the disproportionate development of a Pig,
causes the fertility of such animal to fall far short of
the maximum fertility of its species, it is more fertile
than (say) an elephant which is perfect in the integrity
of its species.   So, the injury to the physiological integrity, would be erroneously estimated, were not the
criterion of perfection, to be the full measure of pro-
ductiveness, within the same species.   Thus, the Pig
may have twenty, or thirty offspring, at a birth, and
another species have but two.   In the one species,
therefore, the circumstance of having two at a birth,
might consist with perfection, in the animals; whereas,
the fact of having only a dozen, at a birth, would, with
the Pig, imply disproportionate development.   A similar caution obtains, in estimating the degree of advance
towards perfection, by the number of characters regained.   It is not absolutely, the number, of characters,
which is necessary to physiological integrity.   It is
the full number of the characters, proper to the given
species.   As before remarked, the tiniest insect which

flies, if possessed of all the characters of its species, is, to the full, as perfect, physiologically, as the elephant, which is of such complex development.

The principle before referred to, respecting the impossibility of an ill-proportioned breed, long continuing its existence, without crossing, or otherwise changing its form, is strikingly displayed in the case of the Pig, whose breeds are, under domestication, all ill-proportioned. To ward off the extinction of the highly-bred breeds of Pigs, crossing has to be resorted to, all the time. In one of the quotations, above given, it is seen that Darwin deems it worthy of note, that a Mr. Fisher Hobbes, by means of "judicious selection," and by "dividing his stock into three separate families," "maintained the breed for more than twenty (!) years."

In this connection, Darwin says (p. 240, Vol. ii, *Animals and Plants, &c.*):

"Our Pigs, as Mr. Carrington remarks, during the last twenty years, have undergone, through rigorous selection, together with crossing, a complete metamorphosis!"

And again, in noting the many breeds, of all species, which "have become extinct," he says: * * *

"At the present time, improved breeds sometimes displace, at an extraordinarily rapid rate, older breeds; as has recently occurred throughout England, with Pigs."

All of the present, cultivated breeds of Pigs, have been produced by crossing. When crossed, the animals start off with a stock of characters, derived from the two old breeds; which enables them to run for awhile,

before sterility and completely shattered constitutions,
are threatened. When these effects occur, the animal
is required again to be crossed, to preserve it; and that
tolls the knell of the old breeds, and rings in the
advent of a new breed. When the individuals of this
new breed, become, by interbreeding, of a dead uni-
formity of character, they must repeat the same process,
and their breed undergo a complete metamorphosis.
Were the characters, which are reduced in these breeds,
all developed, the breeds might run their course, for
centuries, without being driven to a cross. Or, did
breeders give the legs a little show, they would not
be forced to the unpleasant necessity of so frequently
crossing their choice breeds.

Darwin says (page 120, Vol. ii, *Animals and
Plants, &c.*):

"The improved Essex Pig owes its excellence to
repeated crosses with the Neapolitan, together, probably, with some infusion of Chinese blood."

The advantage of crossing with the Neapolitan, and
with Chinese breeds, is due to the fact, that the Neapolitan and Chinese standards do not require the
reduction of so many characters, as does the English
standard of Pig breeding.

"With most of the improved races of the Pig," says
Darwin (p. 120, Vol. ii, *Animals and Plants, &c.*),
"there have been repeated crosses."

He says, that, owing to the great delicacy of constitution, and to the sterility entailed upon highly-bred
animals, a great amount of crossing has been found
necessary, to keep the breeds from extinction.

"Chiefly in consequence of so much crossing" (p. 101, Vol. i, *Animals and Plants, &c.*), "some well known breeds have undergone rapid changes; thus, according to Nathusius, the Berkshire breed of 1780, is quite different from that of 1810; and, since this latter period, at least two distinct forms have borne the same name."

CHAPTER X.

It has been shown, that, with Fowls and Pigeons, the multiplicity of divergent varieties, observable in either of these species, involves great disproportionate development of the individual; and, comformably to the theory adduced in this work, it has been found, by reference to the phenomena recorded by Darwin, that such individuals are peculiarly susceptible to the evils occasioned by interbreeding.

With the Pig, although there is no or very little divergence of character, a failure in proportion of the characters, has been caused, by a process of degeneration, persisted in by Man, through a very mistaken sense of policy. It has, likewise, been shown by Darwin's facts, that very great evil results from the reduction of the characters of the Pig.

It is now designed to show, that with those species, under domestication, whose individuals approximate the true type of their respective species, there is an almost complete exemption from the evils of lessened fertility, and of lessened constitutional vigor, however long and closely, the individuals may be interbred. It must be remembered, that it is not necessary to show

(298)

a total absence of evil; for, even individuals of the same family, differ, in some degree, from each other; and, that necessarily implies, that all but one of the individuals, are measurably degenerate.

The true ratio of the development of the characters of a species, or due coördination, is realized more in the Horse, in the Cow, and in the Sheep, than in any other animals upon which man has bestowed any degree of care. Though the individuals, of each of these species, may lack one or more of the characters of their respective species, and may vary, to some extent, the just relation of their parts; they are, comparatively, proportionately developed. With them, there is no such division of features, among the different varieties, as is met with, in the case of the Pigeon and of the Fowl. Neither, is there such a reduction and suppression of parts, as are observed in the Pig.

With Cattle, with Sheep, and with Horses, all of the characters, of the respective species, are retained, in each of the varieties. True it is, especial care may be given, in each of several varieties, to some one excellence; and, the true proportion may be thus, in some degree, affected; yet, such proportion is not much altered, because, together with the special feature, the other parts are suffered to develop themselves:—to which development accidental circumstances often contribute, such as the exercise which the animals are permitted, and the degree of self-feeding, to which they are accustomed. This concurrent bringing-up of all the characters, in each individual, has precluded that divergence of character, which is so observable, in Pigeons and Fowls, and, which is so prolific of evil, by reason of its entailing, in each individual or variety, the absence of the important, positive peculiarities of others of the same species.

The fact, of individuals of each of the Horse, Sheep, and Cow species, falling thus so little short of the original type of their respective species, leads to the expectation, that little, or no evil is the outcome of their interbreeding. This expectation, with respect to Cattle, and to Sheep, is amply fulfilled by Darwin's facts.

With respect to the Horse, it may be said, that it is, manifestly, of all animals, the most proportionately developed. Race-horses, and dray-horses, are very distinct; but very distinct, only, for breeds of Horses. What constitutes a great difference, between breeds of Horses, is, compared with the differences between breeds of other species, a very slight distinction. In the Horse, all or nearly all of the characters maintain the true relation. The theory of reversion, then, requires, that the facts should show the possibility of the highly-bred animals, of this species, being long and closely interbred, with impunity. It would be an occasion of surprise, if the horse was not a most striking instance, of exemption from the injurious results of this process.

Yet, strange to relate, there is, notwithstanding the fact that the evidence, obtainable upon this subject, is both most abundant and widespread, a remarkable absence, in Darwin's works, of all mention of the experience of breeders, respecting the crossing and the interbreeding of Horses. Could it have been,—what there is so much throughout his books, to warrant one in suspecting,—that Darwin guessed the true secret of the in-and-in breeding process, and feared lest, if he noted the Horse's exemption from the evil results, the current conception of symmetry, which attaches, peculiarly, to the Horse, would evoke the truth, namely, that the proportionate development of the characters of a species, is the *sine qua non* of perfect physiological condition ?

The stipulation, with which we started,—viz., that both the Refutation and the Converse Theory, would be based exclusively upon Darwin's facts,—precludes any detailed reference to the evidence, showing how the Horse does withstand in-and-in breeding. It is a matter of such common notoriety, however, that, possibly, any such evidence which Darwin might have furnished, would be esteemed by the reader, as needless, furnished as the reader now has been with the light afforded by the idea of Reversion.

With respect to Cattle, and to Sheep, Darwin says (p. 146, Vol. ii, *Animals and Plants, &c.*):

"WITH CATTLE, THERE CAN BE NO DOUBT, THAT EXTREMELY CLOSE-INTERBREEDING MAY BE LONG CARRIED ON; *advantageously, with respect to external characters, and with no manifestly apparent evil, as far as constitution is concerned.* THE SAME REMARK IS APPLICABLE TO SHEEP.

"Whether these animals have gradually been rendered less susceptible, than others, to this evil, in order to permit them to live in herds,—a habit which leads the old and vigorous leaders to expel all intruders,

26*

and, in consequence, often to pair with their own daughters, I will not pretend to decide." (!)

How coolly, Design is here invoked, to extricate this brilliant disciple of Bacon, from the quandary he is now in. When our heterodox friends fancy, that some secondary law which they have discovered, or some apology therefor, which they have deftly devised, contravenes the doctrine of Final Causes, they take care to acquaint the world, in tones of dignified severity, that they esteem such doctrine, a monster of most frightful mien, born of the distempered imaginations of the superstitious; but, when this principle,—so much abused in the houses, both of its friends and of its foes,—will alone, they conceive, subserve the purpose of patching up their ragged, and flimsy theories, with what charming suavity, they court and embrace it! We believe in the doctrine,—not in such an application, as is above made of it however;— but, we do not deem ourselves bound therefore to believe every absurdity which is adduced in evidence thereof. It is ignorance alone, which holds itself constrained to fall back upon the doctrine of Final Causes. There is, never, need to invoke the doctrine, to solve any difficulty. For, wherever its operation, in any instance, may be definitively settled; there are always secondary laws which wholly preclude the necessity of any reference to it. Where such secondary laws are not positively known to subserve it,—however proper it may be to admit it as an element of moral evidence,—it has no title to admission within the domain of positive science. So, in either contingency,

it has no concern to be mixed up in scientific contro-
versies.

Darwin's beautiful tribute to the efficacy of Divine
Government, will avail him, or his theory, not a jot,
in the presence of the facts.   It is to be lamented, that,
when Darwin does essay a little orthodoxy, it should
be so palpably misdirected.   The simple solution, of
the phenomenon to which he refers, is, that, for whatever disproportion resides in any individual, that
individual must pay the penalty, in the evils, usually
incident to close-interbreeding: But, as with Cattle,
the violation of structural symmetry, has been little,
the physiological penalty is correspondingly small.
Could an explanation be more satisfying? or, could
any assigned cause be more readily and easily adjustable to actual and possible variations in the quantity of
the effects?

Continuing, Darwin says:

"The case of Bakewell's Longhorns, which were
closely interbred for a long period, has often been
quoted; yet, Youatt says, the 'breed had acquired a
delicacy of constitution, inconsistent with common
management,' and 'the propagation of the species
was not always certain.'   But, the Shorthorns offer
the most striking case of close-interbreeding: for instance, the famous bull, Favorite (who was himself,
the offspring of a half-brother and sister from Foljambe),
was matched with his own daughter, granddaughter,
and great-granddaughter; so that the produce of this
last union, or the great-great-granddaughter had fifteen-
sixteenths or 93.75 per cent. of the blood of Favorite
in her veins.   This cow was matched with the bull
Wellington, having 62.5 per cent. of Favorite blood

in his veins, and produced Clarissa: Clarissa was matched with the bull Lancaster, having 68.75 per cent. of the same blood, and she yielded valuable offspring. Nevertheless, Collings, who· reared these animals, and was a strong advocate for close-inter-breeding, once crossed his stock with a Galloway, and the cows from the cross realized the highest prices."

These animals approached very close to the perfect form of their species. They needed, perhaps, little more than a greater development of their horns (which were short), to enable them to withstand, forever, the closest interbreeding.   With respect to the Longhorns; the reason, that evil results began eventually to tell upon them, was due, perhaps, to their horns being pushed to a development, far out of proportion to the size of their other characters (which is a defect as se-rious, as where the error lies in the other direction, viz.: of inordinate decrease in size of such a feature); and, due to other defects in proportion.   The absence, in an animal, of the many slight, positive differences which characterize others of the same breed, and of other breeds, occasions defects which a long continued course of in-and-in breeding will cause to tell palpably upon the organization.   Even, when the true theory of development is accepted, as a standard, an individual may be esteemed the very ideal of proportionate de-velopment, yet, when a minute comparison is made of the animal, with others of its species, it will be dis-covered, in how many little points, here and there, improvement remains to be effected.

For, as Darwin says (p. 10, Vol. 2, *Animals and Plants, &c.*):

" Probably, no two individuals are identically the same:" no two "are of a face:" "the shepherd knows each sheep, and man can distinguish a fellow-man, out millions, upon millions, of other men:" and "Shepherds have won wagers, by recognizing each sheep, in a flock of a hundred, which they had never seen, until the previous fortnight."

Now, this power of discrimination,—based as it is, upon the conscious, or unconscious perception of features, peculiar to the individuals so distinguished,—generally implies, that there are many positive points of structure, which even a seemingly perfect and symmetrical individual must lack. Many, therefore, of these little features,—just recognizable by a practiced eye,—when added up, make a sum of defects, which is calculated to tell, after many generations of close-interbreeding.

In a cow, for instance, in which it would be difficult to see, wherein the animal was in any wise deficient, there may yet be some slight detail of proportion, wanting, in every one of the following characters : in the horns, in the legs, in the hoofs, in the ears, in the eyes, in the tail, in the nostrils, in the muzzle, in the coating of hair, in the neck, in the chest, in the ribs (defected slightly, for instance, from the true curve, or arch), in the shoulder, in the rump, in the vertebræ, and in numberless other characters, both internal, and external.

When two individuals, which are similarly defective in these almost infinitesimal points, are matched, they will not be susceptible, to any appreciable degree, of evil ; but will, for many generations, rather, go on improving. But, after (say) twenty, or thirty generations of interbreeding, between (say) brothers and sisters, the evil will begin to manifest itself; unless, the capacity for reversion, in these slightly deteriorated parts, has been able to outstrip the exacerbation, consequent upon the community of defects, in the individuals paired; or unless the brothers and sisters were dissimilar in these little points,—which would not be unlikely.

When regarded by themselves, it is apparent, from what is known of the diversity prevailing among the different breeds of cattle, that the individuals vary much from what can be estimated to be the true ratio of the development of the characters of the said species. But, such departure from the true type, implied from their diversity, seems scarce worthy of thought, when the great disproportion of Pigs, Pigeons, and Fowls (especially of the high fancy breeds thereof), recurs to the mind.

Again Darwin says, respecting Cattle :

" Mr. Bates's herd was esteemed the most celebrated in the world. For thirteen years, he bred most closely in-and-in; but, during the next seventeen years, though he had the most exalted notion of the value of his own stock, he thrice infused fresh blood into his herd; it is said, that he did this, not to improve the form of his animals, but on account of their lessened fertility. Mr. Bates's own view, as given by a celebrated breeder, was that ' to breed in-and-in from a bad stock, was ruin and devastation; yet, that the practice may be safely followed, within certain limits, when the parents, so related, are descended from first-rate animals.' We thus see that there has been ex- tremely close-interbreeding with Shorthorns ; but Na- thusius, after the most careful study of their pedi- grees, says that he can find no instance of a breeder, who has strictly followed this practice, during his whole life. From this study, and his own experience, he concludes that close-interbreeding is necessary to ennoble the stock; but that, in effecting this, the great- est care is necessary on account of the tendency to in- fertility and weakness."

Had the defect, which the name, Shorthorns, con- notes, been supplied, the animals just mentioned, could go on interbreeding, for double, treble the time; aye,' forever, were there no positive differences, possessed by other cattle,—thereby implying that, in some details, the former were deficient. The evil, of the shortened horns, is indirectly, but surely shown, by the following remark of Darwin:

"It may be added" (p. 174, Vol. ii, *Animals and Plants, &c.*), "that another high authority asserts, that many more calves are born cripples, from Shorthorns, than from any other and less closely interbred races of Cattle."

This effect is due, to the fact, that the horns and the legs are correlated, in all animals; and, therefore, when one, of two parts which are so tied or correlated to- gether, is absent or reduced, the other is, in some degree, weakened. This injury to the balance of the organization, is, of course, augmented by the mating of two individuals in which the said defects similarly obtain; and, this is the reason of the strange phenome- non which Darwin notes.

With respect to the interbreeding of *Sheep*, Darwin says:

"WITH SHEEP, THERE HAS OFTEN BEEN LONG-CON-TINUED INTERBREEDING WITHIN THE LIMITS OF THE SAME FLOCK; but, whether the nearest relatives have been matched so frequently, as in the case of Short-horn Cattle, I do not know. *The Messrs. Brown, during fifty years, have never infused fresh blood into their excellent flock of Leicesters.* Since 1810, Mr. Barford has acted on the same principle, with the Foscote flock. He asserts, that one half a century of experience, has convinced him, that when two nearly related animals are quite sound in constitution, in-and-in breeding does not induce degeneracy; but, he adds, that he 'does not pride himself on breeding from the nearest affinities.' *In France, the Naz flock has been bred, for sixty years, without the introduction of a single, strange ram.* Nevertheless, most great breeders of sheep have protested against close-interbreeding prolonged for too great length of time. The most celebrated of recent breeders, Jonas Webb, kept five separate families to work on, thus retaining the requisite distance of relationship between the sexes."

And, then continuing, Darwin says, that:

"By the aid of careful selection, *the near interbreeding of Sheep may be long continued, without any manifest evil.*"

It is a noteworthy fact, that all of the breeders, quoted by Darwin, unlike Darwin, seem to have hewn their opinions, close to the line of the facts. They formulate no "great law of nature!" Darwin doubt-less calls it a "*law*," upon the *lucus a non lucendo* principle;—because it governs nothing.

It may be thought strange, that Darwin, who so

economizes facts which are " ugly" in the aspect they
wear towards his theory, should have adduced these
phenomena, respecting Cattle and Sheep, which militate so strongly against his "law."

There is one explanation, which needs not any conjecture, to establish its soundness. It is,—that he is bent
upon showing, that the whole subject of fertility is so
completely "muddled," that it is unfair to draw any
inference, against his theory, from the sterility of hybrids. As before intimated, it shall be demonstrated
how little such an ingenious device avails him. Another reason, which may explain why he adduces the
evidence of the exemption, of these proportionately
developed animals, from the evils of interbreeding, is,
that he doubtless deems the strength and validity of
his "law," in question and in doubt, until he shows
exceptions to its operation;—upon the principle, that
"the exceptions prove the rule." If such be the case,
his readers have a perfect Bonanza of assurance upon
that point.

On page 175, Vol. ii, *Animals and Plants, &c.,*
he again reiterates his "great law of nature," and
adds :

"*The rule applies to all animals*, EVEN TO CATTLE AND
SHEEP, WHICH CAN LONG RESIST BREEDING IN-AND-IN
BETWEEN THE NEAREST BLOOD RELATIONS."

The fact, of his here being necessitated to note, that
the rule applies "even to Cattle and Sheep," is not
without its significance.

Again he says (p. 213, Vol, ii, *Animals and Plants,*
&c.), referring to Cattle and Sheep, and, doubtless, to

27

those individuals of each species, which have all the
characters of their species, well developed:

"With some animals, close-interbreeding may be
carried on, for a long period, with impunity, by the
selection of the most vigorous and healthy individuals;
but, sooner or later, evil follows."

The questions, however, for Darwin to answer, are,
Why sooner? and, Why later?

The experience of breeders shows unequivocally,
that extremely long-continued, close-interbreeding is
possible with Cattle and Sheep. This is an occasion
of no surprise, when it is remarked, how proportionately developed these animals are, in comparison
with other species.

The testimony also acquaints us with the fact, that,
although this process may be long carried on, evil at
length begins to manifest itself. Nor, is there room
for marvel, in this connection. For, although all of the
characters of each species, have a passably fair chance
to become developed, there is always some one character, in each breed, to the development of which the
breeder devotes especial care. Besides this, some defects in the true proportion, are frequently occasioned
by blind conformity to certain standards existing in the
breeder's mind; or, to a certain standard prescribed
by fashion; or, defects are present, through breeders
having deemed it politic to continue a certain, defective arrangement, of characters, which originally and
accidentally accompanied the special excellence of
the breed, as the preservation intact of the build as
originally discovered (inclusive of such defects), would

be deemed a guaranty of purity of blood. They are moved to this, frequently, by the fancy that, in some mysterious way, the special excellence is dependent upon such peculiar build. To preserve this peculiar ratio of the characters, the breeder is forced to inter-breed the individuals, and, of course, after a time, short or long, according as the proportion has been impaired, the consequent evil becomes manifest.

It is apparent, that, when it is an object with each breeder, to preserve the type of his breed, there is little attempt to remedy any defects in structure.

As Darwin remarks (page 195, Vol. i, *Animals and Plants, &c.*):

"Any visible deviation of character, in a well-estab-lished breed, is rejected as a blemish."

Is it any wonder, that evil effects do eventually result, when, not only are many little points of struc-ture left to continue defective, but, when the point aimed at, by breeders, is to bring all of the animals, of a breed, which are to be interbred, to a dead uni-formity of character, which is replete with defects?

"Youatt urges the necessity," says Darwin (p. 236, Vol. ii, *Animals and Plants, &c.*), "of annually draft-ing each flock (of sheep); as many animals will cer-tainly degenerate, 'from the standard of excellence which the breeder has established in his own mind.'"

Breeders, in pursuance of this course of preserving what they have seen fit to regard as the proper type, for any variety, even discard, and "weed" out (as they say), many *positive* points of structure, which are sorely needed, to fill out the proportion.

As before marked, the undue development of the special excellence of a variety, is the principal element, in the evils which ultimately manifest themselves. Where the horns are the peculiarity of a breed, they are pushed to a development, out of all proportion. The extreme development of the udders, and mammary glands, in many breeds, is not without its deleterious effect. It will be, doubtless, fully understood, that this extreme development, referred to, is not an absolute evil; but an evil, only relatively to the lesser development of the other characters. Then, the immense coats of wool, which many small sheep are forced to produce, mar the proportion.

Darwin says (page 239, Vol. ii, *Animals and Plants, &c.*):

" Sheep are bred and valued, almost exclusively for the fineness of the wool."

It remains a question, to be settled by future experiments in close-interbreeding, whether coarseness is not the normal condition of the wool. If so (which is probable), the quality of wool, produced for Man's benefit contributes its quota to the evil.

Of course, it would never do, for Man to forego the production of fine wool, in order to perfect the physiological integrity of the Sheep. Nor, would there be any adequate occasion ; for, the effect of reduction, in size, of the threads of wool, would not manifest itself,— if all other characters of the sheep were fully and proportionately developed,—until after fifty generations, perhaps, of the closest possible interbreeding.

The fault to be found with Man's processes of breeding, is not, that he subordinates the health and fertility of the animal or plant, to the special object in view ; but that he ignorantly reduces and suppresses parts, in the organisms, and suffers them to remain reduced or suppressed, when no purpose of his is to be subserved thereby ; and, when the ends he aims at, are thereby eventually defeated, and toil and trouble occasioned him, by the lessened fertility, the sterility, and delicacy of constitution which, after all he has done to provoke them, appear so mysterious to him. The same remark is applicable to the extreme development of the udders, in cattle : Let man but see that points in the structure of the animals, are developed, which it is now a matter of indifference to breeders, whether they are developed or not; and he will find no material obstacle in the effect on the fertility and vigor, produced by such undue development of the udders. Not only does Man, in his breeding of Cattle and of Sheep, produce the evil results of close interbreeding, by carrying a special excellence to excess, and by continuing the false proportion, of characters, which existed when such special excellence was assigned as the peculiarity of a breed; but he also, from misguided policy, reduces some characters which, he fancies, are in no wise profitable to him. How far profitable, they may be, to the animal, he never stops to consider. He considers a little, when the results of interbreeding occur to vex him ; but, so blinded is he, and so imbued with the idea, that all organisms were assigned to his care, to mould, as he lists, that this element,—the reduction of which he has effected,—never enters into

27*

any conjecture he may make as to the cause of the evil.

Not only are characters directly reduced by the breeder; but other characters, also, are degenerated, either, owing to the adverse conditions in which the animals are placed, or owing to correlation with features which, from any cause, do not attain to proportionate development.

An example of this, is given by Darwin, in the following remark (page 361, Vol. ii, *Animals and Plants, &c.*):

"With respect to Cattle, Professor Tanner has remarked, that the lungs and liver in the improved breeds, 'are found to be considerably reduced in size, when compared with those possessed by animals having perfect liberty;' and the reduction of these organs affects the general shape of the body. The cause of the reduced lungs, in highly-bred animals which take little exercise, is obvious; and, perhaps, the liver may be affected by the nutritious and artificial food on which they largely subsist."

It is likely, also, that the reduced size of the liver may be due, either to direct correlation with the comparatively little exercised legs, or to correlation with the head and its several appendages, which are, themselves, immediately correlated with the legs.

Of the reduction of characters, by Man, the Pig affords the most notable instance. With the Sheep, however, it has been deemed, in some instances, desirable to make the bones of the leg, as thin as possible; such being considered a "*saving!*" The legs have also been divested, as far as possible, of any woolly covering; and the flesh thereon, it has been a point, to reduce to a minimum. The animals are even placed upon a table, as mentioned below by Darwin; and, it is thus ascertained, how far a "saving" may be had, in the internal organs; and, how far the fat (which is tissue which has undergone a retrograde metamorphosis) may be extended. These things ascertained; the relatives of those animals esteemed worthy of commendation, are interbred; and (some of), the results desired, thereby attained—and some, results, too, which are not desired.

Darwin says (p. 33, *Origin of Species*):

"Sheep are placed on a table, and are studied, like a picture by a connoisseur; this is done three times, at intervals of months, and the sheep are each time marked and classed, so that the very best may ultimately be selected for breeding."

Even Darwin sees that the reduction of characters is injurious; but he does not extend the induction,— doubtless, because he perceived that, if he did, his "great law of nature" would lose in dignity, by thus becoming less mysterious and inscrutable.

"Youatt believes," says he (p. 293, Vol. ii, *Animals and Plants*, &c.), "that the reduction of bone, in some of our Sheep, has already been carried so far that it entails great delicacy of constitution."

The reason, for instance, that Merinoes have a tendency to barrenness, is because, among other defects, their legs are small in the bone, their breasts and backs are narrow, and their sides are somewhat flat; and because their foreheads are low, and there is under

the throat, a singular looseness of skin, or hollow-
ness in the neck. Everything is sacrificed to fineness
and quantity of wool, in them. This is the criterion;
and, however deformed, or miserable the carcase is, it
always passes muster, if the special excellence be superior, or up to the average of the breed. The consequence is, invariably, the eventual ruin of the animals,
which die out, unless crossing is resorted to; which re-
plenishes the organic stock, and saves the individuals
from sterility and extinction. The proportion of the
carcase, is not even a secondary consideration, with
breeders; the most radical defects, in structure, being
often relied on, as assuring the purity of the breed.

Bakewell, of Leicestershire, in the middle of the
last century, seems to have been the only breeder who
ever had a glimmering of the correct principle of
breeding. His aim was, to procure the proportionate
development of all the characters, in his Sheep. The
effects of this policy, are observable to the present
day, in the .descendants of his breed. It is they, to
which Darwin refers, as being the animals which are
exceptionally exempt from the evils of long-continued,
close-interbreeding! Darwin also remarks, respecting
them (p. 236, Vol. ii, *Animals and Plants, &c.*):

" Lord Somerville, in speaking of the marvelous
improvement of the New Leicester Sheep, effected by
Bakewell, and his successors, says, 'It would seem, as
if they had just drawn a perfect form, and then given
it life.' "

Yet, breeders, whilst admiring the perfection of form,
and the almost complete exemption from evil, attend-

ant thereon, will go on breeding animals, and make no attempt to repair such defects, as legs reduced in size, and in bone, and void of wool ; a head hornless, small, concave or too abruptly tapering ; body either diminished in width, towards the rump, or, with chest and barrel narrow and shallow; the ribs, forming but a meagre arch from the spine ; the back, hollow ; the ears, small; the withers, depressed; the tail, short and small ; and other variations from the true symmetry of build.

Blackwell made, what must be considered, in theory, as a mistake; although, practically, it was not such. Reference is had, to the small size at which he aimed, in all his animals.   He was governed, in this, by perceiving, that smaller animals are of more profit to the breeder, because they consume less food, as the same amount of pasture, which feeds a smaller number of large animals, will suffice a larger number of small ones.

Upon even the strictest, practical principles of breeding, he was justified, in this course.   For, if the proportion of the characters be maintained, it matters but little, within certain limits, how the general size may be reduced ; and, as the very little evil entailed by mere reduction in size, would be made manifest, only after many generations of the closest interbreeding, the gain, resulting to the breeder, would more than outweigh any consideration of the slight and remote injury to the animals.

That some evil, though, generally, inappreciably small, does result from reduced size, is manifest, *a*

posteriori, by actual observation; and *a priori*, from
the loss of interstitial tissue, necessarily involved; from
the fact, that many organs must be measurably impaired, in function, when their size is reduced; and,
from the fact, that, when dissimilarly developed animals, of a species, are crossed, increase in size results,
and when disproportionately developed animals are
interbred, decrease in size is occasioned. The small
size of many Horses (Ponies, &c.), is due to their close
interbreeding, which was incompetent, by reason of the
animals' little disproportion, to work much loss of fertility, or of constitutional vigor; but, which elicited the
evil of disproportion, chiefly by means of reduction in
size. This view is confirmed by the fact, that, when a
small number of animals, much disproportionately developed, are restricted within a narrow range, such
as an island, or a valley enclosed by impassable moun-
tains, thus necessitating their interbreeding, the animals die out; but, when animals but little disproportionately developed (such as Horses), are so confined, and constrained to interbreed, they do not so die
out, but become, instead, much reduced in size,—the
reduction being caused by the little disproportion
which is insufficient much to affect their fertility and
vigor. Jersey and Alderney breeds are also instances
of the operation of this principle.

They are too little disproportionately developed to
have entailed upon them the evils of much lessened
fertility and of much lessened constitutional vigor, from
interbreeding not very close ; but the defects in structure which they have, entail, instead, reduction in size.

If an organism has all of its features, proportionately reduced, the evil entailed, will be less, than if some only of its characters are reduced; for, the balance is, in the former case, immeasurably less disturbed. But, even when the proportion is preserved as well as may be, in the reduction of the animal's size, evil results, because perfect proportion is incompatible with any reduction; for, the tissue which filled the interstitial spaces, is wanting, and full functional play of the several organs of the body, is inconsistent with any reduction. The evil effects, entailed by a measurably proportionate reduction of all the characters, are inappreciable, and infinitesimal, when compared with the injury effected by disproportionate development, such as is occasioned by the loss of some characters, or the greater, or less reduction of some only of the features. In the first case, viz., of proportionate reduction, the evils would begin to manifest themselves, only after long-continued (say, a score of generations of) close-interbreeding of the nearest relatives. In the second case, viz., of disproportionate development, the evils would begin to display themselves, in the first stage of interbreeding, either, with the furthest removed individuals of the same variety, or with individuals in the relation of cousins, or of father and daughter, or of brother and sister; or after several generations of interbreeding, in any of the degrees of relationship; according to the degree of such disproportionate development.

An individual may be twice, or thrice, the size of its fellows, and have most of its organs twice, or thrice the size they are, in others of its species; yet, if one of its organs, be not of proportionate size, with the other features (—and the disproportion may lie, either, in being smaller, or larger, in proportion, than the other organs, and, even though the organ, out of proportion, be greatly superior in size to the same organ, as it exists in the other individuals—), the evil manifesting itself in interbreeding, will, other things equal, be many fold greater, than in the smaller, well-proportioned individuals.   There is, however, a limit which may be reached, to the size to which some organs,—notably those obviously of vital importance to the organic economy,—may be proportionately reduced, with but little evil resulting.

It is therefore, evident, that, breeders need not fear to reduce the size, if they have retained, as far as possible, the proportion of the characters.   The interests of the breeder, and of the animal, are, generally, in the long run, identical.   But, where the gain to the breeder, is so great,—as, in the instance of Bakewell's breeding small Sheep, for the purpose named, in the case of pushing the development of the wool in Sheep to an advanced degree, and in the extreme development of the udders in a small breed of Cattle, say, the Alderney,—and the injury to the animal is so little and so remote in its manifestation, the animals' interests may justly be made subordinate.   Breeders, however, in their ignorance of the true laws of growth, and of interbreeding, work adversely to their own, and to the animals' interests, by suffering disproportion to exist in parts and organs which it is a matter of indifference, with them, whether they are developed or reduced, but the development of which is necessary to fertility and vigor.

"In 1791," says Darwin (p. 126, Vol. ii, *Animals and Plants, &c.*), " a ram-lamb was born, in Massachusetts, having short, crooked legs, and long back, like a turn-spit dog. From this one lamb, the otter, or Ancon semi-monstrous breed, was raised. As these sheep could not leap over the fences, it was thought, they would be valuable," and it was deemed desirable to increase their number indefinitely.

But, this semi-monstrosity,—as it was so violative of the true proportion of the characters of its species,—could not but inevitably fall a victim to the extinction occasioned, always, under like circumstances, by inter-breeding. As a matter of fact, the breed, as Darwin records, did become extinct. That their dispropor-tion was the cause of the extinction of this "valuable" breed, is clearly evidenced by the fact, that their ex-tinction was not owing to their being supplanted by crossing with other breeds, or to any failure of theirs to transmit their peculiarities ; for, first, they were esteemed " valuable," according to Darwin, and, there-fore, pains must have been taken, as Darwin implies, to preserve the type ; and, secondly, because they were peculiarly capable of breeding true to their kind, so far as they were capable of breeding at all ; for Dar-win says:

" These sheep are (were) remarkable from transmit-ting their character so truly that Col. Humphreys never heard of 'but one questionable case' of an Ancon ram, and ewe, not producing Ancon offspring," and "when they crossed with other breeds, the offspring, with rare
28

exceptions, instead of being intermediate in character, perfectly resemble either parent; and this has occurred, even in the case of twins."

It is possible, however, that this monstrous peculiarity might have been retained, and that without inducing lessened fertility; if only care had been taken that no other features of disproportion remained.

It is susceptible of a very easy explanation why Darwin, in his exposition of the process of Natural Selection, failed to record this factor, viz., of the gradual extinction of all organisms which departed far from the type of the sum of all the positive characters of their respective species; and, conversely, viz., of the assured perpetuation of their kind, by individuals which realized or approximated such perfect type. Had the phenomenon been in accord with his theory, he would not have ignored it, as he has done; but would have rung all the changes upon it, *ad nauseam.*

The conditions of nature seem to be more propitious to the development of Cattle and of Horses, than to that of most other species. Most other species, have had many of their characters reduced or suppressed, but, with Cattle, especially, the existing state of nature seems to afford a better *habitat*, than does domestication. The wild cattle not only present, to the eye, an almost perfect symmetry of development, but the close-interbreeding which they withstand, with no or little evil effect, is a proof of their proportionate development. As Darwin has before remarked, they are generally sired by only one bull, which, older and stronger than the others, compels the closest interbreeding. The half-wild Chillingham, Pembroke, and other cattle, justify the theory of a one only, perfect type, by the results they afford, of in-and-in breeding. Domestic Cattle, which are,—as compared with the half-wild breeds,—degenerate, so far as symmetry of build is concerned, would, if placed under the same conditions as to their interbreeding, as are the Chillingham, and Pembroke breeds, have never been able to be preserved so long from extinction.

Referring to these half-wild Cattle, Darwin says (p. 148, Vol. ii, *Animals and Plants, &c.*):

"The half-wild Cattle, which have been kept in the British parks, probably, for 400 or 500 years, or even for a longer period, have been advanced by Cully and others, as a case of long continued interbreeding within the limits of the same herd, without any consequent injury."

This instance of Cattle, sired by one bull, at each successive period, during 500 years and over, is a fair test of the truth of the theory of proportionate development. It is the more remarkable, because Darwin says, each herd has of late been kept down by slaughter and by fighting to the average number of fifty. But their appearance, form and size, render their exemption from loss of fertility, and of constitutional vigor, in no wise surprising. They but fulfill the requirements of the theory, propounded in this work. All of their characters are developed, and proportionately developed, in marked contrast with those of domestic breeds. Their horns (which in domestic animals are kept down, by man), are of enormous

size, and their hoofs and legs are well developed by
exercise, which aids also the growth of all the features
to which these are correlated. The close interbreeding is manifest, for it is probable, that one dynasty of
autrocratic bulls, has ever been dominant.

Darwin remarks that, of late, it has been discovered,
that they are bad breeders. But, this was to be expected, ultimately ; for, it was natural, that such close
interbreeding, for 500 years, within a breed, of late
kept down to the number of fifty, would eventually
augment the evil due to those slight defects of structure, which are implied by the very capacity, of man,
to discriminate between the individuals. Darwin con-
trasts their alleged, present, bad breeding, with the fertility of the wild herds of South America. But, the
individuals of the wild herds of South America, occasionally repair their slight deficiencies, in structure,
by intercrossing with other individuals, possessing
slight, positive differences, due to their being reared,
under slightly different conditions.

The principle, that animals, but little defective in
proportion, display, when interbred, the evil of the
little defects they have, by means of decrease in size,
is confirmed by what is known of these half-wild
Cattle. Darwin says (p. 149, Vol. ii, *Animals and
Plants &c.*):

" The decrease in size, from ancient times, in the
Chillingham and Hamilton cattle (wild), must have
been prodigious, for Professor Rütimeyer has shown
that they are almost certainly the descendants of the
gigantic Bos *primigenius.*"

This Bos, from which, also, all our domestic Cattle have descended, is described by Cæsar, as being not much inferior to the elephant in size.

The decrease in size, from interbreeding, is due to the reverse reason of that of the increase in size, attendant upon crossing. The latter namely, increase of size resulting from crossing two breeds, is owing to room having to be made, in the offspring, to allow of the combination of the characters contributed by both parents. The decrease in size referred to, is due to the saving of interstitial space, due to the augmentation of the similar defects of the parents interbred.

The principle of the decrease in size, from interbreeding animals, with but slight defects of proportion, is further illustrated by the case of the Sebright Bantam (Fowl). This animal was produced by many very complicated crosses, until, at least, the bases of all or nearly all the characters of the Fowl, were united in it. Then it was closely interbred for a long period, which gradually reduced its size, so that it now weighs but one pound!

It is clear, that, when the different breeds cross, some of the deficiencies of each, are corrected by the positive differences, or by the special excellence, of another; and that such result must, *ex hypothesi*, bring, with it, increased fertility and constitutional vigor. This is shown by Darwin's facts. But, the increase in fertility is less, in the case of Cattle, and of Sheep; because they are little divergent in character, and because there is little room for improvement. The crossing of varieties of the Pigeon, and of varieties of the Fowl, is

28*

attended with the greatest increase of fertility, because the many widely divergent varieties of these species, necessarily imply great disproportionate development, of each variety. They are, therefore, extremely susceptible to improvement, because they lack so many characters; and, when two varieties, of one of those species, cross, there results, to the offspring, the accession of some important character which one of the parents lacked.

The different breeds of Cattle, and of Sheep, on the other hand, approximate closely to the sum of all the characters of their respective species. There is, therefore, comparatively little, to be gained, by any one of these breeds, from a cross. The positive differences, distinguishing the other varieties, are very few, very slight, and of comparatively little importance.

Strikingly in harmony with this interpretation, is the fact, that the more highly-bred the Pigeons are, the greater, is the gain, from a cross. The reason is, because the more highly-bred the breeds are, the more divergent they are; the more distinct they are; and the greater is the need for each to possess the characters which, in the others, have been pushed to an extreme point.

Equally congruous, is the converse fact, namely, that the more highly-bred, generally, that the breeds of Cattle and of Sheep, are, the less is the gain from the crossing of two varieties of one of the species. This is because, the more highly-bred the breeds of Cattle and of Sheep, become, the more, generally, do they all converge to the full and proportionate development of all the characters of their species, and, therefore, the less are the differences between them. It is, only when each variety lacks very much that the other crossed variety possesses, that great good results. There is but little margin, for increase of good, with varieties of Cattle and of Sheep, because those varieties, generally, have nearly all the development, which is required for perfection. The results from crossing varieties of these last-named species, are generally shown, mainly, in increase of size, and in some accession of vigor.

Darwin says (p. 149, Vol. ii, *Animals and Plants, &c.*):

"Although, by the aid of careful selection, the near interbreeding of sheep, may be long continued, without any manifest evil, yet it has often been the practice, with farmers, to cross distinct breeds, to obtain animals for the butcher, which plainly shows that good is derived from this practice. Mr. Spooner sums up his excellent Essay on Crossing, by asserting, that there is a direct pecuniary advantage, in judicious cross-breeding, especially, when the male is larger than the female. A former celebrated breeder, Lord Somerville, distinctly states, that his half-breeds from Rye-lands and Spanish sheep, were larger animals than, either, the pure Ryelands, or pure Spanish sheep."

The reason of the increase of size, attendant upon crossing, is not only because of reversion to the original type (which was of a size, sufficient to cover any at present existing individual of the given species), but, also because greater size, or room, is demanded in the offspring of a cross, in order to accommodate the peculiarities of both parents. The reason, increase of size from a cross, is especially observable, when the male is

larger than the female, is, as we shall see, when treating of generation, because the formative capacity of the
male element is of an exogenetic character, and has a
peculiar, but not an exclusive influence, over the development of the periphery of the organism.

With respect to the Crossing of Cattle, Darwin says
(p. 147, Vol. ii, *Animals and Plants &c.*):

" Although, by carefully selecting the best animals,
close-interbreeding may be long carried on with Cattle,
yet the good effects of a cross between almost any two
breeds, is at once shown by the greater size and vigor
of the offspring; as Mr. Spooner writes to me, 'crossing distinct breeds certainly improves Cattle, for the
butcher.' Such crossed animals are, of course, of no
value to the breeder, but they have been raised
during many years, in several parts of England, to be
slaughtered; and their merit is now so fully recognized,
that at fat-cattle shows, a separate class has been formed
for their reception. The best fat ox, at the great show
at Islington, in 1862, was a crossed animal."

The reason why, as Darwin asserts, such crossed
animals, though "their merit is now so fully recognized," " are of course of no value to the breeder," is,
because they will not persist in one type, but drop offspring, of every variety of improved types, though with
no one excellence predominant. They have, united, in
them, the peculiarities of two varieties, and this combination stimulates all the other centres of growth.
The breeder desires to develop each excellence, in a
different variety. In one, he wishes to have fine meat-
producing qualities; in another, quantity of milk; in
another, good butter-making capacity, &c. On the

other hand, the offspring of a cross, whilst it abates the extreme degree of each excellence, is bent upon the proportionate development of all its characters and capacities; and that is why it and the breeder cannot agree. It is, perhaps, the only fair show, that the poor animal has had, for " millions of generations," to regain the proportionate development of all the characters of its species; and, it endeavors to avail itself of the golden opportunity. But, the breeder, disgusted with such " *Vielseitigkeit*," and imbued with the wisdom of that sound, old English proverb, that " Jack of all trades can be master of none," ships the poor wretch off to the butcher ; and individuals, only, which respectively restrict their improvement to the special quality which the breeder has assigned them ; which patiently suffer their other structural, and functional points, to remain little developed ; and which do not aspire to become Goethes, are allowed to propagate their kind.

The breeder desires persistency of type, in his animals. However good, the product may be, he does not want offspring of one and the same cow, to possess, the one, the excellence of a Durham, the other, the peculiar excellence of an Alderney, another that of a Jersey, and another to be like a Chillingham. He desires to be able, to count upon the character, of the calves which his cows will drop. Mongrels are too diversified ; they yield too many characters to suit the breeder. Each mongrel-calf seems bent upon regaining its lost integrity, in a different way, from the others. This, to the breeder, is positively disgusting.

He would have them, to be all alike, in some one character, so that he may give them a name, and form a breed of them. He cannot count, with any confidence, upon a mongrel-cow, with a fine butter-making capacity, dropping a calf of its kind. For aught he knows, the offspring may wantonly forego the character of an Alderney, and develop, instead, fine meat-growing qualities. Such results occasion emotions, within the breeder, similar to those indulged by a bow-legged man, driving a pig to market. The breeder is so imbued with the love of order, and of regularity, that it positively piques him, to have one animal, with one set of characters, producing offspring each of which has started a different ratio of characters for itself; or producing several calves which have, more or less, succeded in acquiring all the peculiarities of every breed. How is he, in such a case, to give them a name? to call them a certain breed? His desire, is that they shall be content, with one special peculiarity alone; whereas, every individual, which is dropped, seems to be pushing on, to the recovery of the mould of "some ancient progenitor," in a different direction, or in all directions; which direction, or sum of them all it will not even adhere to, but it, in its turn at this confusion worse confounded, drops offspring, with some different character slightly in the ascendant, or with an altogether different ratio from them all. What cares the breeder for their repaired integrity? What he aims at, is to get them with one special character, only, developed. The capacity of these mongrels to withstand close-interbreeding, for dozens of generations, without injury, pleads in vain for their lives. The butcher closes the last scene of all.

Is it any wonder, that crossing is regarded, with aversion, by every breeder?

"Until quite recently," says Darwin (p. 122, Vol. ii, *Animals and Plants, &c.*), "cautious and experienced breeders, though not averse to a single infusion of foreign blood, were almost universally convinced, that the attempt to establish a new race, intermediate between two widely distinct races, was hopeless; 'they cling with superstitious tenacity, to the doctrine of purity of blood, believing it to be the ark in which alone true safety could be found.'"

And again he says, not of Cattle and Sheep especially, but of all animals (p. 122, Vol. ii, *Animals and Plants, &c.*):

"As cross-bred animals are, generally, of large size and vigorous, they have been raised in great numbers, for immediate consumption. But, for breeding, they are found to be utterly useless; for, though they may be themselves uniform in character, when paired together, they yield during many generations, offspring astonishingly diversified. The breeder is driven to despair, and concludes that he will never form an intermediate race. But, from the causes already given, and from others which have been recorded, it appears that patience alone is necessary; as Mr. Spooner remarks 'nature opposes no barrier to successful admixture; in the course of time, by the aid of selection and careful weeding, it is practicable to establish a new breed.' After six or seven generations, the hoped-for result will, in most cases, be obtained; but even then, an occasional reversion, or failure to keep true, may be expected. The attempt, however, will assuredly fail, if the conditions of life be decidedly unfavorable to the characters of either parent breed."

It is for this object, namely, the formation of new varieties, that crossing is resorted to. It is also resorted to, as seen above, to procure fine animals for immediate consumption. The other reason that it is adopted, is to ward off the evils which have accrued, from interbreeding. This motive seldom obtains with respect to Cattle and Sheep, unless there has been very long-continued and very close-interbreeding. With animals, like the Pigeon, the Fowl, and the Pig, as has been already shown, breeders of the high fancy breeds are constantly compelled to have recourse to crossing. Yet, even with Cattle and Sheep, the breeder, in pushing the peculiarity, of a breed, to an extreme point, needs must interbreed the individuals; this leads to its natural, evil results; and crossing is then required. The criterion, generally, with breeders, of the good resulting from a cross, is, whether the offspring has improved or deteriorated, in the quality precious to the breeder. It may have improved most wonderfully, in a physiological sense, and have regained every character of its species, in a comparatively high degree of development; yet, if it has abated the least, in the special excellence required for the breeder's purpose, it is esteemed shamefully deteriorated; although all immunity from danger, for tens of generations, from the closest interbreeding, may have succeeded previous loss of (nigh) all fertility.

When a breed is suffering from the results of close-interbreeding, there is no necessity to cross with a very distinct breed. The slight, positive differences of a near variety, or of a different strain, will frequently suffice to ward off the evils of disproportion ; and by this crossing with a different strain only, the special excellence of the breed is saved from injury, or from abatement, while sufficient vigor and fertility are acquired.   It is even possible, to bring up the individuals, to the original, perfect type, by merely taking advantage of the slight, positive differences which present themselves at times in the individuals of the same variety. As Darwin's facts show, breeders have learned, that it is not necessary to cross the animals of a variety, with a very distinct variety, in order to stave off the evil of interbreeding.   Breeders, however, are just as likely as not, in crossing, to select those individuals of a different strain or sub-variety, which have *negative* differences distinguishing them, as they are to cross their animals with the individuals of such different strain, which have positive peculiarities to contribute to the offspring.   Breeders, together with Darwin, fancy, that the good resulting from a cross, is due to difference, *per se ;* whereas, it is solely *positive*, differences, from which the favorable result accrues.

CHAPTER XI.

In Chapter vi, on the processes by which races have been formed under nature, and varieties have been formed, under domestication, it was shown, that Plants have been greatly modified. Not only do the improvements which arise, under domestication, imply the previous loss and reduction of many organs and features; but, this conclusion is incontestably established by Darwin's testimony, to the effect, that,

"With species in a state of nature, rudimentary organs are so extremely common that scarcely one can be mentioned which is free from a blemish of this nature;"

And, in Chapter iii, authority from Darwin has been adduced to the effect, that nearly every species of Plant has had organs, either reduced, made rudimentary, or completely suppressed, with no vestige of their past existence left. These organs, he asserts, have first become of less and less use and ultimately superfluous. He shows, in detail, that there is scarcely an individual plant, under nature, which has not some of the features of its species, absent. Some one, or several, of the following characters, viz., Stamens, stems, tendrils, tubers, roots, leaves, fruit, flowers, pistil, calyx,

(334)

corolla, anthers, ovules, stigma, ovaries, seeds, seed-capsules, medicinal qualities, &c., are, save in a few exceptional cases, found to be wanting, in each Plant, as it exists under nature. Besides the loss of one, or of several of these characters, there is a false ratio of the development of those remaining. Frequently, too, though developed, in structure, characters are rudimentary, in function.

Nor is this degeneration, in structure (necessarily resulting, *ex hypothesi*, in lessened fertility and sterility), at all remedied, when the plants are placed under domestication. The physiological injury has only been augmented, by the " *improvements*," which Man has effected. As Darwin confesses :

" Cultivated races of Plants often exhibit an abnormal character, as compared with natural species ; for they have been modified, not for their own benefit, but for that of Man " (page 14, Vol. i, *Animals and Plants, &c*).

Man even augments the degeneration, commenced by the adverse conditions of nature :

"With cultivated Plants," says Darwin (p. 380, Vol. ii, *Animals and Plants, &c.*), " it is far from rare, to find the petals, stamens, and pistils represented by rudiments, like those observed in natural species. So it is, with the whole seed, in many fruits. * * In certain varieties of the gourd, the tendrils, according to Naudin, are represented by the rudiments, or various monstrous growths."

In fact, it is not possible to mention any organ, or part of a plant, which has not, in some species, under cultivation, been systematically or unintentionally reduced by Man; under the ignorant impression that it is useless.

Together with the reduction of certain characters, by man, there ensues a reduction of other features, to which the first are correlated. With respect to these, Darwin speaks most learnedly, of "a *natural tendency*, in certain parts, to become rudimentary."

"In the Broccoli and cauliflower," says he, "the greater number of the flowers are incapable of expansion, and include rudimentary organs. In the Feather hyacinth (Muscari *comosum*), the upper, and central florets are rudimentary; under cultivation, the tendency to abortion travels downwards and outwards, and all the flowers become rudimentary. * * In these several cases, we have a natural tendency (*sic*) in certain parts, to become rudimentary, and this, under culture, spreads either to, or from, the axes of the Plants. * * According to A de Jussieu, the abortion is only partial, in Carthamus *creticus*, but more extended in C. *lanatus*; for, in this species, two or three alone, of the central seeds, are furnished with a pappus, the surrounding seeds being either quite naked, or furnished with a few hairs; and, lastly, in C. *tinctorius*, even the central seeds are destitute of pappus, and the abortion is complete."

But, not merely by the degeneration, effected under nature, and by the systematic, or the unintentional reduction or suppression of organs, by Man, is the structural and the physiological integrity of Plants, impaired. Man's object, in cultivating Plants, is to increase their development. But, the manner in which he strives to effect this, only adds to the physiological injury. For, he vitiates, the more, the true proportion, by selecting

some one part only, of a Plant, and pushing its development to an extreme point!

This is the dominant feature of Man's Selection, with
Plants,—viz., the disproportionate ascendancy of one
part or organ. All of the modes of Selection may be
discerned, with Plants, but this carrying of one part
alone to an extreme development peculiarly characterizes the cultivation of these organisms.

If it be the fruit, which he values, that character
alone is developed, and all of the other features are retained in *statu quo*, or still further reduced.

If it be the leaves, or the flowers, or the roots, or
any other part which, in a given species, subserves his
pleasure or profit, the same disproportionate development is to be seen; and, the individuals are but the
more injured, in their reproductive power, by the care
which is bestowed upon them. All the parts of the
given species, are not concurrently re-developed, in
each individual.

As Darwin shows (p. 14, Vol. i, *Animals and Plants*,
&c.), cultivated varieties of Plants "show adaptation to
his (Man's) wants and pleasures."

In order to disclose the cause of the greatly lessened
fertility of Plants, after they are placed under domestication, it may be advisable, again to quote Darwin's
description of the manner which Man adopts, in the
cultivation of plants. Under the heading of "*Tendency in Man to carry the practice of Selection to an
Extreme Point*," he says (p. 290, Vol. ii, *Animals and
Plants, &c.*):

"It is an important principle, that, in the process
29*

of selection, *man almost invariably wishes to go to an extreme point,*" *i. e., with some one character only.* "On the whole" (p. 266, Vol. ii, *Animals and Plants, &c.*), "we may conclude that *whatever part or character is most valued,—whether the leaves, stems, tubers, bulbs, flowers, fruit, or seed of Plants   *   *   *—that character will, almost invariably, be found to present the greatest amount of difference, in kind, and degree.* And, this result may be safely attributed to man having preserved, during a long course of generations, the variations which were useful to him, and neglected the others."

And again he shows (page 34, *Origin of Species*), that there are great differences, in the parts which are valued, and no or little differences, in the parts neglected; which is owing to the parts, which are valued, being retained at each stage of their re-development, while the parts, not valued, occupy a common level of degeneration!

"Compare," says he, "the diversity of Flowers, in the different varieties of the same species, in the Flower-garden; the diversity of Leaves, Pods, or Tubers, or whatever part is valued, in comparison with the Flowers, of the same varieties; and the diversity of the Fruit, of the same species, in the Orchard, in comparison with the Leaves, and Flowers, of the same set of varieties. See how different, the Leaves of the Cabbage are, and how extremely alike the Flowers; how unlike, the Flowers of the Hearts-ease are, and how alike the Leaves; how much the Fruit of the different kinds of Gooseberries, differ in size, color, and hairiness, and yet the Flowers present very slight differences. It is not, that the varieties which differ largely, in some one point, do not differ at all in other points.   *   *   *   The laws of Correlation of growth, the importance of which should not be overlooked, will ensure some differences, but" (the exclusive and continued selection, by man, of those parts only, which he values, in the Plants, be it) "the Leaves, the Flowers, or the Fruit, will produce races differing from each other, chiefly in those characters."

Again he says (page 509, Vol. ii, *Animals and Plants, &c.*):

"The best proof of what selection has effected, is perhaps afforded by the fact, that whatever part or quality, in any animal, and more especially in any Plant, is most valued by Man, that part or quality differs most, in the several races. This result is well seen, by comparing the amount of difference between the Fruits, produced by the varieties of the same Fruit tree ; between the Flowers of the varieties, in our Flower-gardens ; between the Seeds, Roots, or Leaves of our culinary and agricultural plants, in comparison with the other, and not valued parts of the same plants."

Each species, under cultivation, departs from its degenerated type under nature, only in that way which will be serviceable to man. If it should essay the re-development of any other part, than that for which it is valued, it will be destroyed. As Darwin says:

"With all improved Plants * * they examine the seedlings, and destroy those which depart from the proper type" (p. 242, Vol. ii, *Animals and Plants, &c*).

Is it any wonder, then, considering the many characters, which are reduced and suppressed, in each plant, and the false ratio which is established with the characters remaining, which is increased in proportion as the one part valued is pushed out of all proportion, that (as

Darwin notes, in profound ignorance of the reason, p. 9, *Origin of Species*), "STERILITY HAS BEEN SAID TO BE THE BANE OF HORTICULTURE;" and, that so many plants become self-impotent?

Strange, mysterious, and inexplicable seem, to Darwin, to be the many phenomena of self-impotent Plants, recorded by him; but, the disorder is resolved into the fullest harmony, when it is observed, THAT THE LESSENED FERTILITY AND LESSENED VIGOR, ATTENDANT UPON INTERBREEDING AND UPON SELF-FERTILIZATION, ARE EVER PROPORTIONATE TO THE PLANTS' DEPARTURE FROM THE TYPE OF THE SUM OF ALL THE POSITIVE PARTS OF ITS SPECIES; AND THAT GAIN IN FERTILITY AND IN CONSTITUTIONAL VIGOR FROM CROSSING, IS DUE TO EITHER OF THE CROSSED PARENTS CONTRIBUTING A CHARACTER OR CHARACTERS WHICH THE OTHER PARENT LACKS, AND TO THE CONSEQUENT REMOVE WHICH IS MADE TOWARDS THE ORIGINAL, PERFECT TYPE OF THE GIVEN SPECIES.

It is not by the exclusive development " of the part valued," to the neglect, or suppression of the other characters, that any Plant may progress toward perfection. The further such culture is carried, the worse it becomes, physiologically, for the plant; for, the more is its balance disturbed.

Darwin talks about "serious defects in structure," and about the policy of not violating "the mutual relation of the parts." If he had but availed himself of such ideas, to resolve the phenomena which he records, he would have spared himself the mortification of confessing his ignorance of the many phenomena of sterile, and of self-impotent plants. Those ideas,—viz., "serious defects in structure," and "mutual relation of the parts,"—are the threads which will lead the inquirer, safely through the labyrinth of plant-sterility.

As the development, of the different varieties of Plants, differs; and, as positive characters are generally found, in each, which are absent in the other varieties, it becomes matter of little surprise, that good,—viz., constitutional vigor, and fertility,—flows from the crossing of two varieties.

To show, that the reproductive organs are not necessarily implicated, in this good resulting from a cross, it is necessary only to refer to the phenomena, which Darwin gives, showing that the good, from the union of two varieties, is displayed, even when the union is effected by Grafting!

In order to improve in fertility and vigor, nothing more is needed, than the accession, to the individual, of characters which it lacked. It is immaterial, how this may be effected. The gain to physiological integrity accrues, whether the return, to the sum of all the positive characters of the species, be secured by means of Reversion, of Crossing, or of Grafting!

The following are proofs, from Darwin, showing the evil, entailed by the reduction of characters to a rudimentary condition, and entailed by the disproportionate development, effected by Man, in attending exclusively to the culture of some one part which he values, in a Plant. It must be noted, in connection with these proofs, that Darwin is, confessedly, in profound ignorance, both of their cause, and of the reason of the many variations in the quantity of the effects. He traces many of the phenomena to the action of the conditions; but, he truly recognizes that such are but *conditions.*

On page 136, Vol. ii, *Animals and Plants, &c.,* he says :

"I raised a number of purple-flowered, long-styled seedlings (of Primrose) from seed, kindly sent me by Mr. Scott, and though they were all in some degree sterile, they were much more fertile, with pollen taken from the common Primrose, than with their own pollen."

To understand the philosophy of this, we need only turn to Darwin's statements, showing that, in plants, valued alone for their flowers (as is the Primrose), the development of this especial excellence, is pushed to an extreme point, while the other portions of the organism, viz., the seed, seed-capsules, ovules, ovaries, leaves, roots, &c., are neglected, reduced, or suppressed. The true ratio of the development of the characters, is vitiated by the abnormal disproportion of the flowers. When a cultivated variety of the Primrose is crossed with the common Primrose, good results, because some of the characters which, in the cultivated plant, are reduced or suppressed, are supplied; and the evil is also remedied, by means of the abatement, in the extreme and disproportionate development of the Flowers, which ensues.

Again he says (page 164, Vol. ii, *Animals and Plants, &c.*) :

"It has recently been discovered, that certain plants,

whilst growing in their native country, under natural conditions, cannot be fertilized with pollen from the same plant. They are sometimes so utterly impotent, that though they can readily be fertilized by the pollen of a distinct species, or even distinct genus, yet wonderful as the fact is, they never produce a single seed by their own pollen. In some races, moreover, the plant's own pollen and stigma mutually act on each other, in a deleterious manner."

In all of these plants, so self-impotent, and of injurious self-action, there are to be found many of the organs reduced to a rudimentary condition; in some cases, with the rudiments still traceable; and, in others, with not, as Darwin shows, a single vestige of the lost characters, discernible.

Darwin fancies, that these parts which are wholly lost, and these rudimentary parts, have "first become of less and less use and then absolutely valueless." But, valueless as he may esteem them, they, by their absence, work serious effects upon the constitution, and upon the capacity of the reproductive elements, which can never regain their full potency and vigor, until these lost and rudimentary characters are fully re-developed. The perfect type alone, is consistent with physiological integrity; and, the various degrees of lessened fertility and of sterility, which are empirically noted by Darwin, are but the registers of the several degrees of departure from such type.

Even in Plants, seemingly very much alike, there are positive differences which, if united in an individual, or united in the reproductive elements, will frequently, where the parents are but little prolific, enhance the fertility; or, where the parents are self-impotent, restore the reproductive power.

As Darwin has said:

"It is not that the varieties which differ largely in some one point, do not differ at all in other points. The laws of Correlation, the importance of which should not be overlooked, will ensure some differences."

The slightly different conditions of plants, growing along side of each other, will entail a dissimilarity of development, which will furnish occasion for good from a cross between them. This applies, not merely to different plants, but even to the different sets of reproductive elements, growing upon the same plant! By the following remarks, Darwin shows, what little differences, in the conditions, entail different modifications of the specific type:

"Even the seeds," he says (p. 304, Vol. ii, *Animals and Plants, &c.*), "nurtured in the same capsule, are not subjected to absolutely uniform conditions, as they draw their nourishment from different points."

This explains the reason of cases like the following, where the action of the same pollen is widely different, according as it is placed upon the stigma of the same flower, upon the stigma of a flower on the same twig, upon the stigma of a flower on another bough, or upon the stigma of a flower on a different plant. It is possible for Darwin to see, that, in many such cases, the good derived, is in proportion to the differences between the organisms, or to the differences between the parts, of organisms, contributing the reproductive elements.

But he does not see, that this distinction is required, only where there is disproportionate development; nor does he perceive, that the difference works fertility, merely because it implies the contribution, by each parent-form, of the forces of some characters which are wanting in the other.

"Sixty-three flowers," says Darwin (p. 164, Vol. ii, *Animals and Plants, &c.*), "of Corydalis *cava*, born on distinct plants, were fertilized by Dr. Hildebrand, with the pollen from other plants of the same species; and fifty-eight capsules were obtained, including, on an average, 4.5 seed, in each. He then fertilized sixteen flowers, produced by the same raceme, one with another, but obtained only three capsules, one of which alone produced any good seeds, namely two in number. Lastly, he fertilized twenty-seven flowers, each, with its own pollen; he left also fifty-seven flowers to be spontaneously fertilized, and this would certainly have ensued, if it had been possible, for the anthers not only touch the stigma, but the pollen-tubes were seen by Dr. Hildebrand to penetrate it; nevertheless, these 84 flowers did not produce a single seed capsule. This whole case is highly instructive, as it shows how widely different the action of the same pollen is, according as it is placed on the stigma of the same flower, or on that of another flower on the same raceme, or on that of a distinct plant."

Here, Darwin wisely and grandiloquently asserts, that the fact of "the widely different action of the same pollen," "is highly instructive," because (*sic*) "it shows how widely different the action of the same pollen" is! This is a clever device, by which Darwin frequently conceals his inability to explain the phenomena which he records. The student is naturally solicitous to know the reason of this widely different action of the same pollen. Darwin, by a dexterous re-statement of the very facts which were to be explained, insidiously conveys the idea that, by so re-stating them, he has achieved a full solution.

This is on a par with the explanation, he affords, of the reason why animals and plants vary,—Because, they possess an "innate tendency to vary!"

But, if he had revealed the true reason of the widely different action of the same pollen; if he had shown, that the reason sterility existed, was because of the evil due to the disproportionate development of the plants, which evil self-fertilization but augmented; and had shown that the regain of the lost fertility, was due to the different reproductive elements having added together their slightly different coördinating forces, and thus secured the complement necessary for reproduction; the result would have been disastrous to his hypothesis of the Origin of Species; for, it would have proven the normal immutability of each species, and the impossibility of any organism's departure from a certain set of characters, peculiar to its species, save at the cost of its physiological integrity.

On page 174, Vol. ii, *Animals and Plants, &c.*, he speaks of "Plants becoming, under culture, self-impotent. A cutivated plant, in this state," he continues, "generally remains so during its whole life, and from this fact, we may infer that the state is probably congenital." The breeder has but to abate the abnormal development of the part which he values, and to develop the parts reduced, or suppressed, to have the self-impotence "vanish like a morning cloud" (as Tyndall has it), "into the infinite azure of the past." "Kolreuter, however," continues Darwin, "has described some plants of Verbascum, which varied in this respect, even during the same season." If the plants had suffered a change, from comparatively favorable, to poor conditions, of light, heat, electricity, chemical elements, &c., and this change had lessened the vigor of the neglected parts of the plants, this variation from fertility to sterility, during the same season, would be explicable. Or, if the favorable conditions were peculiarly propitious to the advanced development of the special excellence of the plants, this improvement in one character alone, would, through affecting the proportion, induce self-impotence. In corroboration of this last remark, is the following from Darwin (p. 380, Vol. ii, *Animals and Plants, &c.*):

"In the Compositæ, the so-called doubling of the flowers consists in the greater development of the corolla of the central florets, generally accompanied with some degree of sterility."

This sterility results, because the corolla alone, of the central florets, and the central florets alone, have been greatly developed, without the concurrent development of the other florets, of the other parts of the central florets, and of the several leaves, racemes, stamens, branches, pistils, anthers, and other characters normally proper to the given species. As a consequence, the true coördination has been impaired,—all the parts have not been brought into harmony with each other. If the parts valued are pushed any further, out of proportion, or if the less-valued or neglected parts are any further reduced, the "some degree of sterility" will be succeeded by self-impotence.

According to Darwin's own showing, there are many plants which are capable of self-fertilization, without any apparent evil resulting to them from the process.

It is manifest, to the reader, that these owe their fertility, to the absence of all reduction, in them, of any of the characters of their respective species ; or to such reduction, as they may have, being too little, in degree, to have much effect upon their reproductive powers.

Then, there are many plants which display lessened fertility, from self-fertilization.

These are disproportionately developed, to an extent sufficient to effect their fertility, but not sufficient to render them self-impotent.

Again ; there are many plants which are wholly self-impotent.

These have many of their characters reduced to a rudimentary condition, or so completely suppressed as not to leave a vestige of their past development. From these two latter classes, namely, of plants self-impotent, and plants with their fertility lessened, Darwin has empirically generalized the conclusion, that self-fertilization is radically injurious. Those, however, among the more intelligent of botanists who are sufficiently well disciplined in scientific habits of thought, to see that his "great law of nature" is manifestly an incomplete induction, have openly questioned the validity of Darwin's conclusions; and to warrant their skepticism, have appealed to many plants, of the first-class,—namely, those which are very fertile, though self-fertilized,—which conclusively show, that, however much evidence Darwin may accumulate to justify his "law," there is an immense array of evidence which obviously militates against any such induction as he would fain draw.

Darwin, piqued by the distrust displayed, in many quarters, towards his "law of nature," resolutely determines to·confound all of the incredulous, by the results of a series of experiments which he has partially made, and which he intends to continue.   He declares, that he intends to *"settle forever"* the question, by means of the experiments he is now conducting, with many plants of a certain species.

It will, doubtless, be the occasion of some amusement to those who find that the theory of proportionate development reconciles all of the vast array of seemingly conflicting evidences, on this point, to see Darwin patiently experimenting with many plants of one species, in the full confidence, that his results will confound all of those who dared to draw into question what he, the autocrat of the world of natural history, had declared to be a "law of nature."

The cream of the joke lies in this, That the results, of his experiments, depend entirely upon the structural condition of the species, which, he fixes upon, with which to experiment !   If the species he were to determine to use, had, as its individuals, ones which had no characters reduced to a rudimentary condition, or had no character pushed to the extreme of develop-

30*

ment, whilst the others remained reduced, his "great law of nature" would be completely negatived. If, however, the individuals of the species, were, comparatively, little disproportionately developed, his heart would be rejoiced, to find that some evil did result from self-fertilization, and that, on the other hand, good resulted from a cross between varieties of such species. If again; he chose a species that had many of its characters reduced to a rudimentary condition, and had one or two only of the remaining characters pushed to an extreme of development, the results of his experiments, would be, in his eyes, so signal and conclusive, as to cause him regret that he had suffered himself to be ruffled, for a moment, by mere quibblers who had not taste enough to recognize the implicit deference they owed to genius so transcendant.

The following quotation, in which Darwin gives assurance that he intends "forever (to) settle the question," is rich.

"Experiments have not been tried," says he (pp. 157–8, Vol. ii, *Animals and Plants, &c.*), "on the effects of fertilizing flowers with their own pollen, during several generations. But, we shall presently see that certain plants, either normally or abnormally, are more or less sterile, even in the first generation, when fertilized by their own pollen. Although nothing is known on the evil effects of long-continued close-interbreeding, with plants, the converse proposition, that great good is derived from crossing, is well established.

"With respect to the crossing of individuals belonging to the same sub-variety, Gärtner, whose accuracy and experience exceeded that of all other hybridizers, states that he has many times observed good effects from this step (crossing), especially with exotic genera, of which the fertility is somewhat impaired, such as Passiflora, Lobelia and Fuchsia. Herbert also says, 'I am inclined to think that I have derived advantage from impregnating the flowers from which I wished to obtain seed, with pollen from another individual of the same variety, or at least from another flower, rather than with its own.' Again, Professor Lecoy asserts that he has ascertained that crossed offspring are more vigorous and robust than their parent.

"General statements of this kind, however, can seldom be fully trusted; consequently, I have begun a series of experiments which, if they continue to give the same results as hitherto, *will forever settle the question* of the good effects of crossing two distinct plants of the same variety, and of the evil effects of self-fertilization. A clear light will then be thrown (*sic*) on the fact that flowers are invariably constructed so as to permit, or favor or necessitate the union of two individuals."

With respect to this last statement, he has been a little negligent in the use of the word "invariably;" for, he himself gives cases of flowers so enclosed as to preclude all possibility of a cross. These enclosed flowers, too, are perfectly fertile, notwithstanding that their structure forbids the supposition, that there ever was anything, with them, but self-fertilization!

But, to accompany Darwin, in the experiments which are "forever to settle the question" of his "great law of nature:"

"The plan," continues he, "which I have followed, in my experiments, is to grow plants in the same pot, or in pots of the same size, or close together in the open ground; to carefully exclude insects; and then to fertilize some of the flowers with pollen from the same flower, and others on the same plant with pollen from a distinct, but adjoining plant.   In many, but not all, of these experiments, the crossed plants yielded much more seed than the self-fertilized plants; and I have never seen the reversed case. * * * Now, I have carefully observed the growth of plants raised from crossed and self-fertilized seed, from their germination to maturity, in species of the following genera, namely, Brassica, Lathyrus, Lupinus, Lobelia, Lactuca, Dianthus, Myosotis, Petunia, Linaria, Calceolaria, Miranda, and Ipomœa, and the difference in their powers of growth and of withstanding, in certain cases, unfavorable conditions, was most manifest and strongly marked." * * * * *

"I will briefly describe the two most striking cases as yet observed by me.   Six crossed, and six self-fertilized seeds of Ipomœa *purpurea* from plants treated in the manner above described, were planted as soon as they had germinated, in pairs, on opposite sides of two pots, and rods of equal thickness were given them to twine up.   Five of the crossed plants grew from the first more quickly than the opposite self-fertilized plants ; the sixth, however, was weakly, and was for a time beaten, but at last its sounder constitution prevailed, and it shot ahead of its antagonist.   As soon as each crossed plant reached the top of its seven foot rod, its fellow was measured, and the result was that when the crossed plants were seven feet high, the self-fertilized had attained the average height of only five feet, four and a half inches.   The crossed plants flowered a little before, and more profusely than the self-fertilized plants.   On opposite sides of another small pot, a large number of crossed and self-fertilized seeds were sown, so that they had to struggle for bare existence; a single rod was given to each lot: here again, the crossed plants showed from the first their advantage; they never quite reached the summit of the seven foot rod, but relatively to the self-fertilized plants, their average height was 7 feet to 5 feet 2 inches." (This is a good instance of Darwin's Natural Selection. Although stronger and more vigorous than the other lot of plants in the same pot they were,—relatively to the plants, in the other pot, which had, each, a pole,to itself,—rather degenerated. If the conditions were made more unfavorable, they would— even whilst retaining their character of being stronger and more vigorous than those succumbing—be degenerating. Yet, Darwin, in his argument of Natural Selection, would have his readers believe, that the mere fact that they were stronger and more vigorous than those of their fellow lot, argued a net advance in development for the species). " The experiment was repeated in the two following generations, with plants raised from the self-fertilized and crossed plants, treated in exactly the same manner, and with nearly the same result. In the second generation, the crossed plants, which were again crossed, produced 121 seed-capsules, whilst the self-fertilized plants, again self-fertilized, produced only 84 capsules.

"Some flowers of the Mimulus *luteus* were fertilized with their own pollen, and others were crossed with pollen from distinct plants, growing in the same pot. The seeds after germination, were thickly planted on opposite sides of a pot. The seedlings were at first equal in height ; but, when the young crossed plants were exactly one-half an inch, the self-fertilized plants were only a quarter of an inch high. But, this inequality did not continue, for when the crossed plants were four and a half inches high, the self-fertilized plants were three inches, and they retained the same relative difference, till their growth was complete. The crossed plants looked far more vigorous than the un-

crossed, and flowered before them; they produced
also a far greater number of flowers which yielded
capsules (judging, however, from only a few) containing more seeds. As, in the former case, the experiment was repeated in the same manner during the next
two generations, and with exactly the same result.
Had I not watched these plants of the Mimulus and
Ipomœa during their whole growth, I could not have
believed it possible, that a difference, apparently so
slight as that of the pollen being taken from the same
flower, and from a distinct plant growing in the same
small pot, could have made so wonderful a difference
in the growth and vigor of the plants thus produced.
This, under a physiological point of view, is a most
remarkable phenomenon."

It is to be lamented, that such experiments, so carefully and patiently conducted, and so faithfully re-
ported, should add not a jot of weight to his " great
law of nature;" that, such a simple idea, as the want
of full structural integrity, should explain the lessened
vigor, and the lessened fertility of self-fertilized plants;
and, that the union of the different structural points,
of the different plants, and the return, thereby effected,
towards the sum of all the positive features of the
species; should account for the good thence resulting.
All of these "most remarkable" phenomena, are
wholly inexplicable to Darwin. Yet, the explanation
is so simple and clear. The self-fertilized plants are
deficient in the integrity of their structural conforma-
tion; whilst, when crossed, the same integrity is measurably repaired, through each parent's supplying structural defects in the other, by means of the positive
differences which distinguish it from the other. The

induced return, to the original type of the species, brings with it vigor and fertility.

Had Darwin but learned the lesson, which is fairly thrust upon him by so many of the facts of breeding,—prominent among which, and most significant, is the fact which he records, that the mere increase, of one-half an inch, to one of the sickle tail-feathers of the Fowl, "brings with it increased probability of increased fertility,"—all of the mystery of the phenomena of fertility, and of sterility, would have been dispelled; and all necessity of his invoking that most senseless of all expedients, a "law of nature," would have been obviated.

There is no occasion for the indulgence of such an idle and ignorant wonder, as that to which Darwin gives expression, when it is observed, that each of the positive differences, in the several individuals or varieties of a species, which it is possible, and practicable, for each plant to obtain, either, directly, by reversion, or by grafting, or, indirectly, through crossing, ensures a measurable return to the type upon which close-interbreeding, or self-fertilization, is incapable of entailing any evil effect. Each slight difference, which enables a person, acquainted with plants, to distinguish one from the others, is of moment to the plant ; for, each such slight, positive difference gained, carries with it a guarantee of exemption from weakness and sterility.

Darwin says, " this, under a physiological point of view, is a most remarkable phenomenon." If he had but paid a tithe of the attention, to the "physiological

point of view," which he has given to the mere anatomical differences; or, if he had but thought, for a moment, what physiological effect must be wrought by
anatomical changes ; and if he had heeded the almost
infinite number of hints which physiology has actually
obtruded, but in vain, upon him ; he would have been
spared the egregious blunders which he has made ;
and, phenomena, instead of being insensately characterized by him, in ignorant wonder, as " remarkable,"
would have been fraught, to him, with knowledge of
laws, the simplest and most beautiful possible.

Instead of being constrained, as he is, to regard his
facts with the awe the savage shows to his fetich, he
would have been enabled, *a priori*, to expect results
which, now, he says, he could not have believed possible.

How any man, with the least tincture of scientific
habits of thought, could range through such varying
phenomena; could ignore the significance of their
almost infinite variations in quantity of effect; could
escape the conclusion, that the modification of a certain ratio of characters, underlies all the evil effects of
close-interbreeding and of self-fertilization; and could
so completely lull all of his scientific instincts, as to
formulate an inflexible "law of nature," in derogation
of such a wide diversity of effects; are mysteries which
can be explained, solely by resorting to the one
hypothesis that, "Motley's the only wear" for this
standard-bearer of modern thought; or, to the other
hypothesis, that the author of the *Origin of Species*
systematically and wilfully ignored the element of

physiology, governed by the conviction, that the least insight, by his readers, into that phase of the problem, would suffice to explode his fanciful notion, that the higher animals are evolved from the lower.

Darwin, in connection with his "great law of nature," that good follows from crossing, *per se*, and evil from interbreeding, *per se*, is proof against any amount of evidence.   In some cases, the evil from close-interbreeding, or from self-fertilization, is manifest; and, then he is exultant.   In other cases, where it is clear, that close-interbreeding, or self-fertilization, may be long carried on, without any evil effects, he finds refuge in the supposition, that the animals or plants must have been crossed, at some time back.

But it is possible, and practicable, to prove even the negation of his gratuitous supposition.   For there is one class of facts, recorded by Darwin, which should suffice to give his "great law of nature," its quietus. It is, viz., that certain flowers are *enclosed!*

These flowers are fertile! and the fertility must have been long continued; for, there is a radical impossibility that they ever were crossed.   The only means, by which crossing, can be effected, is, either, by foreign pollen being conveyed to the stigmatic surface of the flower, by mechanical forces, winds, &c., or by the transportation of such, by bees, or other insects.   But, in the cases mentioned, all ingress for foreign pollen, is absolutely precluded.   The flowers, containing the stigmatic surface, are *enclosed;* and each flower needs must have been ever fertilized by its own pollen.   Of these enclosed flowers, which he recognizes as milita-

31

ting against his "law," he speaks as follows (p. 116, Vol. ii, *Animals and Plants, &c.*):

"The Leersia *oryzoids* produces minute, *enclosed flowers which cannot possibly be crossed*, and *these alone, to the exclusion of the ordinary flowers, have as yet been known to yield seed.* (*!*) A few additional and analogous cases could be advanced. But, *these facts do not make me doubt, that it is a general law of nature*, that the individuals of the same species occasionally intercross, and that some great advantage is derived from this act."

Some great good is derived from the intercrossing of individuals of the same species, because they each have, in them, some positive point of structure, which is needed in every individual of the given species. In presence of facts, like these enclosed flowers, precluding the possibility of crossing, Darwin trims, somewhat, his "law." As he states his "law," elsewhere, it is an absolute necessity, that individuals of the same species should cross. Here, however, in the quotation above, he states it, in a manner which is very little defective.

"Some great advantage" is, undoubtedly, often "derived from this act" of Crossing. But, it is not a great "law of nature." It is due to structural defects in either parent being supplied by positive differences in the other parent.

When individuals of a species are disproportionately developed, a "great advantage is," without doubt, "derived from the act" of crossing. But, there is no "law of nature," requiring a cross. An individual, and its descendants, which have, each, all of the positive characters of their species, need never cross, if their type is never modified. With them, a cross must needs entail evil upon them, instead of good. For, the only variety with which they could possibly cross, must necessarily be one, distinguished from them, by negative features, which ever work evil.

But, when individuals are deficient in some of the characters of their species, it is necessary, in order for good to accrue to their offspring,—in order for the physiological evil, attendant upon their structural defects, to abate,—that they regain the characters they lack. It is a law of nature, that all the characters, of a species, should be developed, in every individual of such species. The good accruing from a cross, is not due to crossing, *per se*, but to that accession, of extra characters, which a cross generally involves. The good flows, from the repair, made to the lost integrity, by the addition, in the offspring, to the one set of characters of one variety, of another set of characters of another variety. Darwin would be correct, were he to say, that an advantage frequently results from the act of crossing two varieties; for, each generally possesses characters which the other lacks. But, when individuals have the complement of characters, necessary to fertility, they may long continue their breeding without crossing.

The instances, which Darwin cites, of the enclosed flowers, which are incapable of crossing, alone being fertile; and, the instances of other plants of the same species, which are sterile, are fully explicable, upon the theory, that the reason why the enclosed flowers are fertile, is because they are fully and proportionately developed; while, the reason the unenclosed flowers are sterile, is because, in the feature of enclosure, and most, probably, in other characters, they are deficient. The smallness of the enclosed flowers, is a feature which weighs but little, in the account of fertility, in comparison with disproportionate development. The mere lack of enclosure, would suffice to make an appreciable difference in fertility only after very long continued self-fertilization. But, this lack of enclosure, is doubtless conjoined with other structural defects.

On p. 229, *Animals and Plants, &c.,* Darwin says, as:

"In several well authenticated instances, already often alluded to; certain species have been affected, in a very different manner, for they have become self-impotent, whilst still retaining the capacity of fertilizing, and being fertilized, by distinct species."

Frequently, individuals only, of a species, are modified in character, and have parts reduced to a rudimentary condition. These individuals, of the species, will of course be sterile; while those, individuals of the species, which are unmodified, or very little modified, will preserve their fertility. Of such cases, Darwin really speaks, in the following remarks (page 168, *Animals and Plants, &c.*):

"We now come to cases clearly analogous with those just given, but different, inasmuch as individual plants alone, of a species, are self-impotent. This self-impotence does not depend on the pollen, or ovules, being in a state unfit for fertilization, for both have been found effective, in union with other plants of the same, or of a distinct species. The fact of these plants having spontaneously acquired so peculiar a constitution, that they can be fertilized more readily by the pollen of a distinct species, than by their own, is remarkable (!) These abnormal cases, as well as the foregoing normal cases, in which certain, orchids, for instance, can be much more easily fertilized by the pollen of a distinct species, than by their own, are exactly the reverse of what occurs with all ordinary species (!) For, in these latter, the two sexual elements of the same individual plant, are capable of freely acting on each other; but are so constituted, that they are more or less impotent, when brought into union with the sexual elements of a distinct species, and produce more or less sterile hybrids. It would appear, that the pollen, or ovules, or both, of the individual plants which are in this abnormal state, have been affected in some strange (!) manner, by the conditions to which they themselves or their parents have been exposed; but whilst thus self-sterile, they have retained the capacity, common to most species, of partially fertilizing, and being partially fertilized, by allied forms. However this may be, the subject, to a certain extent, is related to our general conclusion, that good is derived from the act of crossing."

"Conclusion!" The term is a happy one; for his explanation concludes precisely where it begins,—at the very fact to be explained. If, from the fact, that good results from crossing, he deduces, or induces, a *conclusion*, that good results from crossing, how unique, and ingenious, must have been the process of ratiocination, or of induction, by which he effected the transition from the fact to the conclusion !

He makes a passably good guess at the remote cause
31*

of the self-impotence, of these plants, when he says above:

"It would appear, that the pollen or ovules, or both, of the individual plants which are in this abnormal state, have been affected in some strange (!) manner, by the conditions to which they themselves, or their parents have been exposed."

Had he but eliminated the "strange," and the "remarkable" elements from his problem, he would have found, that the conditions were at the bottom of the sterility, through the reduction, or suppression, of certain parts, in the plants, which they effected. This reduction, or suppression (as he would have found), has rèduced the number of characters, in each plant so self-impotent, below the complement necessary to give the reproductive elements their needed capacity.

Conformably to this idea, it was to be expected, that, when plants of full reproductive power, were placed under conditions which were adverse to the development of certain of their characters, they would become self-impotent, or abate the measure of their fertility, in proportion as they became so modified in their development. The result is due to the absence of certain chemical elements, &c., necessary to the development of some part, or parts, of the organism. Not only may this be the occasion; but, frequently, of a number of plants, which are comparatively fertile, there are some, placed where the conditions are peculiarly favorable to some one, or more parts only. The proportion of the parts being thereby vitiated, injury results to the reproductive organs; whilst it does not result, in the other plants, to all of whose parts, the conditions are unfavorable, in the degree in which they are to most of the parts, in the sterile plants just mentioned. Thus, favorable conditions, if favorable only to one part or organ, will often produce loss of fertility. Darwin in the quotation below, notes the sterility of the plants, and sees that the conditions are, in some way, answerable for the results; yet, he cannot imagine the mode, in which the conditions work the effect; but concludes that the sum of the knowable, in this respect, is that the conditions are "*unnatural.*"

He says (p. 218, *Animals and Plants, &c.*):

"Plants, which have been exposed to unnatural conditions, sometimes become modified, in so peculiar a manner, that they are much more fertile, when crossed by a distinct species, than when fertilized by their own pollen."

This explanation, that the "*peculiar*" manner, in which they are modified, is due to conditions being "*unnatural,*" is to the full as satisfactory, and to the full as scientific, as the explanation, that variations are due to "an innate tendency to vary;" or, as the explanation, that it is a "great law of nature," that evil should attend close-interbreeding, and that good should follow crossing.

When plants, such as these which have been in "unnatural conditions," are changed to other conditions, and these other conditions are favorable to the development of the parts which before were reduced or suppressed, a gain in fertility naturally follows.

"Returning to P. alata," says Darwin (p. 170, Vol.

ii, *Animals and Plants, &c.*), "I have received (1866) some interesting details from Mr. Robinson Munro. These plants, including one in England, have already been mentioned, were inveterately sterile, and Mr. Munro informs me of several others, which after repeated trials, during many years, have been found in the same predicament. At some other places (!), however, this species fruits readily, when fertilized with its own pollen."

At these "some other places," it has found the chemical elements, and other conditions of life, which are essential to the development of those of the parts whose loss, or reduction, produced the sterility of the individuals, found in the bad "predicament." Consequently, the development of these parts, with that of the others, secures the fertility, which attains its maximum, only when a full return is made to the original, perfect type.

In different habitats, different plants receive unlike quantities of the gases, liquids, and solids, necessary to their development. The proportion, therefore, of a Plant varies, according to the place to which it is fixed. The soil, in such cases, possesses, generally, some ingredient which is favorable to the development of some one part. In another place, to which the plant may be transplanted, there may be an abundance of the matter required for a certain other part, or for a certain class of its tissues. When so transplanted, it not only derives a benefit, from the development of these latter portions of its organization, but the high development of the other part, may be sustained for a time, through the capacity for assimilating and making thoroughly available, the ingredient first mentioned, which may or may not be present only in meagre quantities, in its new location. It is therefore, to be expected, that good will be derived from slight changes in the conditions of life.

Under the heading of "On the Good derived from slight Changes in the Condition of Life" (p. 178, Vol. ii, *Animals and Plants, &c.*), Darwin says:

"In considering whether any facts were known, which might throw light on the conclusion arrived at in the last chapter, namely, that benefits ensue from crossing, and that it is a law of nature that all organic beings should occasionally cross, it appeared to me probable, that the good, derived from slight changes in the conditions of life, from being an analogous phenomenon might serve this purpose. No two individuals, and still less no two varieties are absolutely alike, in constitution and structure; and when the germ of one is fertilized by the male element of another, we may believe that it is acted on in a somewhat similar manner as an individual, when exposed to slightly changed conditions. Now, every one must have observed the remarkable influence on convalescents, of a change of residence, and no medical man doubts the truth of this fact. Small farmers, who hold but little land, are convinced that their cattle derive great benefit from a change of pasture. In the case of plants, the evidence is strong that a great advantage is derived from exchanging seeds, tubers, bulbs, and cuttings, from one soil or place to another as different as possible.

"The belief that plants are thus benefited, whether or not well founded, has been frequently maintained from the time of Columella, who wrote shortly after

the Christian era* (*sic !*), to the present day; and it now
prevails in England, France, and Germany.   A sagacious observer, Bradley, writing in 1724, says, 'When
we once become Masters of a good Sort of Seed, we
should at least put it into Two or Three Hands, where
the Soils and Situations are as different as possible;
and every Year, the Parties should change with one
another, by which Means, I find the Goodness of the
Seed will be maintained for several Years.   For Want
of this Use, many Farmers have failed in their Crops,
been great Losers.'   He then gives his own practical
experience on this head.   A modern writer asserts,
'Nothing can be more clearly established in agriculture, than that the continual growth of any one variety
in the same district, makes it liable to deteriorate either
in quality or quantity.'   Another writer states that he
sowed close together, in the same field, two lots of
wheat-seed, the product of the same original stock,
one of which had been grown on the same land, and
the other at a distance, and the difference in favor of
the crop from the latter seed was remarkable.   A gentleman, in Surrey, who has long made it his business
to raise wheat to sell for seed, and who has constantly
realized in the market, higher prices than others, assures me that he finds it indispensable continually to
change his seed; and that for this purpose, he keeps
two farms differing much in soil and elevation."

(Darwin thinks, that the good derived is due to the
change, *per se !*)

If, on the other hand, plants are changed to a locality, wanting in some of the conditions, present at the
former habitat, and which supplies none of the conditions which may have been absent, or in meagre

---

* The impression, with the writer, has ever been, that the " Christian era" lasted, *at least*, until the *Origin of Species* was published.

quantity, at the former locality, the plant must, instead of gaining in fertility, become of lessened fertility or sterile; on account of the reduction or suppression of those parts the conditions whereof, are wanting. Such is the case.

Darwin says (p. 182, Vol. ii, *Animals and Plants, &c.*), under the heading of "Sterility from Changed Conditions":

"I will now attempt to show, that animals and plants when removed from their natural (!) conditions, are often rendered in some degree infertile, or completely barren, and this occurs when the conditions have not been greatly changed. It is notorious that many animals, though perfectly tamed, refuse to breed in captivity."

The animals, which refuse to breed in captivity, are those which have been taken from a state of nature, and subjected to close confinement. They are barren, because,—though their new conditions may be incapable of reducing any of their features,—those new conditions are yet capable of suspending the functions of some of the organs, which is next injurious to their being divested of those parts; inasmuch as the absence of this activity, bereaves the respective organs of that influence upon the aggregate, which is essential to the balance of the whole. Consequently, those organs have not their due influence upon that portion of the system, from which the reproductive element is differentiated. This reproductive element is the reflex of the forces of the aggregate, and when the latter is modified, the reproductive power is impaired. Fancy a monkey, taken from the wild state, wherein he so disported himself as to keep his cerebellum constantly on the *qui vive* in order to coördinate every fibre and muscle in his body; and placed in a cage, three feet by three, where he is constrained to a quiet, modest behavior. If the reproductive element derives its capacity, from the coördination of all the parts, is it any wonder, that the animal refuses to breed? Of course, the conditions of food, of drink, of air, etc., enter into the problem. But, in every aspect of the case, the cause of the sterility resolves itself into the want of perfect coördination of the parts—be those parts suppressed, reduced, or only measurably atrophied; be the reduction in characters, structural, or merely functional.

But, in these cases, where animals, in captivity, refuse to breed, there has often been an actual reduction and suppression of some of the features of the animals; —doubtless due to correlation with those parts constrained to unwonted inactivity. On page 193, Vol. ii, *Animals and Plants, &c.*, Darwin notices many cases, where the sterility of captive animals has been attended with the loss of characters of the individual. He does not discern the relation between the two, but he states the facts as severally existing.

Darwin says (p. 337, Vol. ii, *Animals and Plants, &c.*):

"Slight variations, of many kinds, * * * are retained as long as plants are grown in certain soils, of which Sageret gives, from his own experience, some instances."

If such plants are removed to another soil, wanting

in the conditions necessary to retain such variations; and if, in addition, the new soil is not capable of developing some other characters which the plant has lacked, and which may serve to keep up the complement of developments, necessary to any degree of fertility, the plant will manifestly become sterile.

Darwin says, that, "Any two self-impotent plants can reciprocally fertilize each other." This conclusion of his is supported by an immense array of facts. But, when the cause is known, the said conclusion is seen to be a little too broad. Self-impotent plants can, and generally do, fertilize each other. But, this is, because the plants are somewhat different in structure. Where two self-impotent plants are similarly defective in structure, they cannot fertilize each other. Plants are self-impotent, because they are defective in structure, and because, in the self-impregnation, each reproductive element supplies the forces, of exactly the same number (and no more) of characters, which the other element does. But, when two individual plants, with any positive differences distinguishing them, cross, the reproductive element of each has some positive character or characters to contribute to the formation of the seed, which the other plant has not; and, between the two of them, they make up the forces of the number of parts requisite for successful fertilization. To Darwin, the fact of the capacity of two self-impotent plants to fertilize each other, is simply anomalous.

He says (p. 174, Vol. ii, *Animals and Plants, &c.*):

" It is interesting (!) to observe the graduated series,
32

from plants which, when fertilized by their own pollen, yield the full number of seeds, but with the seedlings a little dwarfed in stature,—to plants which, when self-fertilized, yield few seeds,—to those which yield none, —and, lastly, to those in which the plant's own pollen and stigma act on each other like poison."

One would presume, that this "graduated series" of effects, instead of being "interesting," would be rather disheartening, to a scientist who had given nearly a half century to the study of plants, without making one step towards a solution which could give a quantitative explanation of these phenomena! His "law of nature" is no explanation—it is a farce, in the light of the many exceptions there are to it, and in the light of this "graduated series." It does not allow such exceptions; it permits no such "graduated series;" nor does it contemplate such infinite variations in the quantity of effect. This "law of nature," of his, is but the formula of the re-statement of an observed general effect. It is an insult to the very name of science to formulate such a "law." His "law of nature" is born of an order of thought, no higher than that which ascribes results to a fetich. It would have been the occasion of little surprise, that Darwin assigned such a "cause," had his acquaintance with the phenomena of lessened fertility, been a meagre one. But, to perpetrate such an absurdity, after noting such a diversity of effects (a diversity, plainly intimating, that a *vera causa* exists, and that it lies within easy reach of discovery, at the recurrence of each variation in the effects), betrays habits of thought of the most slovenly character. Darwin has genius;

but, it is for this, principally: For exalting convertible platitudes into "explanations!"

Darwin, while gazing, contemplatively, upon this "graduated series" of effects, which stands as a monument to his well-nigh phenomenal obtuseness, ejaculates, with all the impressiveness of Pickwick, How "interesting!" It is "interesting" to him (mark), because it is inscrutable.

It may be "interesting," so to indulge a barbarous wonder; to regard phenomena as due to chance, or some innate tendency; and to obviate the incongruities of his theory, by recourse to the proverbial idea that Nature is capricious; but, it should be infinitely more "interesting," to a scientist, to resolve this "graduated series;" to discover the *vera causa* thereof; and to note how this seemingly fortuitous diversity of effects, corresponds most faithfully, in every instance, and degree for degree, to like gradations in the quantity of a given cause. It is more gratifying, by far, to be able to place, side by side with this "graduated series" of effects, a similarly graduated series of departures from a normal type; than, to be lost in dumb wonder, as Darwin is, at phenomena which, with silent eloquence, tell him, who is so fertile in "great laws of nature," to obey the injunction which follows Pope's request to teach Omnipotence how to rule.

A man, of "liberal" ideas, may, when it subserves his purpose, repose with perfect confidence, upon the hypothesis, that there are phenomena which it is never for Man to solve. But, woe betide the unlucky sprite,

tinctured with the faintest trace of orthodoxy, who may
have the effrontery to entertain or propound such a
view!

When, in times past, before was waged that "fearful
Struggle for Existence," of which "Natural Selection"
was the outcome, all of the chemical elements and conditions essential to the full and proportionate development of a plant, were adequately supplied; all the features and organs of the plant, were in full and harmonious proportion. When fertilized by its own pollen,
its fertility was at its maximum, and the flowers yielded
their full number of seeds.   When the species became
modified,—when parts of the plant became somewhat reduced,—the plant "when fertilized by its own
pollen," had its "flowers to yield the full number of
seeds, but with the seedlings a little dwarfed;" When
the plant, "in the terrible battle of life," had departed
further from its primitive, and normal type; when the
loss and reduction of parts, became more pronounced,
the plant, when self-fertilized, yielded "few seeds;"
When the departure from full integrity, grew greater
still; when many organs had been reduced to a rudimentary condition; the plant yielded "no seed;"
When the degeneration progressed, the reproductive
elements found not, represented in them, the forces
of that number of characters of the species which
was necessary to the reciprocal play of their functions
of integration.   Self-impotence, then, characterized the
plants: When this, or a greater, departure from the
original mould had ensued, the reproductive elements,
being incapable of any integration whatever, under-

went a retrograde metamorphosis; "the surface of the stigma, in contact with the pollen, and the pollen itself, becoming   *   *   dark brown and then decaying;" When the plant became still more modified, the vigor of the plant was gone; and the individual died. The individuals of each species of plant are at present to be seen in one, several, many, or all of these stages. This is the explanation of the "graduated series." This is more than "interesting:" It is a complete, quantitative solution of all the diverse phenomena.

Speaking of those species, which have but some individuals self-impotent, Darwin says (p. 174, Vol. ii, *Animals and Plants, &c.*):

"This peculiar state of the reproductive organs, when occurring in certain individuals alone, is evidently abnormal."

What a wealth of knowledge, is here conveyed. He can but mean, that exceptions to the general rule for a given species, are (*sic*) evidently exceptions! He cannot intend anything else; for, he is precluded from using the words "normal," and "abnormal" in any other sense, by his theory, viz., that there is no fixed *status*, for any organisms, because the law of their development is constant change. The above, is but another of his re-statements of what he affects to explain.

The self-impotence, of which he speaks, and all cases of sterility and of lessened fertility, are abnormal. It matters not, whether they occur in certain individuals alone, of a species; or whether they occur in all of the individuals of a species. It is not the fact, that they contravene an observed, general result, which makes them abnormal (although it does in one sense; but that sense is so obvious, that no one, unless he was solicitous to give an impression that he was not passing by facts without *explaining* them, would ever think of imparting what it needs no ghost, come from his grave, to tell). They are abnormal, by reason of the fact, that they prevail, only when there is a breach of the true coördination of the characters of the given species. "This peculiar state of the reproductive organs," is the consequence of the absence, or reduction of characters; which, also, is abnormal. It is the penalty, entailed upon the organisms, for their departures from the true integrity of their respective species.

Referring to the self-impotence of many plants, Darwin remarks (p. 111, *Origin of Species*):

" How strange are these facts! How strange, that the pollen and stigmatic surface of the same flower, though placed so close together, as if for the very purpose of self-fertilization, should, in so many cases, be mutually useless to each other. How simple are these facts explained, on the view of an occasional cross with a distinct individual, being advantageous or indispensable !"

"How simple ?" aye, how idiotic! to *explain*, that the cause of the bane, is the existence of the antidote! We are lost in wonder, at this evidence of how great an amount of cerebral phosphorus, some of these highly-developed Quadrumana may secrete.

To paraphrase Darwin's statement: Men frequently fall sick ; " How strange are these facts! How simple are these facts *explained*, on the view of an occasional" dose of medicine "being advantageous or indispensable !"

Darwin, in striving to explain the causes of the lessened fertility of plants, essays the very ingenious surmise, that "their sexual functions are disturbed." But, it is to be remarked, that he gives not the remotest approach to a conjecture, as to what is the reason for this disturbance ; how it is brought about; nor why the disturbance is absent in one case, is great in another, is less in a third, and but slight in a fourth. He says, respecting these phenomena (p. 231, Vol. ii, *Animals and Plants, &c.*):

"We are far from knowing the cause; nor is this surprising, seeing how profoundly ignorant we are in regard to the normal and abnormal action of the reproductive organs."

It has been shown, with respect to animals, that varieties are generally incapable of long continuing the same form; that, unless crossing is resorted to,—which varies the form,—or reversion occurs in some of the parts, such varieties die out, and give place to others ; owing to the evil effects resulting from their incomplete, or disproportionate development. The same holds good, with plants. Varieties, either die out altogether, after a time, or they vary somewhat their form.   To this principle, is due the degeneration which, as Darwin has shown, requires that there should be frequent exchanges of seed, or change of conditions.   A variety which long remains " genuine," may be relied upon, as being comparatively propor-

tionately developed. The evils which result to plants
from disproportionate development, are encouraged by
the process which planters have of "roguing" (*i. e.,*
weeding out) those individuals, of a variety, which depart from the type prescribed by their owners. Darwin says (p. 34, *Origin of Species*):

"When a race of Plants is pretty well established,
the seed-raisers do not pick out the best plants, but
merely go over their seed-beds, and pull up the 'rogues,'
as they call the plants that deviate from the proper
standard."

As this "proper standard," generally requires the
monstrous development of some one character only
(that character, which is valued); and suffers, or has
compelled, the reduction of other characters to a rudimentary condition; it is impossible for the plants, long
to continue their kind. To remain constant long, to a
a given type; either that type must approximate the
sum of all the positive characters of its species; or it
must deviate from such "proper standard," by abating
the abnormally developed part; by increasing the development of one or more of the other (*i. e.,* the not
valued) parts; or by restoring some of the parts which
were wholly suppressed or rudimentary; or it must
supply some of these defects of structure by crossing
with individuals of another variety.

So imperative is this alternative, of either extinction,
or change of form, where plants are defective in structure, that Darwin comments upon it, with some surprise. The change of form is effected, generally, unconsciously to man. For, those plants which persist

in a varietal type which is of defective structure, become of lessened fertility, and of lessened vigor.
These, man, for obvious reasons, rejects; and selects
those which are hardier and most fertile.   The latter
owe this vigor and fertility to such slight successive increments of growth in various parts, that the change
escapes man's eyes, until he awakes, with surprise, to
the fact of how different the variety is, to what it was
but a few years back!   He himself has occasioned it,
by his selection of the strongest and most fertile.
Then; it is very difficult to confine a plant to a given
type, when its seed is distributed and grown in many
places, where the supplies of the conditions of growth,
are so different.   A variety is, very frequently the
outcome both of man's selection, and of a given set
of conditions.   Where this set of conditions, is not
realized, all of man's care cannot prevent a change of
form, in the transplanted variety.

"De Candolle," says he (p. 513, *Origin of Species*),
"has fully discussed the antiquity of various races of
plants."

He then speaks of old varieties of the poppy, of the
almond, of the cabbage, of the turnip, &c., which existed, many centuries back, and which are measurably
like the varieties existing at the present day.

"But," says he, "it does not seem improbable, that
some of these varieties may have been lost and reappeared;" and "whether any of these plants are absolutely identical with our present sub-varieties, is not
certain."

Respecting the changes of form, which are required

to save varieties from extinction, the following assertion of Darwin may be quoted:

"Whether," says he (p. 397, Vol. i, *Animals and
Plants, &c.*), "the incessant supply of new varieties, is
partly due to * * occasional and accidental crosses,
and their fleeting existence to changes of fashion; or,
again whether the varieties which arise after a long
course of continued self-fertilization, are weakly and
soon perish, I cannot even conjecture."

The doubt, in his mind, as to their becoming
weakly, and perishing, arises probably from the fact, of
his having observed several varieties which,—being
proportionately developed,—contravene his incomplete
induction.

The loss, or reduction, of characters, entails loss of
fertility. This fertility may be regained by the restoration of such lost or reduced characters. It matters
not, by what process is effected the addition of characters to a defective variety, to make up the complement necessary to induce fertility, or increase of fertility. If the result be attained by direct reversion (*i. e.*,
by what is called improvement), the fertility ensues:
If by crossing, the same gain follows. Even when ·
à measurable return to perfect type, is secured by that
addition of characters, which is effected by splicing
two varieties together, in Grafting, the good equally
results.

As Darwin remarks (p. 12, *Origin of Species*):

"It is really surprising, to note the endless points in
structure, and constitution, in which the varieties and
sub-varieties," ("of some of our cultivated plants
as the" varieties of the "hyacinth, potato, even the

dahlia," &c.), " differ slightly from each other. The whole organization seems to have become plastic and tends to depart, in some small degree, from the parental type."

Each variety has some positive peculiarity, which is wanting in all the other varieties of the same species, and the absence of which, lessens the capacity of those varieties, for reproduction. A plant, lacking many, and important features will, as has been shown, have its reproductive elements wholly incapacitated for union with each other, or for union with the sexual elements of other plants of exactly the same mould; and yet, the plant will be quite fertile, with other individuals of the species, with forms dissimilar. The reason is; in the former cases, the reproductive elements cannot build a structure, when each lacks so many, and the same, materials. In the latter case, they may build (though each lacks many of the materials), if both make up, with the forces of what characters they have, all, or most, of what is needed. To be functionally perfect, an organism must be, of the full structural integrity, of its species. Man may mould the individuals, of a species, into a multitude of shapes; but each such form (save one), will, of necessity, be in derogation, both of its structural, and of its functional perfection. In such a way, the whole organization may be shown to be "plastic;" but, plastic, in much the same manner a man may be shown to be, by cutting off his leg. May a truncated crystal, with an edge lopped off, be rightly said to be plastic? Or, may a number of such truncated crystals, be said to be plastic, merely because it is possible to arrest each crystal, at a different stage, in its process of reintegrating its lost edge?

Of the three processes, by which lessened fertility is regained, reversion by means of slight accretions of growth, is one.   The evidence from Darwin, on this point,—namely, of increased fertility, concomitant upon the development of structure by means directly of Reversion,—is not abundant; for two reasons.   The one is, that Darwin, not being conscious,—or seeming not to be,—of the connection between the two, has not made it a subject of close observation; and, direct Reversion, not being abrupt, as Reversion, of course, is in Crossing, the resulting gain, in fertility, has just been noticed by Darwin, and left without further remark.

He says (p. 212, Vol. ii, *Animals and Plants*, *&c.*):

"Domestication, as a general rule, increases the prolificness of animals and plants."

Another reason is, that the gain, in fertility, which should ensue from the improvement, or reversion, occurring under domestication, is quite frequently precluded by man's vitiating the proportion, through pushing the development of one or two characters only, to an extreme point.   This, as we have before frequently observed, is often worse, in its effects, than was the comparatively uniform degeneration which obtained, before Man bestowed care upon the individuals.   Another reason is that Man suppresses and reduces organs, as he has done with the Pig.   These are the reasons, why the result required by the theory of reversion, and noticed by Darwin, obtains, as he says, "as a general rule" only.

On the other hand, as Darwin says (p. 144, Vol. ii, *Animals and Plants, &c.*):

"The benefit from a cross, even when there has not been any very close-interbreeding, is almost invariably at once conspicuous."

In the chapters, on Pigeons and Fowls, it will be remembered, that Darwin says, what he repeats, and reiterates in one form, or another, again and again, throughout his works; that:

"The more distinct the breeds, that are crossed, the more fertile, the mongrel offspring." Below, he notices the exceptional excellence of mongrel plants "'of which, the parents were the two most dissimilar varieties, I could select.'"

It will be noticed, that the gardener erroneously terms mongrels, "hybrids;" a fault which Darwin corrects. The other term, "hybridizations," Darwin doubtless thought it needless to rectify.

"With respect to the benefit, derived from crossing distinct varieties" (Vol. ii, p. 160, *Animals and Plants, &c.*), "plenty of evidence has been published; Sageret speaks, in strong terms, of the vigor of melons raised by crossing different varieties, and adds, that they are more easily fertilized than common melons, and produce numerous good seed. Here follows the evidence of an English gardener. 'I have, this summer, met with better success, in my cultivation of melons, in an unprotected state, from the seeds of hybrids (*i. e.*, mongrels), obtained by cross-impregnation, than with old varieties. The offspring of these different hybridizations (?) (one, more especially, of which the parents were the two most dissimilar (!) varieties I could select), each yielded more ample and finer produce than any-

33

one, of between twenty, and thirty established varieties.'"

The mongrels, from a cross between " the two most dissimilar varieties I could select," were remarkably excellent, because the amount of positive differences, is generally greatest, with individuals, or varieties, the most dissimilar; for, the union of the characters which constitute these differences, in the mongrels, secures a great remove, towards the original, perfect type. Each of these varieties, therefore, had much to contribute, which the other lacked. Here, with the varieties of the melon, as with the varieties of all cultivated species, the excellences, which should be compounded, or united, in each individual, of the species, are frittered away, by apportioning them among different individuals and varieties. Hence; the evil effects, which are attendant upon the close-interbreeding and the self-fertilization of the individuals of each variety, which lacks the special excellences of all the other varieties. Hence; the good from Crossing, which remedies such apportionment, by uniting the special excellences, or other positive, peculiar characters, of two varieties, in the one individual, the offspring.

Again he says :

" Andrew Knight believed that his seedlings, from crossed varieties of the Apple, exhibited increased vigor, and luxuriance; and, M. Chevreul alludes to the extreme vigor of some of the crossed fruit trees, raised by Sageret."

" By crossing, reciprocally, the tallest and shortest peas, Knight says, ' I had, in this experiment, a striking instance of the stimulating effects of crossing the breeds; for, the smallest variety, whose height rarely exceeded two feet, was increased to six feet; whilst the height of the large and luxuriant kind, was very little diminished.' "

The offspring was not diminished, or increased, to a mere mean, between the two varieties which were, respectively, large and small; because the capacity for reversion to the greater height, lay ready to be exercised, in the smaller variety; and, doubtless, the latter also made amends, for its small size, by contributing some positive differences, in some of its characters, in which the large variety was deficient. For, the accession of new characters, always,—or nearly always,—brings with it increased size; due, both to the capacity for reversion, and to the room which this accession demands. Crossing, Darwin asserts, increases the size; though, the fact belongs only to his voluminous repertory of things which are "strange," "wonderful," "remarkable," "peculiar," etc., and which obey an "innate tendency." Darwin's *forte* lies in facts; his explanatory sagacity he seems to have exhausted, in devising his "innate tendency," and his "great law of nature." Those explanations (?) contain, within them, the very quintessence of the absurd; but, it is no paradox to assert, that there is ever a greater expenditure of cerebral phosphorus, involved in the conception and application of a fallacious doctrine, than there is, in the discovery of the grandest truths. The hard attrition, of each fact, against the fallacy, is most wearing to the brain; whereas, a true principle evolves itself most gracefully, and courses with perfect ease, in and out, among all of the phenomena.

Continuing, Darwin remarks:

"Mr. Laxton gave me seed-peas, produced from crosses between four distinct kinds; and the plants, thus raised, were extraordinarily vigorous, being in each case, from one to two or three feet, taller than the parent forms growing close along side of them."

On page 161, Vol. ii, *Animals and Plants, &c.*, he says:

"Weigmann made many crosses between several varieties of cabbage; and he speaks with astonishment, of the vigor and height of the mongrels, which excited the amazement of all the gardeners who beheld them. Mr. Chaundry raised a great number of mongrels, by planting together six distinct varieties of cabbage. These mongrels displayed an infinite diversity of character; but the most remarkable circumstance was, that, while all the other cabbages and borecoles, in the nursery, were destroyed by a severe winter, these hybrids (?) were little injured, and supplied the kitchen, when there was no other cabbage to be had."

The height, which was observed in these mongrel cabbages, was due, doubtless, to reversion in the stock which, according to Darwin, in some individuals, has attained an enormous height.

"In the Island of Jersey," says he (p. 389, Vol. i, *Animals and Plants, &c.*), "from the effects of particular culture, and of climate, a stalk has grown to the height of sixteen feet, and 'had its spring shoots, at the top, occupied by a magpie's nest;' the woody stems are not unfrequently, from ten to twelve feet in height, and are there used, as rafters, and as walking sticks."

The great room, for improvement, there is in the cabbage, by means of reversion direct, or reversion by crossing, is here shown (although no useful purpose of Man will be served by effecting such improvement in the said plant); and the "infinite diversity of character," which Darwin notes, is explained, by the fact, that many of the characters of the cabbage species, have been distributed among the different varieties. The above quotation shows one feature, in which most of the varieties have been modified. "Every one," says Darwin, "knows how greatly the various kinds of cabbage, differ in appearance." He then notices the height the plant has attained in the Island of Jersey, and gives many of the forms which the cabbage has assumed, in several parts of the world.

On page 281, Vol. ii, he says, "No variety of wheat is quite uniform, in character." This shows, that, not only do the varieties of wheat differ in character, but so, also, do the individuals of each variety. His observation has doubtless been confined, to the part which man values, viz., the seed; but, together with variations, in the special excellence of that species, there are, also, many variations in the leaves, in the stalks, and in other not-valued parts. When these positive differences are united, in an individual plant, as they are, by crossing, good must, according to the theory of reversion, result. The facts consist with this inference.

"Mr. Maund," says Darwin (p. 161, Vol. ii, *Animals and Plants, &c.*), "exhibited before the Royal Agricultural Society specimens of crossed wheat, together

33*

with their parent varieties, and the editor states, that they were intermediate in character, 'united with that greater vigor of growth, which, it appears, in the vegetable, as in the animal world, is the result of a first cross.' Knight also crossed several varieties of wheat, and he says, 'that in the years 1795 and 1796, when almost the whole crop of corn, in the island, was blighted, the varieties thus obtained, and these only, escaped in this neighborhood, though sown in several different soils and situations.'"

On page 281, Vol. ii, *Animals and Plants, &c.*, he says:

"The straw of the Fenton wheat, is remarkably unequal in height; and, a competent observer believes, that this variety is highly productive, partly because the ears, from being distributed, at various heights, above the ground, are less crowded together."

Doubtless, to this is due some of the effect; but, it is probable, that, with the inequality in height, there is a diversity in the quality of the different classes of tissues, in the proportion of the chemicals assimilated, and in others of the characters; and, that the fertility arises from the interbreeding of the individuals, which is, under the circumstances, tantamount to crossing.

It may be asked, by the reader, unacquainted with the motives which govern seed-growers, in their selection; Why, if such great increase in vigor, size, fertility, &c., is secured by crossing, is not that process generally resorted to? The reason is, that the improvement of the plants is but a secondary consideration, with planters. Their first aim is, to secure uniformity of character, in the individuals of each variety, and this end is frustrated by crossing. Upon a cross, each of the mongrels starts out, in a different direction, towards the perfect type of its species, and there is but little chance, if crossing be continued, of ever getting them uniform again, until they attain their goal.   The case, where the mongrels may be made uniform, is unique.

On p. 121, Vol. ii, *Animals and Plants, &c.*, Darwin says:

"The history of a variety of wheat, which was raised from two very distinct varieties, and which, after six years' culture, presented an even sample, has been recorded on good authority."

In this case, the wheat must have been grown for those six years upon the same piece of ground.   In no other way, could they have been brought under subjection.

Planters are jealous of the development, in their plants, of any characters other than the special excellence.   They even grudge other characters, the chemical elements, and even the carbonic acid of the atmosphere, which are needful for their growth.   The prejudice they entertain, respecting a cross (which starts the development of all the characters of the plant), may, therefore, be appreciated.   Planters have never had more than two ideas, on the subject of the cultivation of Plants, namely, Selection, and "Fertilizers;" despite the fact that every plant, under their care has ever been vocal, with the cry, that the true *Fertilizer* is proportionate development.   Full, proportionate development may, at times, not consist with the profit of the planter; but that degree of proportionate development, which is requisite to stave off sterility, and lessened fertility, is an important item in cultivation.

Darwin says (p. 505, Vol. ii, *Animals and Plants, &c.*):

"I have just said, that the crossed offspring would gain in vigor and fertility. From the facts given in the xviith chapter, there can be no doubt of this; and there can be little doubt * * that long-continued, close-interbreeding leads to evil results. From these various considerations, the conclusion, arrived at in the chapter just referred to,—namely, that great good of some kind, is derived from the sexual concourse of distinct individuals,—must be admitted."

What a brilliant and satisfying conclusion to come to! With what admiration must his readers regard him, thus:

"* * boldly soaring, in sublimer mood,
Through trackless skies, on metaphysic wings."

With what a hush of profoundest awe, must his disciples here contemplate their master, who has just proved that he is capable of discovering, that, in a congeries of effects,—varying, too infinitely in quantity,—there is at work, some mysterious law! Good is observed to recur, at times, from crossing: Then, the scientist (this scientist, *par excellence*) frames a "great law of nature," viz., that good recurs! Truly, the following tribute should be paid, to Darwin's genius, as it was to that of his grandfather, the author of "*Loves of the Plants*":

"Willing Nature to thy curious eye,
 Involved in night, her mazy depths betray."
                  *   *   *   *   *   *
"And Nature in primordial beauty seems
 To breathe, inspired by thee, THE PHILOSOPHIC SOUL !"*

Again does Darwin say (p. 175, Vol. ii, *Animals and Plants, &c.*) :

" These facts all point to the same general conclusion, namely, that good is derived from a cross between individuals which, either innately (*sic*), or from exposure to dissimilar conditions, have come to differ in sexual constitution."

Why, (1) good should be derived from a cross; (2) what this " innate " tendency is, which causes the individuals to differ in sexual constitution; (3) What are these differences in sexual constitution; (4) and Why exposure to dissimilar conditions produces these sexual differences, are conundrums which are not solved upon Darwin's theory, doubtless because it was deemed that to attempt their solution would be in derogation of the respect due to " a great law of nature."

Darwin is mistaken, not only when he refers the phenomena to "a great law of nature," but also when he contends, that the good from crossing, has any necessary connection with any sexual features, or sexual constitution.   The good accrues, whenever there is an increase of the number of characters of the individual,

---

* These chaste effusions, by admiring friends of Dr. Erasmus Darwin, are to be found incorporated within an edition of the latter's " *Botanic Garden.*"   It is to be regretted, that those works of the imagination, " *The Origin of Species,*" and " *Animals and Plants under Domestication,*" which are much superior, in poetical merit, to " *The Loves of the Plants,*" were not also set to metre.

however such increase may be wrought. In Grafting, the condition is supplied, and the good results; and, there, the element of sex, and that of reproduction, are wanting. Each variety possesses some peculiar or other feature which it is necessary, for perfect physiological integrity, that the others should have. The fact of the good results being occasioned also by the process of Grafting, is strikingly out of harmony with his idea, of the good being due to some quality, resident in the sexual organs. Crossing is not the cause, but merely one of the occasions, of the good. The ultimate reason of the good effects, is, that the union, or addition, of characters, supplies a deficient integrity, and brings the individual receiving such an accession of features, back to the type, from which it should never have departed. As frequently remarked, difference, *per se*, is not the cause; the beneficial effect is wrought, only when there is some positive difference capable of covering, or of supplying, a deficiency.

Darwin says (p. 174, Vol. ii., *Animals and Plants, &c.*):

"The self-impotent *Passiflora alata*, which recovered its self-fertility, after having been grafted on a distinct stock, shows how small a change is sufficient to act powerfully on the reproductive system."

This case of the self-impotent Passiflora *alata* becoming again capable of self-fertilization, shows clearly that no matter how the lost integrity of an individual, is repaired; or how the individual regains the characters, lost by itself, or by its ancestors, the recompense, due a return to the original type, is always paid.

The above quotation reveals another of his ingenious

fallacies. By introducing the remark, that the grafting acts powerfully on the reproductive system, he wishes to insinuate the idea that the phenomena incident to grafting, are not inconsistent with the view he previously propounded, to wit, that the good from crossing is due to some peculiarity in the sexual constitution. The fallacy lies in this, that in either of his two propositions, cause and effect are transposed, when compared with the relation the good effects and their cause bore to each other in the other proposition. His first proposition is to the effect that some peculiarity in the sexual constitution is the cause, and the good observed is the effect. His latter proposition, however, is to the effect that the good observed is the cause, and the peculiarity in the sexual constitution is the effect!

On page 437, Vol. ii., *Animals and Plants, &c.*, he speaks of the "facts which render it, to a certain degree probable, that when the tissues of two plants, belonging to distinct varieties, are intimately united," in Grafting, "the characters of the two forms are united."

On page 180, Vol. ii, *Animals and Plants, &c.*, he gives many instances of the good derived from Grafting.

It is a matter, of supreme consequence, to understand the reason of the lessened fertility, and of the sterility, among individuals of the same species; for, it is by the test of sterility, that botanists determine what are and what are not species. Where this is not the test, with them, structural difference is; and the consequence has been, that the classification of species of plants is most absurd. How can they safely make sterility, *per se*, a test, when individuals of the same species are frequently sterile with each other! How safely make structural difference, *per se*, a test, when there are many cultivated varieties, and many natural races, of the same species, distinguished from each other, by differences, greater than those which mark even genera from each other! It has been popular faith in this idea, of mere structural difference, which has hitherto secured Darwin's theory against confutation. As soon as the idea is broached, that structural difference is of little account, compared with physiological difference, the main stay of his theory is gone.

The result of the test of structural difference, and of the ignorant application of the test of sterility, has been, to make the science of classification, chaos worse confounded. The true test, of a species of plant, is the capacity for long-continued self-fertilization, without abatement in fertility, vigor, or size. All plants capable of indefinitely-continued reproduction with one capable of such self-fertilization, belong to the same species, however structurally different such plants may be. Each plant, which is self-impotent, or of lessened fertility, falls short of the full structure of the species. Plants, of the same, and plants of different species, may be discriminated, by breeding them each with another. If they are capable of long-continued fertilization, they are of the same species. If, however, they are sterile with each other, it is not conclusive evidence of their being of distinct species. For, that may occur with individuals of the same species; in fact, those most alike in structure, if wanting in any

character, will be generally, the most liable to sterility, *inter se.*

Agriculturists, and horticulturists, with Plants, and
breeders, and fanciers, with animals, may count confi-
dently upon an individual being susceptible of improvement, or of increase in structure, whenever such individual suffers any loss of vigor or fertility when self-
fertilized, or when closely interbred. The margin of
improvement, still possible, will be susceptible of ascertainment, by noting the degree of the evil resulting from
(say) the animal mating with one of its own kind; or, if
it be a plant, from the degree of evil resulting from
its self-impregnation. If it be a plant, and it be self-
impotent, it will ever be found, either that it has many
organs, in a rudimentary condition; or, that some one
organ has become extraordinarily dominant. In estimating, however, whether a plant with perfect, or but
little impaired fertility, is fully and proportionately developed, or nearly so, security must be had against
such possible crossing with other varieties, or with
other individuals, as may be effected through the
agency of bees, and other insects. If, however, there
are no varieties, or individuals of the same species,
which have any positive differences distinguishing
them from the given individual, it may be safely con-
cluded, that the full fertility and vigor of the individual,
truly imply its full and proportionate development;
for, if those varieties, with which it is possible for it to
cross, have no points of structure, other than those
also possessed by the individual in question; it is clear,
that the fertility cannot be due to crossing. There is
34

still another consideration, which obtains, in connection with this subject. A plant may be very degenerate in structure; possess very many organs in a rudimentary condition; may not have crossed with another variety of the same species; and yet such plant may be, at least for one generation, very fertile and vigorous. Such conditions would well consist with a state of facts, where the plant had been crossed by an individual of a distinct, but allied species. It is frequently possible, as Darwin shows, for an individual which is wholly self-impotent, to cross with a distinct species, and be very prolific.

On page 297, *Origin of Species*, Darwin says, that he is led:

" To refer to a most singular fact, namely, that there are individual plants, of a certain species of Lobelia, and of some other genera, which can be far more easily fertilized by the pollen of another, and distinct species, than by their own pollen. * * For these species (Lobelia and Hippeastrum) have been found to yield seed to the pollen of a distinct species, though quite sterile with their own pollen, notwithstanding that their own pollen was found to be perfectly good, for it fertilized distinct species."

It may be asked: is the fertility and vigor acquired, for one generation, by a cross with a distinct species, due to a return to the perfect type? In a measure, or, *sub modo*, it is. It is not, however, a perfect type common to both species. The reason, why fertilization may be effected, for one generation, by the pollen of a distinct species, is because, in the reproductive element of the foreign, but allied species, the given individual finds many characters, either like its own, and with which its characters may isochronize; or (as in the case given above, where the plant was self-impotent), like the characters, of its species, which it has lost, and which fail to be represented in its own pollen.

With the characters of another species, it may, for one generation, make up its lost integrity. But, the escape of the line of such individuals from extinction, by means of crossing with a distinct species, is only a temporary and slightly deferred one. For, on account of such a cross, their hybrids become irremediably sterile. Had the individual crossed with one of its species, it might have continued indefinitely fertile. The sterility of an individual, whose ancestors have never been crossed with a different species, is not absolute. All that makes such individual sterile, is the loss or reduction of characters; which may be remedied, and the fertility of the individual restored, either by reversion, crossing with an individual of the same species, differing positively in structure, or by grafting. But, when a cross is had with a distinct species, a definite, and inevitable failure of issue, is entailed upon the offspring. There exists a barrier to further reproduction. When two individuals of different species cross, the reproductive element of each is capable of the process of integration, because such element has been normally secreted by a pure species! If the forces of such element, are isochronous with the forces of the other reproductive element, as is the fact generally in the case of closely allied species, the two may concur in building up an organism. But, though the forces

of each element are not so far wanting in rhythmical
harmony as to prevent such a coördination as is required for the production of a hybrid, yet that hybrid
has in it the characters of the two species, so compounded or coalesced as to preclude its possession of
the power of spontaneously exuding a new organism;
or in other words, of impressing its coördinating force
upon a part of itself, so as to make such part capable
of reproducing a likeness of itself.

This is the reason of the good resulting from a
cross with a distinct, but allied species, viz.: The
plant, in question, is wanting in some of the characters of its species. In the distinct species, it finds
characters, like those which are wanting in itself; and,
it is possible for it to avail itself of them to amend its
lost integrity. But, the line of descent is not capable of being carried any further; and, there is no
means possible of averting the extinction which occurs
in the succeeding generation, as there is, when an individual of a pure species, becomes self-impotent, or
sterile. Two self-impotent individuals of the same
species, may be fertile together; and they are fertile,
because they have made up, together, the complement
of the characters necessary for reproduction; but they
are different from distinct species, for these characters
are perfectly in harmony with each other, when joined
in the mongrel; and, therefore, there is no impedi-
ment to the offspring, and its line, continuing indefinitely fertile. All such offspring need do, to continue
the fertility, is to keep up the requisite number and
proportion of the characters of its species.

To the theory of the necessity for the full and proportionate development of all the characters of a species, it might possibly be objected that the law of Compensation, propounded by Gœthe and the elder Geoffroy, shows that "in order to spend on one side, nature is forced to economize on the other side." Darwin says, respecting this law of balancement of growth, "I think this holds true to a certain extent with our domestic productions;" but doubts the universality of the rule.

The fact is, that the rule holds good only where the organism is impoverished; where, either, it is denied food, chemical elements, &c., in amount sufficient for the needs of all parts of the system; or, where having them to hand, it lacks the capacity for assimilating enough for all of its parts. In either case, the reduction of some parts will benefit the growth of other parts of the organism.

This interpretation, however, is not needed to obviate the objection to the theory of full and proportionate development of all the parts, being necessary to perfection; for, even when by economy on the one side of an organism, an impulse is given to the growth of the other part, physiological injury accrues in proportion to the extent to which the normal ratio of the characters has been vitiated. Quite frequently, by keeping down the growth of some of the parts of a plant, other parts,—say, the reproductive organs, the reproductive elements, and the fruit thereof,—will be greatly augmented in structure. But, this augmentation in structure, even in such parts, will lessen the fertility

34*

and vigor of the organism instead of enhancing them; because such growth violates the proportion. Thus, you may cut away the leaves in a plant, and thereby much increase the size of the seed, but the seed will have its vitality lessened, instead of increased, by augmentation in size, so occasioned.

FERTILIZATION OF ORCHIDS.

In this connection, it may be well to notice Darwin's work, on the Fertilization of Orchids, which was written, with the design to prove the truth of his "general law of nature," that evil results from close-interbreeding, *per se*, and from self-fertilization, *per se*, and that a cross with another individual or variety, is absolutely necessary.

This "law," Darwin, as we have shown, promulgated first, in his Origin of Species. Of course, his "law" was demurred to, by every breeder and fancier, horticulturist and agriculturist, who knew of the great variation in the quantity of the effects of interbreeding, and of fertilization; and, who had noted, that, frequently, there resulted no evil whatever from such a process.

Darwin says, on page 1, of the *Fertilization of Orchids:*

"Having been blamed for propounding this doctrine, without giving ample facts, for which I had not in that work (*Origin of Species*) sufficient space, I wished to show that I have not spoken without having gone into details. I have been led to publish this little treatise, separately, as it has become inconveniently large to be incorporated with the rest of the discussion on the same subject."

In this work, he shows that many of the species of Orchids, are incapable of self-fertilization, and are compelled to be fertilized by means of insect agency, to which the structure of the flower, is very elaborately adapted. His argument is, that as these plants are mechanically incapable of self-fertilization, and as the contrivances of the flowers so manifestly subserve insect agency, it follows, that there must be something radically injurious in the process of self-fertilization; and that an advantage is derived from a cross, with a distinct flower. The whole argument presses upon the fact, that the flowers are incapable of self-fertilization. The adaptation to insect agency exists in other flowers, which are able to fertilize themselves; and, with these, no presumption therefore arises, that there is a necessity for the cross which insects effect.

But, the whole significance of his facts, is taken away, when it is observed, that the original form of the flowers, and of the plants, has been modified, in a number of ways; that many characters, as he shows, have been reduced to a rudimentary condition, and that the incapacity for self-fertilization (which is a mechanical, or structural incapacity, and not a physiological incapacity) has arisen (as may be shown, by analogy with the forms of other species of the same genus), from the reproductive organs, of the plants, having become partially rudimentary in structure. The whole structure, of the flowers (barring, the slightest, possible modification), is consistent with adaptation to self-fertilization, as well as to insect agency. The only detail wanting, is but a little more efficiency in the working of the mechanism. The pollen-mass does not slip, of itself, from the anther-cells but requires force, *ab extra*, to be torn therefrom. *Were the anther-cells and the pollen-mass to proceed a little further in their development, so as naturally to disengage the latter from the meshes of the former*, the flower could well be self-fertilized, by means of the very beautiful adaptations which facilitate the action of insects.

Now, this is the case with one of the species of Orchids, and such species, so self-fertilized, is exceptionally fertile and vigorous !

" Robert Brown," says Darwin (p. 65, "*Fertilization of Orchids* "), "first observed that the structure of the Bee Ophrys is adapted for self-fertilization. When we consider the unusual and perfectly adapted length, as well as the remarkable thinness, of the caudicles of the pollinia; when we see that the anther-cells naturally open, and that the masses of pollen, from their weight, slowly fall down to the exact level of the stigmatic surface, and are there made to vibrate to and fro by the slightest breath of wind, till the stigma is struck; it is impossible to doubt, that these points of structure and function, which occur in no other British Orchid, are specially adapted for self-fertilization."

Now, although the different species of Orchids have certain specific differences of structure, they were originally all capable of self-fertilization; and it has been but a slight modification of their structure, which has deprived them of such capacity. Did space permit, it would be possible, to take up each species, and point out the modification mentioned. In the first species, mentioned by Darwin, the failure of the flowers to

fertilize themselves is due to the anther-cells lacking the power to open naturally, and to the consequent inability of the pollen-mass to release itself and
fall to the level of the stigmatic surface. The modification is very slight. It is simply a case of slightly ar-
rested development of the pollen-mass, and of the
anther-cells where they cohere. And, as to the possibility of the modification's having been induced; Darwin shows (chap. vii) that, many great modifications
have occurred, in almost every individual of this genus,
in many and important characters.

Robert Brown, who "first observed that the structure of the Bee Ophrys is adapted for self-fertilization,"
"believed" (though "erroneously," as Darwin contends), "that this peculiarity (of self-fertilization) was
common to the genus." Darwin's only answer to this
induction of Mr. Brown, is, that "this one alone of the
four species" of British Orchids, shows this capacity.
But, this is no objection, as the assumption is, that the
other species originally fertilized themselves, and subsequently becoming modified, thus lost the power so
to do.

The test, by which to ascertain, whether they have
so become modified, and by which to ascertain whether
the process of fertilization, *per se*, is injurious, is to be
found in a comparison of the fertility of the self-fertilized plants, with the fertility of those which depend, for
their reproduction, upon the crossing which is effected
by insect agency. The test is the fairest possible; for,
Darwin's principal criterion, by which to judge of the
injurious effects wrought by self-fertilization, or by

close-interbreeding, has ever been (in his "*Origin of Species*," and in his "*Animals and Plants under Domestication*") the lessened fertility, or the sterility, of the individuals so impregnated. And, the test is also that, required by the theory of reversion. Such theory, of Reversion, maintains, that, where there is little, or no modification, there are no, or very little evil effects occasioned by the process, in question. If, then, there is, in some of the Orchids, the modification which entails the mechanical incapacity for self-fertilization; and, if there is an absence, of such modification, in others of the Orchids, the test of fertility—which is the test with either theory—should, upon Darwin's theory, show that the modified plants (which are ever crossed) are superior, in fertility, to the plants capable of self-fertilization; whereas, upon the theory of reversion, or proportionate development, it should show, that it is the less modified plants (which, in this case, are the self-fertilized ones) which are more fertile than the ones which are crossed, and which have parts which are structurally and functionally rudimentary.

Darwin, as above remarked, has, in his works to which this "*Fertilization of Orchids*" is merely supplementary, clearly defined what he means, by the evil effects of the process of close-breeding. He there ever states, and states explicitly, that those effects are, principally, lessened fertility, and sterility. In all of the phenomena, adduced in his former works, his test has not, to his mind, conclusively failed him. With the light, derived from the theory of reversion, the phenomena mentioned may be proved (as already shown), to confound, completely, all of his views. But, evil has, in the main, been shown (however much it has varied in character), to be, in some way, occasioned by close-interbreeding. In those instances, even, where good has resulted, the gratuitous supposition has ever appeared open to him that, if the interbreeding were only continued long enough, the evil would manifest itself. And, his "law" has had a semblance of support from the good resulting from crossing; because, each crossed variety had some feature, to contribute to the offspring. Consequently, he has hitherto been pleased and satisfied with the test of lessened fertility, and of sterility.

He finds, however, that the crucial test—admissible on both theories—reveals, that, with Orchids, *the self-fertilized plants are much more fertile, than the crossed plants!* Such a result is the very antithesis to what Darwin's theory requires, and fully refutes his "great law." The reason, to the reader, is plain, and exactly what was to be expected. The self-fertilized plants are,—at least in the reproductive features above mentioned,—unmodified and therefore just that much less provocative of sterility; whereas, the plants, incapable of self-fertilization, and which are crossed, are rudimentary in such features, and therefore just that much more susceptible of lessened fertility.

Here is the proof. He says (p. 66, "*Fertilization of Orchids*"):

"I have often noticed, that the spikes of the Bee Ophrys *apparently produced as many seed-capsules as flowers;* and, near Torquay, I carefully examined many dozen plants, some time after the flowering season; and, on all, I found from one to four, and occasionally five, fine capsules; *that is, as many capsules, as there had been flowers (!); in extremely few cases* (excepting a few deformed flowers, generally on the summit of the spike), *could a flower be found which had not produced a capsule (!). Let it be observed, what a contrast this case presents, with that of the Fly Ophrys,* WHICH REQUIRES INSECT AGENCY, *and which* FROM FORTY-NINE FLOWERS, PRODUCED ONLY SEVEN CAPSULES!

"From what I have seen of other British Orchids, I was so much surprised at the self-fertilization of this species, that, during many years, I have looked at the state of the pollen-masses in hundreds of flowers, and I have never seen, in a single instance, reason to believe that pollen had been brought from one flower to another. Excepting in a few monstrous flowers, I have never seen an instance of the pollinia failing to reach their own stigma."

These results stare him in the face. Not only, as he admits, does it "seem conclusive, that we here have a plant which is self-fertilized for perpetuity;" but, these plants even exceed—and enormously exceed—the crossed plants, in fertility! The test of fertility, here flatly contradicts his "law."

After such a blow at his law, he concludes to abandon such a dangerous test. He falls back upon one of those mysterious, occult factors, which he evokes, whenever he is in a dilemma, and vaguely declares that "*some* great good" is derived from crossing, and *some* kind of evil from self-fertilization. He even says (p. 71), respecting the "*some* great good" (which the reader will remember has, with him, ever been increased fertility), resulting from the crossing of the plants incapable of self-fertilization :

"But the good, in the case of the Fly and Spider Ophrys is gained at the expense (*sic !*) of much lessened fertility !"

And immediately thereupon, he says :

"In the Bee Ophrys, great fertility is gained, at the expense (*sic !*) of apparently perpetual self-fertilization."

Such self-stultification (so coolly, and complacently committed, too!) is unparalleled, in the annals of thought.   Naught but itself could be its parallel.   We have known of a humorous individual, who upon being confronted with a fact signally confounding the view he took, then coolly maintained the proposition contended for by his adversary.   But, we never knew of such a device being resorted to, in all seriousness, as it has here been, by Darwin.

His argument, the reader will remember, has always been the direct converse of this.   When he specified, what the evil of close-breeding was, his argument was, viz., Self-fertilization, or close-interbreeding, is at the expense of much lessened fertility !   Here, however, he shows increase of fertility; and, as if he were bent upon starting the ghosts of Aristotle, Bacon, and Comte, horror-stricken, from their graves, he coolly deduces the proposition, that the *fertility is gained at the expense of self-fertilization !*   His argument also was: .Crossing, *per se*, is productive of the good of ˙much increased fertility !   Here, he shows crossing occasions loss of fertility ! and, then, notwithstanding that he has shown evil, where his argument required

35

good, he says, "*The good* * * *is gained at the expense of much lessened fertility!*" The reader will appreciate the difficulty of dealing with a theorist, to whom all results are apparently welcome, as well those which seemingly favor his theory, as those which signally confute it.

Well, may he say, that the above case is, to him, "perplexing, in an unparalleled degree." Upon the theory of reversion, or proportionate development, the phenomena are perfectly explicable. Some of the plants have had their reproductive organs modified. Hence the incapacity for self-fertilization. Their crossing does not much improve their fertility, because all those, with which they cross, are similarly modified. Other plants are not modified; hence, physiologically, their great fertility; and hence, physically, their capacity for self-fertilization. Their great fertility is not due to their self-fertilization, but to the fact that they are not, or but little, modified.

With respect to the facilities afforded to insects, Darwin, if he lists, may invoke his doctrine of Final Causes, and contend, that such apparent adaptations were constructed, in anticipation of the sterility which would accrue from the modification of any parts of the plants, and in view of the necessity there would then exist for crossing the plants. The light of science has as yet scarce begun to dawn, in that wide department of nature, wherein lie the many beautiful correlations which subsist between different organisms, and between organisms and the physical world.

A chick, with its advent into the world, scarce

accomplished, yet beautifully concentering its muscles and sight, with a view to the capture of a passing insect, is a phenomenon which is to be seen, just within the portals of a world of knowledge, which needs as yet a Columbus to explore.   But, unresolved as such coadaptations may be; and, however much they may subserve physiological purposes—as they unquestionably do, for many species which are ill-proportioned would long since have become extinct, were not crossing effected, with them, by means of insects—the truth remains, that no crude, empirical inferences from such unexplained data, will avail against the law, that physiological integrity is consistent, only with full development, in any individual, of all the characters of its species; and that neither self-fertilization, nor close-interbreeding, can in any way affect such integrity where the above condition, proportionate development, is fulfilled.

CHAPTER XII.

An objection, which has ever obtained, to Darwin's theory, is the fact of the sterility of species, when crossed, or the sterility of the hybrids from a cross between two species. This has ever precluded the idea of the evolution of one species into another.

Since varieties cross readily, and their offspring are fertile, this feature, of the sterility of hybrids, clearly appears to be a fundamental distinction between varieties and species.

Darwin admits the fact, of the sterility of species when crossed, or of their hybrids, and recognizes the antagonism it bears to his hypothesis.

He says (p. 293, *Origin of Species*):

"Hybrids * * have their reproductive organs functionally impotent, as may be clearly seen in the state of the male element in both plants and animals; though their formative organs themselves are perfect in structure, as far as the microscope reveals."

Again, on p. 299, *Origin of Species*, he says:

"I doubt whether any case of a perfectly fertile hybrid can be considered as thoroughly well authenticated."

On p. 27, *Origin of Species*, he says:

"It is difficult, perhaps impossible, to bring forward
    (408)

one case of the hybrid offspring of two animals, clearly distinct, being themselves perfectly fertile."

On page 327, *Origin of Species*, he says:

"The perfect fertility of the many domestic varieties differing widely from each other in appearance, for instance those of the Pigeon or (those) of the cabbage, is a remarkable fact; more especially when we reflect, how many species there are which though resembling each other most closely, are utterly sterile, when crossed."

On page 126, Vol. ii, *Animals and Plants, &c.*, he says:

"The domestic races of both animals and plants, when crossed, are with extremely few exceptions, quite fertile. * * The offspring, also, raised from such crosses, are likewise generally more vigorous and fertile than their parents. On the other hand, species when crossed, and their hybrid offspring are almost invariably, in some degree sterile; and here there seems to exist a broad and insuperable distinction (*sic*) between races and species."

On page 213, Vol. ii, *Animals and Plants, &c.*, he says that, where species are crossed, "though size is often gained, fertility is lost."

On page 490 of same volume, he says:

"There is, however, one important constitutional difference (!) between domestic races and species. I refer to the sterility which almost invariably follows, in a greater or less degree, when species are crossed, and the perfect fertility of the most distinct domestic races, with the exception of very few plants, when similarly crossed. It certainly appears a remarkable fact, that many closely allied species, which in appearance differ extremely little, should yield, when united,

35*

only a few more or less sterile offspring, or none at all; whilst domestic races, which differ conspicuously from each other, are when united, remarkably fertile, and yield perfectly fertile offspring."

He finds it impossible to reconcile this sterility, with his theory. But, he has endeavored to show, that the objection may not be so conclusive against his theory, as it appears to be. He essays this, in two ways, each of which betrays about as cool a device as may be conceived.

He argues, (1) that the objection should not be deemed conclusive, because there is an infinite number of degrees of fertility, and of sterility, among even individuals of the same species, all of which phenomena, he says, are inexplicable; and argues that, therefore, our ignorance of such phenomena, deprives us of a full assurance, that the obvious and conceded import of the sterility of hybrids, is the true one!

He argues further, (2) "that the invariable sterility of first crosses between species, and of their hybrids, is not a special endowment, but is incidental on modifications slowly impressed, by unknown means, on the reproductive systems of the parent forms."

1. It is on page 327 of his Origin of Species, that he advances the first argument (?). He there exclaims, "how ignorant we are on the precise causes of sterility;" and asserts, that, in presence of all the cases of lessened fertility, and of sterility, among individuals of the same species, "we must feel how ignorant we are, and how little likely it is, that we should understand, why certain forms are fertile and other forms are sterile when crossed."

It is in pursuance of this design, to show "how ignorant we are," and thus to weaken the force of the principal objection to his theory; that he, in his different
works, devotes such an amount of space, to the many
instances of crossing and of close-interbreeding, of
which "we are so ignorant."

It is with this same design, that he says (p. 462, Vol.
ii, *Animals and Plants, &c.*):

"With respect to the sterility of hybrids, produced
from the union of two distinct species, it was shown in
the xixth chapter, that this depends exclusively on the
reproductive organs being specially affected; but, why
these organs should be thus affected, we do not know
any more (*sic*) than why unnatural conditions of life,
though compatible with health, should cause sterility,
or why continued close-interbreeding, or the illegitimate union of dimorphic or trimorphic plants should
induce the same result."

The idea he wishes to convey, is, that the whole
subject of sterility and of fertility, forms such an inextricable maze, that it is presumption, in any one, to
say, that any aspect of the question, either rebuts, or
confirms, any theory. In other words: instead of explaining anything to his readers, he demands of them
to give up, for his gratification, the little positive knowledge they have upon the subject, merely because there
is quite a number of similar orders of facts which seem
inexplicable! It is a curious feature, discernible
throughout all of Darwin's works purporting to prove
the evolution of the species, that his hypothesis absolutely demands, that an embargo should be laid on the
acquisition of any knowledge of the cause of any class

of facts he has in hand.   His theory requires, that all of
the phenomena of Variation, of Reversion, of Correlation, of Crossing, of Close-Interbreeding, of Generation, &c., be deemed inscrutable, ultimate in their
character, and absolutely inexplicable.   True it is,
that his theory demands this, not without reason; for,
as the reader sees, knowledge of the causes of these
phenomena, explodes his theory.

The answer, to be made to his argument of an
appeal to every person's ignorance of the causes of
the evil effects of close-interbreeding, and of the good
resulting from crossing individuals of the same species, is,—that there is no such ignorance!—all of the
phenomena, to which he appeals, as being inexplicable, are susceptible, as has been fully shown in previous chapters of this book, of a full qualitative and
quantitative explanation.   Evil effects flow from the
interbreeding of individuals of the same species, because such individuals have characters of their species,
reduced or suppressed.   Those differences in the quantity of effects, which make Darwin so confident, that
the subject is hopelessly confused, are simply due to
corresponding degrees of defective development, in
the individuals so interbred.   The good resulting from
the crossing of varieties, is, as has been shown, due to
the fact, that one variety contributes, to the offspring,
a character or characters which the other variety
lacks; and the physiological gain, evidenced in the
fertility resulting, is because, by such contribution of
characters, the mongrel offspring has removed the
nearer to the perfect type of the species.   Those dif-

ferences in the quantity of these good effects, which Darwin similarly accounts as phenomena the cause of which " no fellow can find out," are due to the different degrees, in which each such pair of varieties, contribute characters to such offspring. There is no phase of sterility, or of fertility, which is not susceptible of clear explanation, by means of the theory of reversion.

Therefore: his argument of an appeal to other things of which we are assumed to be ignorant, must fall to the ground, when it is found that we are *not* ignorant of those things. We shall show below, that this appeal of his, to the different degrees of fertility and of sterility, with individuals of the same species, instead of getting him out of one difficulty, only causes him to put his foot into another, infinitely worse. The explanation of those things of which he assumes we are ignorant, is replete with disproofs stronger, by far, than is even the fact of the sterility of hybrids.

2. It is on page 330, of his *Origin of Species*, that he advances his other argument, viz., That the sterility of species, and of their hybrid offspring, is not " a special endowment," but has been slowly acquired. He there repeats his argument from ignorance, and adds his second reason why the objection, founded on sterility of hybrids, should not obtain. He says:

"The general fertility of varieties, considering how entirely ignorant we are on the causes of both fertility and sterility, does not seem to me sufficient to overthrow the view taken" (by himself) "that the invariable sterility of first crosses between species, and of

their hybrids, is not a special endowment, but is incidental on modifications slowly impressed, by unknown
means, on the reproductive systems of the parent
forms."

There are three answers to be made to this view,
that the sterility of hybrids "is not a special endowment, but is incidental on modifications, slowly impressed, by unknown means, on the reproductive
systems of the parent forms."

(1.) It is a barren assumption. Not the faintest intimation, or conjecture, does he give of the manner in
which this sterility might have been acquired. The
phrase, "unknown means" (a twin brother of "innate
tendency," of "nature and constitution of the being,"
of "a great law of nature," and of that legion of other
metaphysical entities which serve him in good stead,
whenever he is in a dilemma), proves conclusively,
that he had as little idea of what he meant, when he
propounded his "view," as his readers may derive
from his proposition.

(2.) There is not a scintilla of evidence, in his
works, which, upon the most liberal construction, can
be tortured into proof, that the sterility of hybrids was
ever acquired by modifications slowly impressed.

(3.) There are modifications, which have been impressed, and are still being impressed, by *known means*,
however, on the reproductive systems of the varieties
which he terms "incipient species," or "species in the
process of formation;" but, these modifications, so far
from accounting for the sterility of hybrids, consistently with his hypothesis, demonstrate most clearly,

that the sterility of hybrids was never slowly acquired, but that it is "a special endowment;" that varieties are not "incipient species," nor ever can become distinct species; and that each species is physiologically fixed.

Now, let us see, what the facts should be, to meet the requirements of his hypothesis (what, indeed, by the above argument of his, he intimates that they should be); and then observe what the facts really are, by his own showing. It will then be seen, that the sterility of hybrids is not the only physiological argument, in favor of the fixity of the species; but that the fertility and sterility of individuals of the same species, add arguments of even superior weight, in demonstration of the same fact, of the immutability of the species.

Here is what it was absolutely requisite, that Darwin should have shown, to obviate the objection of the sterility of species, and of their hybrids:—

Seeing, that hybrids,—the result of a cross between different species,—are invariably sterile, it is clear that if the conception, that the varieties of a species were "incipient species," or species in the process of formation, were a true one, we should expect, that the more marked, distinct, and widely divergent such varieties became, they would grow sterile, in proportion, when crossed with each other; as sterility is the characteristic of distinct species:

If the differences, between varieties, do really become augmented into the greater differences between species, all fertility, among the mongrels of such varie-

ties, should grow less and less; and those mongrels
should acquire, by degrees, the sterility characteristic
of hybrids:

Furthermore; as it is generally characteristic of individuals of the same species, to be fertile with each
other, the fertility of the individuals of each variety,
when bred, *inter se*, should grow greater, and greater,
in proportion as the variety, to which they belonged,
diverged:

Long continued domestication, or this divergence of
character which according to Darwin evolves the
varieties into species, should eliminate any tendency
to sterility, with the individuals of the same variety;
and eliminate any tendency to fertility, with the mongrels between such varieties:

The individuals of different varieties should grow
mutually sterile, and the individuals of the same variety, should grow more fertile:

The greater the structural differences, between varieties, the more sterile should be their mongrels.

Such are *not* the facts.   The facts are diametrically
at variance with those required by Darwin's hypothesis.

On page 162, Vol. ii, *Animals and Plants, &c.*, he
says :

"It deserves especial attention, that mongrel animals and plants which are so far from being sterile,
that their fertility is often actually augmented, have, as
previously shown, their size, hardihood and constitutional vigor generally increased."

Again, he says, p. 326, *Origin of Species* :

"Varieties, however much they differ from each

other in external appearance, cross with perfect facility, and yield perfectly fertile offspring."

On page 200, *Origin of Species*, he says :

" How can we account for species, when crossed, being sterile, and producing sterile offspring, whereas, when varieties are crossed, their fertility is unimpaired !"

Again he says, page 236, Vol. i, *Animals and Plants, &c.*:

" * * The more distinct the breeds, the more productive are their mongrel offspring." !

In divers other portions of his works, he has, as has already been shown, also declared, that the more divergent the breeds, the less fertile are the individuals of each variety, when bred *inter se*.   He says, that individuals of divergent varieties are extremely liable to sterility, degeneration, and death, when bred *inter se ;* and that crossing needs must be resorted to, all the time, with such individuals, in order to remedy such sterility, and prevent their extinction.

So, it is manifest, that the " modifications which are slowly impressed on the reproductive systems," tell a tale, not only in refutation of his " view," but also infinitely more significant of the falseness of his theory, than is even the sterility of hybrids.   The facts prove, that the sterility of hybrids has not been acquired, as the varieties diverged.   The facts, on the contrary, prove, *that varieties grow more and more unlike distinct species, the further they diverge.*   The facts show, that the varieties not only do not acquire sterility, in their crosses, as they diverge in character; but *that, as they*

36

diverge, they actually grow more fertile when they cross, and that, by means of crossing, they eliminate whatever tendency to sterility has been produced by divergence, in their individuals !

So far from any difference, however great, inducing sterility in the varieties, or in their mongrels, that circumstance it is, which gives the crossed breeds, and their mongrels, the greatest increase of fertility ! This shows, that the structural differences of varieties, are not being augmented into the greater differences which distinguish species. Not only is the assumption negatived completely, that varieties are " incipient species," and that the sterility of species, and of their hybrids, has been acquired, as the varieties grew, by divergence, into species; but the very converse obtains. There are modifications slowly impressed upon the reproductive systems of animals and plants, by the reduction or suppression of their characters, but those modifications add additional force to the objection founded on the sterility of hybrids. Independently of this fact of the sterility of hybrids, and even though the question of a limit to variation, had not been resolved, as it has been ; the fact that the varieties, of a species, are incompetent to become distinct species, would have been shown, by the phenomena of the lessened fertility, and of the sterility of the individuals of such a modified species. The explanation of variations, by means of reversion, disproves Darwin's theory. The sterility of hybrids disproves Darwin's theory : And,—to perfect the demonstration,—the phenomena of the close-interbreeding and crossing of the indi-

viduals of the several varieties of a species, disprove
Darwin's theory.

If the reader will reflect on the steps by which lessened fertility and sterility, among individuals of the
same species, are acquired, he will appreciate the
blunder which Darwin made, when he sought to obviate the objection of the sterility of hybrids, by asserting that such sterility might have been slowly acquired. *Darwin says, that divergence of character, in
varieties, leads to the evolution of distinct species. He
then shows, that the further such divergence of character
is carried, the nearer do the individuals of each such
divergent variety, approach complete sterility and death!
and that the only way that this sterility and extinction
may be staved off, is by the individuals of such variety,
crossing with individuals of another of the varieties of
that species,*—WHICH PROCESS UNDOES THE VERY DIVER-
GENCE OF CHARACTER, UPON WHICH DARWIN DEPENDS
TO SHOW THE EVOLUTION OF THE VARIETIES INTO DIS-
TINCT SPECIES!

As divergence of character is occasioned by the exclusive possession, by each variety, of some positive peculiarity which (being a peculiarity) needs must, therefore,
be absent in all of the other varieties of the same species; and, conversely, is occasioned by the absence, in
each variety, of all the positive peculiarities of the other
varieties; evil effects result from close-interbreeding.
As these evil effects become intensified, degree for degree, with the divergence of such varieties, it is clear,
that distinct species cannot be evolved from such varieties, for those varieties are fast verging on death and

extinction.   This death and extinction may be escaped, by doing what?—by crossing the varieties!
which is, joining the characters of different varieties,
in an individual, the mongrel.   This mongrel is fertile
and constitutionally vigorous, because it is not divergent,—because it has more of the characters of its
species, than have the divergent individuals.

Very great structural differences may mark the varieties of a species.   The characters of such species may
be variedly modified, reduced, suppressed, retained in
every stage of degeneration, or every stage of reversion, and apportioned among the different varieties, so
as to make those varieties most widely divergent and
more distinct in character, than are many species, or
than are some genera.   But, these diversities can subsist, within a species, only by impairing a physiological bond which normally ties together all the positive
characters of the species.   The further, therefore, any
apportionment, or division, of the characters, among
different varieties, is carried, the worse impaired becomes such bond; the weaker, and less fertile, grow
the individuals of the divergent varieties; until, at last, .
that degree of impairment of the bond, is reached,
which is incompatible with the function of the reproductive element, and with even the existence of the
individual.

How, then, is it possible, for varieties to diverge into
distinct species, when Darwin's own facts show demonstratively, that the only redemption possible, from
death and sterility, is in returning to the full and proportionate development of all the characters of the

given species,—in acquiring, by reversion, or by crossing (or by grafting), the positive peculiarities of the other varieties. Is it not a farce, for him to adduce the pouter pigeon, the fantail, and the tumbler, as "incipient species," becoming distinct species by divergence of character, when the poor animals are almost completely sterile, and of a delicacy of constitution, due to the absence, in each individual, of the other organs and features possessed by the other varieties, and due to the peculiarity of the variety, having been carried to the extreme of development, without the concurrent development of the other characters?

The degrees of lessened fertility, and of sterility, among individuals of a species, trend in the wrong direction for Darwin's conception of the sterility of hybrids having been acquired. If the facts would but course, in exactly the opposite direction, Darwin's theory might have some semblance of probability, or vestige of support. If, for instance, the sterility had characterized the crossing of varieties, instead of the interbreeding of the individuals of each variety; and, if increase of fertility had marked the interbreeding, instead of the crossing, of individuals of the varieties, Darwin might have been justified in making light of the objection of the sterility of hybrids.

Professor Huxley (the gentleman who inculcates Darwinism, as an axiom, to the workingmen of England, and who teaches them resignation to their hard lot, by revealing to them, that their misery is but a beautiful exemplification of the grand, scientific principle of Natural Extinction, which is so necessary to
36*

the Selection of the Plutocrats and land-holders), says, in an article in No. LII, of the *Popular Science Monthly:*

"What is needed for the completion of Darwin's theory of the origin of species, is, first, definite proof that selective breeding is competent to convert permanent races into physiologically distinct species."

As the reader has already been shown, the very antithesis to such proof is to be found in Darwin's facts. Darwin's facts show, that such definite proof, as Huxley requires, is absolutely impossible ever to be supplied. These demonstrate, that selective breeding (so far as it has any effect) endows permanent races with a physiological character, more and more unlike that of distinct species, inasmuch as it makes the individuals of each such race, sterile *inter se* (*i. e.* with other individuals of the same race), and gives them an increase of fertility and of constitutional vigor, when they are crossed with individuals of other races of the same species: a result, the direct converse of the character marking distinct species, whose individuals are, in the main, fertile with the individuals of their own species, and sterile with individuals of other species.

As has been mentioned, Huxley further says:

"What is needed for the completion of Darwin's theory, is, * * * secondly, the elucidation of the nature of variability."

Darwin's facts show, also, that there is an elucidation of the nature of variability; but such elucidation, equally with the solution of the physiological problem, militates against Darwin's theory, inasmuch as it shows, that there is a definite limit to such variability, and that such limit precludes the possibility of the evolution of "permanent races," into distinct species. Huxley says, that Darwin starts with an incontestable assumption, viz., "the existence of living matter endowed with variability." Incontestable it is; but, Darwin essays, at the next stage in his argument, an assumption which is contestable, viz.: General ignorance of the law of such variability; and the absence, therefore, of any law forbidding his next gratuitous assumption, that variability is unlimited. This assumption is not tenable, for, (1) there is a law governing variability, and (2) such law completely imposes a limit to positive variations, while (3) the law of proportionate development imposes a limit to negative variations. All variability, of a positive character, is limited to the regain of characters, once lost by the species; and variability, of a negative character, is confined within a narrow range in each species, by the sterility and extinction which await the loss of a given number of the organs and features of such species.

The cause of the sterility, and of the lessened fertility, among individuals of a variety deficient in features of its species, is, that there are not sufficient characters in those individuals, to impress their reproductive tissue with due, formative power. The reason of the sterility of hybrids, is because the hybrid is formed of characters belonging to two different species, and, therefore, the result of the coördination of the characters of the organism is not directed to the required point. The influence of the aggregate is not centered upon that tissue which is specially prepared for exudation from the organism, for reproductive purposes.

An individual, with all the characters of its species fully and proportionately developed, may be likened to a perfect, symmetrically-formed "burning lens," with all of the rays, which pass through it, determining to the center. An individual, belonging to a divergent variety deficient in some of the characters of its species, may be likened to the same lens, but notched, and with a ragged edge. The force, therein coursing, does but imperfectly converge; and the degree of the imperfection determines whether the effective concentration of the rays may at all be attained. If the imperfection be very great, the said effect will be wholly precluded. So, if the reduction of characters, in an individual, be great, the reproductive power is wholly absent, upon interbreeding with another individual similarly deficient. On the other hand, a hybrid,—the product of a cross between two distinct species,—may be likened to a glass, made in the similitude of a "burning lens" *with two foci.* The forces, contained therein,—which would be competent to the production of a given effect, were the rays converged to one point,—are, as there are two *foci*, rendered wholly inoperative for such a result. So; the hybrid would be fertile, were the point, or points, to which the influence of its aggregate determines, susceptible of being exuded. But, as there is but one point, viz., the site of the reproductive organs, where the structure contemplates exudation; and as the influence of the aggregate is not concentrated there, the hybrid needs must be sterile. The above remark, that there is but one reproductive point in that individual, has reference solely to the animals highest in the scale of development. A plant has many such reproductive centers, and so have many animals low in the scale of development. But, *mutatis mutandis*, the principle also obtains with them. Strictly stated, it should be said, that in a hybrid, the influence of the aggregate determines to a point or points *other than those devoted to purposes of exudation.*

The reason, why closely-allied species produce at times hybrid offspring, is because they possess organs and features somewhat alike; and their reproductive forces, having come, severally, from pure species, need only to be sufficiently isochronous, to coalesce and concur in the mutual formation of an organism. The question, with the reproductive elements, in this case, is not one of formative power; for each, having been derived from a pure species which concentrated the influence of its aggregate upon the tissue which was physically adapted for exudation, they have, other things equal, the power of integration. The question is one, simply of the possibility of their uniting and working to the same end. The reason, why very distinct species are absolutely sterile with each other, —not capable even of the formation of a hybrid,—is not because of the reproductive elements of the two lacking the usual formative power, but because there is a physical impossibility of the two forces uniting, through each of them pursuing an absolutely different rhythm.

The hybrid, produced by the union of the two closely allied species,—though capable of coördinating within itself, the coalesced forces of the characters of the two species,—is incapable of reflecting the result of that coördination, to that point, or those points, where the process of exudation of tissue, is possible. If the forces of the whole organism are converged, as in a hybrid, to any point, and the tissue, there, be modified into a miniature likeness of the whole, such tissue is incompetent, by reason of the nature of the mechanism, to become exuded, *i. e.*, to sever the correlation in which it stands with the rest of the structure; and therefore cannot serve as a reproductive element. The hybrid, then partakes of the character of a crystal. It has all of its parts correlated; each of such parts, if exuded or detached, and if the environment were propitious, would be capable of reintegrating the whole; but the crystal has not the power of detaching a portion of itself, for the purpose of such reintegration. Each portion of a crystal is capable of reintegrating the whole. But, the crystal is not capable of exuding, or of detaching, a part of itself, for such a purpose. For a crystal to accomplish such reintegration, a part must be detached by force applied *ab extra*. Were it capable, by itself, of this detachment, it would be, in all essentials, like an organism. Another characteristic of an organism (possessed by a crystal, but in small degree if at all), is that susceptibility to the influence of its environment, which entails that ebb and flux of the coördinating force, which is displayed in the waste and repair of its tissue. This recurrence of alternate degeneration and reintegration, is a general characteristic of life; but it is absurd to pronounce it Life itself. It is more in keeping with the phenomena, to term the coördination of actions, Life. This Herbert Spencer has done; but he has made an egregious mistake, when he fancies, that the coördination, peculiar to any species, is susceptible of any normal modification.

As before remarked, there is no necessity more imperatively felt, than that of a test by reference to which, the precise nature and bounds of the several species, may be susceptible of ascertainment; and, as the absence of all explanation, both qualitative and quantitative, of the varied phenomena of sterility and of fertility, has heretofore lain in the way of attaining such a test, the importance of the solution herein given of such varied phenomena, cannot well be over-estimated. The hybrid is the sole possible element of confusion, in the practical classification of species. Such organism, whilst in theory affording no difficulty, may be often, to the naturalist, a temporary source of confusion. But, its sterility will preclude the possibility of its confusing specific distinctions. Although; when an individual, of one species, with some of its characters reduced or suppressed, crosses with an individual of another species, which has characters so like those which the former lacks, that they may serve to repair, in a measure, the defect in the coördination of the former; gain in constitutional vigor results to the hybrid offspring of such a cross; the hybrid will, however, be sterile, and the line of descent from either parent-form,

CHAPTER XIII.

To recapitulate, the controversy stands thus:

1. Darwin says, that variations or improvements arise among animals and plants, under domestication.

This has been conceded.

2. Darwin's next proposition, is, Descent with Modification: That is, that when a modification is acquired by an individual, the law of Inheritance generally transmits the acquired character to the offspring.

This, also, has been conceded.

3. Another proposition of Darwin, is, That many organs, or characters, after having been in a state of full development, have been so wrought upon by the adverse conditions of Nature, as to become, viz., some of them, slightly reduced; others of them, greatly reduced, having the character of rudiments merely; and others of them, completely suppressed, leaving not a vestige of their past development.

This proposition, also, has been fully conceded.

4. A proposition, which Darwin formulates respecting these reduced and suppressed organs and characters is, viz., That, given, favorable conditions these reduced and these suppressed characters are competent to reappear, and on many occasions have reap-

37   (429)

peared, even after having lain latent for millions of generations.

This, too, has been conceded.

5. Darwin's next point, is, viz., That it is competent and allowable to take the amount of variation or improvement, positively known to take place during (say) the last hundred years, or during the historical period, and therefrom to estimate the amount of variation or improvement possible to occur within a million of years, or other long interval of time. This proposition has been demurred to, because such a proposition necessarily involves

6. The further proposition, viz., That variations, or improvements may proceed without any limit to them, or multiply to an indefinite extent.

This assumption, of his, of No Limit, has been shown to be, both intrinsically erroneous, and conclusively negatived by Darwin's most important factor.

It is intrinsically erroneous, because it is both gratuitous and illegitimate.

First: It is gratuitous, because no evidence whatever is adduced by Darwin, showing that the variations, or improvements, are without a limit, or that they may proceed to an indefinite extent. In fact, the most curious feature in Darwin's theory, and in every theory of Evolution which has been propounded, is that this assumption of No Limit remains a tacit assumption throughout all of his works, and throughout all works on the subject; notwithstanding that it is an indispensable point in such theories, without which they could not be constructed.

Second: This assumption of No Limit, is illegitimate, because the sole, possible warrant which might have been urged to sustain it,—viz., the presumption that, as variations are now seen to go on multiplying, they may still go on multiplying forever, or indefinitely, or may have, in the past, gone on multiplying indefi- nitely,—is invalidated by reason of Darwin's prece- dent (alleged) failure to resolve the law or the cause of variations, which law or cause, if discovered, would, presumably, have determined whether there was or was not a limit.

Third: This assumption of No Limit is, on the other hand, negatived by the fact, that the law of Variations is actually resolved by Darwin, and that law,—namely, Reversion, or the principle of the regain or re-development of characters which were previ- ously lost or reduced,—imposes a definite limit to the Variations;—no more characters may be regained than were originally lost by the respective, varying species.

7. Darwin's next proposition is, that it is possible, upon principles of analogy, that Variations now arise, under Nature, and that they may, in the past, have there arisen, in much the same manner that Varia- tions arise under domestication; and that those Varia- tions may have frequently given their owners such an advantage, in their competition with their fellows, as to secure to them a prolonged existence, and the opportunity of leaving offspring in whom the said variations would be continued.

No exception has been taken to this proposition,

save this, viz., that he has not resolved the law or cause of such possible variations, and thereby ascertained whether the variations are amenable or not to any limit; and that he has illegitimately referred them to an "innate tendency" which he has the grace to confess, is but a name for his ignorance.

8. Darwin's next proposition is, that there is, and has ever been, a fearful Struggle for Existence waging almost incessantly under Nature, among the different animals and plants.

No exception has been taken to this proposition.

9. His next proposition is, that the effect of this Struggle for Existence, is the Natural Selection of "the strongest and most vigorous" individuals, and the extinction of the weakest and least fitted to live; and he implies that, by this Selection of "the strongest and most vigorous," slight increments of development are secured, in each generation.

Exception has been taken to this proposition, because there is a fallacy resident in the terms "strongest and most vigorous." Viewed with reference to the hard conditions of the Struggle for Existence which he pictures, to which even these elect are subjected, the terms to be used, should have been, the least weak and the least degenerate. When these terms are used, no implication of any advance in development arises, as it does, when the terms, "strongest and most vigorous," are used. The implication of advance in development, from the Selection of the best of any one generation, may arise only where exist, both, Selection, and favorable conditions. Under domestication, these two requisites generally concur. Under nature, they do not,—even according to Darwin's showing. Selection is present, there; but, by the very terms of Darwin's argument, the other requisite—viz., favorable conditions,—must be absent, in order to effect the Natural Selection. According to the very terms of his argument, if this requisite of advance in development—favorable conditions—were present, the other requisite—Natural Selection—would necessarily be wanting; for unfavorable conditions are required (according to Darwin) to work off the weakest and most degenerate, and thus occasion the Selection of the others.

Subject to this qualification, the principle of Natural Selection has been recognized. *The argument from Natural Selection, however, is a different matter.*

10. Darwin's next proposition, is that those slight variations which are assumed to arise occasionally, under nature, "in the course of thousands of generations;" and those slight increments of development which are assumed to be the outcome of the Natural Selection of "the strongest and most vigorous" of each generation, may be accumulated by Natural Selection to an indefinite or unlimited extent: in other words, that by means of the accumulation of such occasional variations and of those slight increments of development, the higher animals have all been evolved from the lowest forms of life.

Exception has been taken to this proposition for the same reasons which were urged against the assumption of unlimited variation, when it was considered

37*

will (so far as this hybrid is concerned) forever end. There is a definite and absolute failure of issue, with the hybrid; unlike the failure of issue, in the case of an individual of a pure species, whose sterility is caused solely by its reproductive element being modified by the forces of an inadequate number of the characters of its species. As Darwin has noted, from observations made, the sterility of this individual is not absolute: As Darwin, however, has failed to note, the reason its sterility may be remedied, is because it needs only to mate with another individual of the same species, which has the complement of characters required for the purposes of reproduction, or which (failing to possess such complement) can contribute other characters which the former lacks, the addition whereof to the number it already possesses, may make up the number which is necessary to restore fertility.

sion—which constitutes his most prominent factor, really explains those variations, and imposes a definite limit to them.

If the theory that variations are due to Reversion;* that the improvements arising under domestication are due to the reappearance of characters lost or reduced under nature; and that the variations or increments of development which are preserved and accumulated by Natural Selection, under nature, are but the regain of what was lost by the respective species, at some former period; be true, then Darwinism, and every theory of Biology, of Psychology, and of Sociology, which is based upon the assumption of the unlimited accumulation of those slight increments of development, known as Variations, must be false.

But is the theory of Reversion true?

---

* Of course, the positive features which are due to Reversion, and which are essential to the integrity of a species, do not comprise pathological characters where (for instance) inorganic, or foreign, or misplaced, organic processes of integration have effected a coalescence with the normal forces of growth. Nor do they include the features of local hypertrophy, or other monstrous growths.

The perfect type, of any species, is not the sum of all the modifications of which all the characters of such species, are susceptible, but it is the sum of all the positive characters of a species, as those characters are when fully and normally developed. These words, " fully and normally," do not here beg the question as they would were the theory dependent upon its mere agreement with the facts; for, we have the crucial test of self-fertilization, or of close-interbreeding, by which to determine what is normal and what abnormal. That which is abnormal will ever manifest itself in the evil attendant upon self-fertilization or close-interbreeding.

There is one of the features of species, which may occasion doubt. Reference is had to color. It is difficult, frequently, to tell what color,

It has to recommend it, that it is in full accordance with all the facts of Variation.

It has to recommend it, that the weight of probabilities is in its favor.

It has to recommend it, that there is no converse assumption competent to explain the facts of Variation.

It has to recommend it, that the law of Reversion to which it looks for an explanation, is a well-known scientific factor.

It has to recommend it, that there is no fact which is inconsistent with such explanation.

It has to recommend it, that, in default of such explanation, there is no recourse but to a metaphysical entity, an "innate tendency."

But, great as are the intrinsic defects of Darwin's theory, and overpowering as are the above considera-

---

or variegation of colors is proper and normal to any given species. The difficulty lies in this : When any other feature is abnormal in any way, evil is entailed by self-fertilization, or by close-interbreeding, either immediately or when such process has been long continued. In such way, the abnormal character is ascertained : But, with an abnormal color, the evil entailed thereby, is so inappreciably small, that the test of interbreeding, or of self-fertilization, is practically valueless.

As has been before remarked, the Converse Theory, propounded in this work, has relation, directly, solely to the problem of Variations. Darwin's problem was, How species were evolved. But, in the solution of such problem, he employed these Variations as his *data*, and contended that the species were evolved simply by the indefinite accumulation of such Variations. To confute him, a converse theory of the Evolution of the Species, was not needed, but a converse theory, merely, of his data, namely the Variations. Such theory has here been supplied, showing that the evolution of species was not accomplished by means of Variations ; that each species is normally im-

tions in favor of the theory of Reversion, we have not relied, for the Refutation of Darwinism, upon these points alone. We have not left the theory of Reversion dependent upon its mere agreement with the facts, or sustained by a mere balance of probabilities; nor have we counted, for its acceptance, upon the mere fact that the law to which we look for an explanation of the phenomena, and which alone is competent to explain those phenomena, is a well-established scientific factor, whose additional recommendation is that it is assimilable to other well-known laws, such as that of the reproduction of lost limbs, that of the redintegration of tissue, that of the repair of injuries, and all laws whose operation is to restore the lost integrity of an organism.

Such considerations are amply competent to the

---

mutable; and that each was evolved from a distinct, independent center of inorganic forces. If such converse theory, or History of Variations, be true, it is competent, also, to the refutation of the whole of Herbert Spencer's synthesis, of Bain's hypotheses, and of every theory of Biology, of Psychology, or of Sociology, which assumes that those slight increments of development, known as Variations, may be accumulated indefinitely.

But, although the converse theory of the Evolution of Species, is not needed to the explosion of Darwinism, or other theory of general evolution,—the question of whether or not these are true, being definitively settled by the phenomena of Variation,—a detail of the modes of integration in which the several species were evolved from independent centers, is desirable on other grounds. Therefore, in a future work on The Special Evolution of Species, founded principally, if not exclusively, upon data furnished by Darwin, Bain and Spencer, the evolution of species from independent centers; the differentiation of organisms into sexual, neuter, and otherwise modified individuals; the cause which determines the sex of off-

refutation of Darwinism, but they do not suffice to en-
title the theory of Reversion to a place within the body
of positive truths.

We have, however, supplemented such arguments and
evidences, with adequate, scientific proofs of the truth of
the theory of Reversion, and with positive disproofs of
the theory of Darwin. The phenomena of Crossing
and of Close-Interbreeding accomplish these ends,
with the full, unerring force of demonstration.

These phenomena declare the law, beyond all controversy or cavil, to be, viz., that the positive variations in each species are but the regain of what was
previously lost by such species; that that organic structure which is the sum of all the possible developments
of its species, is alone consistent with full physiological
integrity; that there is a limit to Variation in both directions, in the direction of increase and in the direc-

---

spring; which occasions the transmission to an individual of either
sex of the primary and secondary, sexual characters of the opposite
sex; the philosophy of hydrophobia, of catamenia, of petrifaction, of
the several phases of metamorphosis, and of monstrosities; and the
phenomena of embryology, will receive an explanation as complete as
that which has been given of the phenomena of Crossing and Close-
Interbreeding. This synthesis—the principles of which shall be
evolved from the facts, and descend again to the facts, by as rigorous
processes of induction and deduction, as have characterized the present work—will include the true theory of classification; the explanation of numerous, recondite, psychological problems; an explanation of the history and function of the cæcum; and such a full
and detailed explanation of the function of the cerebellum, as
harmonizes the two seemingly conflicting classes of facts which now
are appealed to by the advocates, respectively, of the two prevailing
theories.

tion of decrease; that there is a limit in the direction of increase of structure, or to positive Variations, for no more Variations can occur in any species, than that amount of characters or features which such species once lost; that there is a limit in the direction of decrease of structure, or to Degeneration, or negative variations, because any organism which falls short of the full organic complement of its species, has thereby entailed upon it, a proportional physiological, evil effect, while if such modification of the specific type be carried beyond what is a comparatively very narrow margin, the effect upon the fertility and constitutional vigor of the individual will be such as to entail the extinction of its line, and death to itself; that the structural degeneration which has taken place under nature, in almost every species, has been in derogation of the physiological integrity of the individuals, and this is evidenced by the evil effects which accompany the close-interbreeding of individuals of each such species; that each and every return which is made towards the full structural complement, viz., the original perfect type,—made, either, by means of direct Reversion, or positive Variation, by means of Crossing (whereby the offspring has, contributed to it by either parent, a character or characters which the other parent lacked), or by means of Grafting,—is fraught with proportional increase of physiological good, or fraught, rather, with proportional abatement of the evil which was caused by the departure from such normal build.

The obvious import of this law, of proportionate development, is that each species is normally immutable.

independently of the question of Natural Selection. Such a conclusion, of indefinite or of unlimited results from Natural Selection, involves the assumption that the accretions of development, represented by the strongest and most vigorous individuals and the variations present in the varying individuals, proceed forever, or without any limit: Whereas, as has been before shown, such assumption of No Limit is both (1) gratuitous, and (2) illegitimate, and (3) is negatived by the fact that the sole law of which such variations and such increments of development are susceptible, viz., Reversion, imposes a limit to such variations and increments, and consequently restricts the extent of the accumulation of such, which is effected by Natural Selection.

Thus the controversy stood, before the positive disproofs of Darwin's theory were developed. Such theory was shown to be untenable because of three salient objections. These were (to repeat):

First: This assumption of No Limit (which assumption is absolutely essential to his theory) is invalidated by being gratuitous; *i. e.,* for want of any evidence to sustain it:

Second: His assumption of No Limit is invalidated by being illegitimate ; *i. e.,* by reason of his precedent (alleged) failure to resolve the law, or the cause, of variations, which, if resolved, would presumably have informed him whether these variations were, or were not amenable to a limit.

Third: His assumption of No Limit is invalidated by reason of the fact that a certain law—viz., Rever-

The state of the individuals, previous to their development of positive variations, is a deficient, physiological
condition, due to their deficient, structural condition.
Their positive variation is a structural return, which is
attended by a return to a perfect physiological condition. The same result is effected by Crossing. By this
process, two individuals which have made structural
returns, in different ways or in different characters,
toward the original mould of their common species,
combine those characters, or the bases thereof, in their
offspring; and the augmented return, so induced, meets
with a proportional response in the gain in fertility
and vigor which is ever then observed.

If the variation, under domestication, be of a negative character, the departure from the normal type is
then evidenced by the lessened vigor and lessened fertility which mark this departure from physiological integrity, which follows fast upon any departure from
structural integrity.

As, then, the reduction, or suppression of any character, is ever observed to entail physiological evil,
the deficient physiological condition of any organisms,
in a state of nature, or when just placed under domestication, must imply the reduction and suppression of
some characters in those individuals; and, it follows
that any development, subsequently under domestication, of positive variations, must be the recovery,
merely, of such lost characters—especially, as it is
observed, that the regain of such lost characters, or the
appearance of such variations, is attended by a like
and proportional decrease of the physiological, evil

effects under which those individuals were observed to suffer.

The following propositions illustrate the manner in which the normal immutability of each species, has been demonstrated by this law, of the complementary nature of the structural integrity, and of the physiological integrity of organisms.

From Darwin's repertory of facts this induction has been made, viz.:

11. That there has been degeneration in each species under nature, to the extent of a margin commensurate with the margin of the possible, positive variation in that species, under Domestication.

Warrant for this induction, is to be found

First: In the conditions of the Struggle for Existence, which needs must have been very adverse, if Darwin's graphic description of them is to be received:

Second: Warrant for the induction, of Degeneration under Nature, is to be found in the many rudimentary organs which, Darwin says, were once in a fully developed state; and the scope of this degeneration may be conceived when Darwin says that these rudiments "imply an enormous amount of modification," and when he says, that "there is scarcely a single species under nature which is free from such blemishes."   •

Third: Degeneration is shown by the many organs which, Darwin declares, have been greatly reduced and simplified by the action of the conditions of Natural Selection:

Fourth: This degeneration is shown by the many
38

characters which, Darwin shows, have been so wholly suppressed that not a vestige of their past development now remains.

Fifth: This degeneration is shown by the many "latent" characters and organs, "proper to both the right and left sides of the body, and to a long line of male and female ancestors," which lie, according to Darwin, within every organism, and which need only the proper conditions, to reappear.

Sixth: This degeneration is shown by the numberless characters which Darwin ascribes to Reversion— Reversion necessarily implying, as Darwin admits, past reduction or suppression of the characters which now revert.

12. The next induction is, That all of the positive Variations, or improvements, in each species, are due to the mere regain of the characters which were lost or reduced in such species, under nature; and that they are limited, therefore, in number and kind to the number and kind of the characters so lost or reduced, under nature.

Warrant for this is found

First: In the previous proposition, and in the proofs adduced in support thereof.

Second: In the numberless instances where Variations are ascribed, by Darwin, to Reversion, the exceptions being rare where he does not thus account for the phenomena of variation.

Third: In Darwin's admission that all Variations are susceptible of such explanation, his only objection being that they must at some time have arisen as new

Variations, and thus formed the species: Such objection, however, is obviously absurd; as that point—viz., that species were formed by the mere accumulation of Variations—is the very conclusion which he is striving now to attain, by means of these very Variations which he admits are most probably the mere regain of what was previously lost. If the mere regain of what was lost, they manifestly stop when all that was lost is regained; and therefore, having a limit, they cannot have formed the several species.

Fourth: Warrant for the assumption that all positive Variations are but the mere regain of what was lost, is found in the fact that Reversion is a well-known, well-established, scientific factor.

Fifth: Warrant is found in the fact that Reversion is, confessedly, the sole explanation of which positive variations are susceptible.

Sixth: Warrant is found in the fact that there are no phenomena which militate against such explanation.

Seventh: Warrant is found in the fact that the sole alternative of the explanation of Reversion, is an "innate tendency," or other metaphysical entities which Darwin admits are but synonyms of ignorance.

Now to the *proofs* of the foregoing propositions.

A proposition of Darwin, is, That self-fertilization, or in-and-in breeding is injurious, and productive of sterility, of lessened fertility, loss of constitutional vigor and loss of size.

An analysis of the facts upon which he professes to found this proposition, discloses :

13. That self-fertilization, or in-and-in breeding is not, *per se*, injurious;

14. That it is the loss or reduction, in the individuals, of some of the characters, proper to their species, which causes the evil results which are so frequently seen to follow self-fertilization and in-and-in breeding:

15. That, when the individuals are fully and proportionately developed in all the positive characters of their species—that is, when the perfect type, which is normally immutable, is realized in the individuals—they may be self-fertilized, or closely interbred in the nearest degree of relationship, without any evil results.

Proof of these propositions is found

First: In the fact that animals and plants in the state of nature, and when first placed under domestication, are susceptible of the evils resulting from close-interbreeding, to a degree corresponding with the amount of reduction or suppression of characters, which either is known to have occurred, or which is implied by the individuals' subsequent development of positive features :

Second: In the fact that these evil results from close-interbreeding abate (other things equal) in proportion as the variations appear under domestication ; or in other words, in proportion as the reduced or suppressed characters which occasioned the evil, re-develop.

Third: In the fact that, where other things are not equal, viz.,—where Man's selection has been so erratic as to preclude the proportionate re-development, in each individual, of all the lost or reduced characters—the evil results from close-interbreeding correspond most faithfully, degree for degree, with the disproportionate development of the individuals—the variations in the quantity of the effects observed, tallying exactly with the variations in the quantity of cause assigned.

The modes of Man's Selection which thus vary the evil results, may be conveniently classed as four: viz.,

a. That mode of Selection which, while it re-developes all or most of the lost or reduced characters of a given species, does not develop them all in the same individuals, or in the same variety; but, instead thereof, apportions or distributes them among different varieties, thereby causing each variety of said species to lack the many important characters which constitute the peculiarities of the other varieties of the same species, and thereby restricting such variety to one only of the recovered characters, which is pushed to an extreme of development which aids the more to mar the true proportion.

This process of Selection is exemplified in the case of the Pigeon, and of the Fowl.

In consequence, therefore, of each variety of either of these species, lacking the characters, which have been appropriated as peculiarities by the other varieties of the given species, and in consequence of the extreme, disproportionate development of the special excellence of each variety, it was to be expected, that the interbreeding of individuals of each such variety, would be prolific of great evil results. This expectation has been fully justified by the facts, from Darwin,

38*

recorded in the chapter on Pigeons and Fowls. These animals not only display the greatest evil upon close-interbreeding, but,—in conclusive refutation of Darwin's theory that the Pigeon and Fowl best illustrate the divergence of character which (he fancies) evolves varieties into species,—the further the varieties diverge, the more sterile and weakened in constitution do they become! proving clearly that divergence of character cannot result in the evolution of distinct species, for the apportionment or separation of characters, which it involves, is in derogation of the fertility and strength of the individuals so diverging, and comes soon to a dead stop within a very short interval, owing to the sterility and excessive delicacy of constitution which the absence in each individual, of the characters which form the peculiarities of the other varieties of the same species, entails.

b. Another of the modes of Man's Selection, which vary the evil results, is that mode which, instead of—or in addition to—re-developing lost or reduced characters, continues the reduction or suppression of characters of the species; thereby greatly modifying the normal type which is the sum of the full and proportionate development of all the positive characters of the given species.

This process of Man's Selection is exemplified in the case of the Pig which—in what are esteemed the best, domesticated breeds—has its snout reduced, the front of its head short and concave, its bristles well-nigh suppressed, its legs reduced to a size often incompatible not alone with locomotion, but with the very

support of the animal, and its tusks almost obliterated.

In consequence of this degeneration, the interbreeding of individuals of the domesticated breeds is pregnant (as has been shown) with very great loss of fertility and of constitutional vigor; greater, in fact (as
Darwin shows, unconscious as he is of the reason), than
in the case of any other large animal; greater, in fact,
than with any other animals, save, perhaps the Pigeon
in which the true principles of development, have been
equally outraged, only in a somewhat different way.
On the other hand, in the interbreeding of the least
well-bred animals of this species (the Pig), the evil
results, owing to the nearer approximation to the normal type of the species, are in a measure absent.

 c. Another of the modes of Man's Selection which
vary the evil results of Close-Interbreeding, is that
mode which, in a great measure, re-develops all or
nearly all of the lost or reduced characters of the
given species; leaving the varieties to be distinguished
from one another, simply by some slight variations in
the ratio of the development of the species' characters.

This process of Man's Selection is exemplified, in a
greater or less degree, in Horses, Sheep, and Cows.

In consequence of this mode of Selection, so favorable to development, the interbreeding of individuals
of each variety of either of these species, is observed
to be replete with very little evil results; the well-proportioned animals often being capable of very close
and long continued in-and-in breeding, without the
slightest apparent prejudice; and, where evil is ob-

served to result, it is ever traceable to the individuals which are paired, being similarly wanting in full structural integrity.

d. Another of the modes of Man's Selection, which vary the evil results of Interbreeding, is that mode which re-develops only one of the lost or reduced characters of the species; the several varieties of each such species being formed by the mere retention of each variety at a different stage of the exclusive development of this one character.

This process of Selection is principally exemplified in the case of Plants, there being, in each species, generally only one character which Man values, and to which exclusively he devotes his attention. In one species, it is, perhaps, the fruit alone which he prizes; in another, it is the flower; in another, the leaves; in another, the roots, &c. The extreme development of this one, valued feature, and the reduction, both positive and relative, of the other characters of the species, have sensibly modified the normal structure of the Plants.

In consequence of this modification of the structural integrity of Plants, there is observed to be an injurious modification of the physiological integrity, which reveals itself when the Plants are self-fertilized, or when two individuals, similarly modified, are interbred; loss of fertility, loss of constitutional vigor, and sterility being the outcome of such self-fertilization, or of such interbreeding, in proportion to the degree in which the parents similarly depart from the full, structural integrity of their species.

All of the species under domestication furnish confirmation to the doctrine that each and every modification of the type of the sum of all the positive characters of a species, is fraught with physiological injury which beyond a very narrow limit entails the extinction of the line of the individuals so modified.

So, even if all the individuals of every species in the world had departed from the types of their respective species, and even if there were no form extant, which realized the perfect type of its species, the type of each species would not be involved in doubt; for it is ever susceptible of ascertainment. Interbreed the individuals, and the evil effects, consequent upon such process, will furnish a perfect register of the amount of departure which they have made from the original, normal form. By careful breeding, modify a human being, until he closely resembles a monkey—in the length and proportion of his arms and legs, in the contour of his head, in his facial angle, in the character of the ribs, &c.,—place the man and a monkey side by side; and if structural differences alone are to be taken into account, as Darwin holds, there would be a close similarity between the two. But, when physiological tests are applied, there is revealed a wide distinction. Breed either of the two, with one of its own kind, similarly modified, and it will respond, and give a faithful register of the distance it has removed from its normal type. The human being will be prolific of the greatest possible evils; thus evidencing the enormous amount of modification which it has suffered. The monkey, on the other hand, will be free from all display of evil effects; or, possibly, will evince a slight degree of evil, after long-continued and very close interbreeding; thereby evidencing that it has departed not at all, or but slightly, from the perfect type of its species.

16. As, then, the loss or reduction of characters, in any individual, is observed to entail physiological injury; and as, previous to their variation under domestication, organisms are observed to be defective in proportion to the number of characters which it is subsequently observed to be possible for them to develop under domestication, it follows that those positive variations which appear under domestication, are but the regain of characters which the given species lost under nature.

17. Further proof is furnished by the fact that the physiological defects, which are occasioned by the loss or reduction of characters, are ever observed to abate in proportion as the individuals develop the variations which appear under domestication; thus proving that such variations are but the regain of the characters whose loss or reduction caused the physiological injury.

18. Warrant for this is found in Darwin's remark that "Domestication, as a general rule increases the prolificness of animals and plants."

19. If, however, further proof be required, it is found in abundance in the phenomena of Crossing, which as it is the converse of the law of Close-Interbreeding, is fraught with more significance than if it were evidence of an independent character. Besides, by means of the several modes of Man's Selection, which have been

before detailed, the good resulting from Crossing is infinitely varied; and the close correspondence which is seen to subsist between such variations in the quantity of the effects, and the like variations which are pointed out as prevailing also in the quantity of the cause assigned, proves the theory of Reversion to demonstration.

20. Darwin says that it is "a great law of nature that good should follow Crossing."

An analysis of the facts upon which he professes to found this law, discloses

21. That Crossing is not, *per se*, beneficial; but is the mere occasion of the good which results;

22. That the cause of the good resulting from Crossing, is to be found in the fact that, in that process, each of the crossed parents contributes, to the formation of the offspring, a character or characters which the other parent lacks; the physiological good which is observed to follow, being consequent upon that induced, structural remove toward the perfect type, which is thus effected by the union in the offspring, of the positive peculiarities of both parents.

Proof of these propositions is found

First: In the fact that the good resulting from Crossing is ever observed to be in proportion to the amount of the positive, structural differences of the crossed parents;

Second: In the fact that where either parent has no positive features to contribute to the offspring, which the other parent lacks, there is, relatively to such last mentioned parent, no increase of good whatever displayed by the offspring.

incontestably that not merely are those phenomena inconsistent with his suppositions, but that the very converse and refutation of them prevails. They show that the sterility of hybrids, *is* "a special endowment," and that, instead of the sterility of hybrids having been induced by slowly acquired modifications, it is the lessened fertility of individuals of the same species, which has been induced by modifications, and that not only do such modifications operate in a way the very reverse of that required by his gratuitous supposition; but, in proportion to his Divergence of Character (which he fain would believe evolves varieties in distinct species), do those varieties become of lessened fertility and of lessened vigor, culminating very soon in death and extinction.

Thus, from four several quarters of the science of Biology—namely, first, from the phenomena of Reversion which fix a limit to positive Variations; second, from the phenomena of Interbreeding which, in the opposite direction, fix a limit to negative Variations, by entailing evil effects upon any organism in proportion to the modification of the perfect type of the given species, which such individual has suffered, which evil effects amount to complete sterility and extinction, at a point which is comparatively a very small remove from such perfect type; thirdly, from the phenomena of Crossing, which show that only in proportion as an individual regains the features which it lacks, and recovers the lost integrity of its species (whether the same be effected by direct Variation, by Crossing, or by Grafting), does it regain its lost physi-

39

ological integrity, its fertility, and constitutional vigor ; and fourthly, from the phenomena of the Sterility of Species, or of their Hybrids which proves that there is an insuperable bar to the admixture of the species—do the facts converge to the following conclusions, viz. :

That there is but one, normal mould or type for any given species :

That such normal type alone is consistent with physiological integrity.

That the several, existing varieties, or races, of any given species, are but negative modifications, or segments of the proper type of such species :

That any departure from the full, structural integrity of the perfect type of the given species, is fraught with proportional physiological evils :

That any return towards the perfect type of the given species, is attended with proportional abatement of the physiological evils under which the individual suffered : and

That each species, although susceptible of countless injurious modifications, is normally immutable.

THE END.

Third: In the fact that where a variety has all of the positive features of its species; or, where it possesses all of the positive features which characterize the other varieties of the species, no advantage accrues from its crossing with another variety.

To these proofs and evidences, has been added the following, which sets an effectual bar to the admixture of distinct species, and shows that there exists "a broad and insuperable distinction between varieties or races and species :"

23. Species when crossed, are either sterile themselves, or produce offspring which are sterile.

The obvious and even the admitted import of this phenomenon is diametrically opposed to Darwin's theory. Darwin, however, has attempted two hypotheses, with which to obviate the force of this objection to his theory. These wholly fanciful hypotheses of his are not only susceptible of signal confutation, but the one, viz., that even individuals of the same species are susceptible of all degrees of lessened fertility and sterility, and that therefore sterility is not distinctive of species; and the other, viz., that this sterility subsisting between different species, may not be a special endowment, but may have been induced by modifications slowly impressed by unknown means, on the reproductive systems of the parent forms; recoil with ten-fold force upon him and his theory, and disclose the full extent of the significance with which the sterility of hybrids is fraught.

The phenomena, of lessened fertility among individuals of the same species, to which he appeals, show